THE COMPLETE IDIOT'S GUIDE® TO

Creating a Graphic Novel

by Nat Gertler and Steve Lieber

ALPHA

A member of Penguin Group (USA) Inc.

To Sara, who put up with me. —Steve
To Lara, who put up with me. —Nat

Copyright © 2004 by Nat Gertler and Steve Lieber

International Standard Book Number: 1-59257-233-2
Library of Congress Catalog Card Number: 2004103236

06 05 04   8 7 6 5 4 3 2 1

Interpretation of the printing code: The rightmost number of the first series of numbers is the year of the book's printing; the rightmost number of the second series of numbers is the number of the book's printing. For example, a printing code of 04-1 shows that the first printing occurred in 2004.

Printed in the United States of America

Note: This publication contains the opinions and ideas of its authors. It is intended to provide helpful and informative material on the subject matter covered. It is sold with the understanding that the authors and publisher are not engaged in rendering professional services in the book. If the reader requires personal assistance or advice, a competent professional should be consulted.

The authors and publisher specifically disclaim any responsibility for any liability, loss, or risk, personal or otherwise, which is incurred as a consequence, directly or indirectly, of the use and application of any of the contents of this book.

Most Alpha books are available at special quantity discounts for bulk purchases for sales promotions, premiums, fund-raising, or educational use. Special books, or book excerpts, can also be created to fit specific needs.

For details, write: Special Markets, Alpha Books, 375 Hudson Street, New York, NY 10014.

Publisher: *Marie Butler-Knight*
Product Manager: *Phil Kitchel*
Senior Managing Editor: *Jennifer Chisholm*
Acquisitions Editor: *Mikal Belicove*
Development Editor: *Jennifer Moore*
Senior Production Editor: *Billy Fields*
Copy Editor: *Susan Aufheimer*
Illustrator: *Steve Lieber*
Cover/Book Designer: *Trina Wurst*
Indexer: *Julie Bess*
Layout/Proofreading: *Becky Harmon, Mary Hunt*

Contents at a Glance

Contents

Foreword

When my wife Barb and I walked down the red carpet at the New York premiere of *The Road to Perdition* (RTP)—the Tom Hanks film based on the book I wrote (and Richard Piers Rayner illustrated)—the reporters called out one telling question. It was a question I would hear at various RTP premieres and functions, and from dozens of reporters. My answer to that question became the basis of articles all over the world—*USA Today* and *Entertainment Weekly* among the celebrated venues.

And the question was … "What's a graphic novel?"

In some respects, I think DreamWorks dreaded hearing people ask me this. The film company had gone out of its way to minimize the comic book roots of their important, *Godfather*-esque crime saga. An early poster credited the source as a "novel" by Richard and me (no "graphic," no reference to "illustrated") and this caused a minor storm in the Internet realm of Ain't It Cool News.

Now, I'm the author of around 30 historical novels—the prose kind—and have won numerous awards for such, and have a reputation for historical accuracy and in particular knowledge about the '30s Chicago crime era. But the DreamWorks publicity machine decided I was an embarrassment, and I was pointedly told I would not be participating in media events, in particular the round-robin of interviews with stars and filmmakers that media mavens world-wide were shipped in to attend. The costume designer would participate; the creator of *Road to Perdition* would not.

The ignoble shadow of comics, it seemed, was not to be cast upon this august event—i.e., a PR flack fest.

But I shouldered my way in to the Chicago premiere—and I must stress that only the DreamWorks PR machine treated me questionably, whereas the actual filmmakers like director Sam Mendes, producers Richard and Dean Zanuck, screenwriter David Self, and exec Steven Spielberg were princes—and it was there that the graphic-novel question was first asked, to echo in New York and London and in Muscatine (Iowa, my home town) through-out the next six weeks.

My answer? Usually a flip one: "A graphic novel is a great big fat comic book."

This usually got a laugh, and as a sound-bite one liner, it served its purpose, principally by being true. You'd be shocked to discover how many people thought "based on the graphic novel written by Max Allan Collins" was an indication that the novel had been graphic, that is, overly violent and/or sexually explicit. (DreamWorks apparently was less troubled by the lat-ter misreading than the notion that the comic-book stigma might attach itself to their film.)

Ironically, the single most covered and discussed aspect of Sam Mendes's wonderful adaptation became the graphic novel roots of the film. I gave more interviews than Hanks or Paul Newman or Jude Law. The guy who'd been consigned to the bench by DreamWorks PR found himself on the playing field pretty much by himself. For a short time, I became America's Graphic Novel Poster Child, and fought the good fight and talked the good talk in the public forum where the concept of comics as a valid narrative form was viewed as an interesting if arcane notion.

My efforts—and those of a number of good writers who did articles on the subject—have seemed to pay off, at least a little. I still get asked the graphic novel question from time to time, but less frequently, and the existence of the book in your hands shows that the term is gaining purchase ... and purchases.

The term "graphic novel" goes back at least as far as a guy named Richard Kyle, who as far as I know coined it for several fine fanzines of the '60s and early '70s (*Graphic Story Illustrated* and *Wonder World*). In those days, in the realm of fanzines, the term got bandied about quite a bit, and such pioneering 1930s efforts as Milt Gross's *He Done Her Wrong* and the wordless woodcut novels of Lynn Ward were cited as artistically successful examples that preceded the graphic-novel designation itself; the gifted superhero/fantasy artist Gil Kane published several self-proclaimed graphic novels, and the real pioneer—the role model for any of us attempting to go down the perditious road of the graphic novel—is of course Will Eisner, whose *Contract with God* walked the same path as mainstream prose. Not a cloak or power ring in sight ....

As an art form, comics is both cursed and blessed. On the positive side, the words-and-pictures vocabulary of comics is universally understood, making sequential narrative the most accessible and populist of storytelling forms, this side of "Once upon a time." But the misnomer of the name—nothing inherently "comic" is attached to sequential narratives—vies with the dominance of superhero material to create a world-class absurdity. From the need to follow the seeming plural noun of "comics" with a singular verb, to the pop-cultural accident of costumed heroes dominating the landscape, the narrative form called comics seems doomed to dismissal as kid's stuff.

Hence the somewhat self-conscious, trying-too-hard term "graphic novel"—a necessary evil, I'm afraid. But the term has its own burdensome aspects. At this point, the bulk of graphic novels falls into two camps: superhero sagas ... some of them very good ... striving for acceptance as something more than adolescent ephemera; and serious, even avant garde works ... some of them very good ... that form a sub-genre of their own.

The battle I've been fighting—with little impact, until *Perdition*, I must admit—is to demonstrate that the graphic novel can work in a mainstream manner. That, for example, a crime novel can be told in comics form and be good and serious and even attract people named Hanks, Zanuck, and Spielberg. Significantly, the movie tie-in edition of *Road to Perdition* got on the *New York Times* bestseller list—comics fans didn't put it there, either.

My heroes were from the comic strips, where the audience was filled with as many grown-ups as kids—guys like Chester Gould and Eisner who spun crime yarns Dashiell Hammett or James M. Cain might well envy; and Al Capp, whose social satire in the twentieth century has few rivals. It should be noted that for a brief shining moment, post-WW II, the comics form was accepted by many adults as a legitimate one. Ex-G.I.s—who'd got hooked on portable, user-friendly comic books—came home with the comics habit, and every genre imaginable was serving up fare to an audience older than the kid stereotype. Any number of great comic-book stories were created in this brief Renaissance, but I remain particularly impressed by those of Johnny Craig, whose 1950s crime-fiction work at EC was adult in the manner that other popular forms—radio at the time, TV, movies, paperback novels—would routinely pursue.

The McCarthy era anti-comics hysteria, fueled by the ravings of psychiatrist, Dr. Fredric Wertham, ended all that—Craig, the ECs, and so much more were replaced by kid stuff ... and significantly, only the superheroes (and just a few of them) survived this purge.

Now we have a second chance: graphic novels. My dream is that we can have *Batman* graphic novels as well as *American Splendor*, that *Hellboy* can thrive along with *Maus* ... but also every other kind of visually interesting story—romances, war stories, westerns, fantasies, historical sagas—and whatever else a gifted storyteller might imagine.

I have hope. That this book exists is a sign that I may live long enough to one day not have to answer the graphic-novel question. It will seem as absurd as the notion that we used to call this wonderful, sophisticated material "kid's stuff."

—Max Allan Collins

March 2004

Max Allan Collins is an award winning novelist and filmmaker who has also made a mark in the world of comics. In addition to *The Road to Perdition*, he has written such graphic novels as *CSI: Serial, Johnny Dynamite: Underworld*, and the forthcoming *The Road to Perdition 2: On the Road*. He wrote the *Dick Tracy* comic strip from 1977 to 1993, and his *Ms. Tree* (co-created by artist Terry Beatty) is considered a key influential work in contemporary crime comics. His prose sequel, *Road to Purgatory*, will be published by William Morrow.

Introduction

You're not an idiot. You're just someone who wants to know more than you do about creating graphic novels. You probably have some ideas about creating graphic novels yourself, and want to know how to go about it. I understand. I've been there myself.

To give you a full picture of the creation process, this book has two main authors. I'm Nat Gertler, and I'll tell you about writing and producing graphic novels, because that's what I do. I've written comic books and graphic novels for literally dozens of publishers. I'm also the one-man company known as About Comics, producer and publisher of graphic novels.

Doing a mighty job showing you the all-important art portion of graphic novels is apple-fritter-eatin' Steve Lieber. Steve is a veteran graphic storyteller, having drawn tales about everyone from the Batman to the inventors of the atom bomb. Between the two of us, we've done just about everything there is to do in comics, and we've even called on the help of a couple of our friends to explain their own specialties.

Sidebar

WHA...?

A **sidebar** is a separate bit of text presented alongside the main text. In this book we use several different types of sidebars. For example, in Wha ...? sidebars like this one we're putting definitions of special terms and graphic novel lingo.

Steve Sez: Sez who?

I'm Steve. If you see a little sidebar like this one, that's me interjecting an artist's point of view into a chapter written by Nat. I might use it to suggest a way of writing that makes things easier for an artist, for example, or I can point out that I don't actually eat apple fritters. Meanwhile, Nat has his own Nat Sez sidebars for pudding-lovin' writer/publisher insight in the chapters that I write.

What the Book Does

This book shows you how graphic novels get made, from the very beginning of the concept to the end result that you can hold in your hands. In **Part 1, "Planning Your Novel,"** we tell you about planning your graphic novel, including how to work out your story concept and how to find collaborators if you need them.

I show you how to write graphic novels in **Part 2, "The Writer's Art."** Here, you learn to plan the details of the plot, work out the dialog, and put things in a script form.

In **Part 3, "Putting It in Pencil,"** Steve shows you the first stage of the traditional drawing process. You'll see how to lay out the page by figuring out where the panels go and composing the content of each panel. You'll learn about drawing comics with a pencil, where you can make plenty of mistakes without causing a real problem, unless there's a worldwide eraser shortage. This part has plenty of tricks you can use and traps to avoid in crafting and telling your story.

In **Part 4, "Polishing the Pages,"** you learn about finishing the art. You learn not only how to ink your pencil drawings to sharpen them and make them reproducible, but also how to add text and colors.

Tip-Top Tips

Check out these sidebars to see tips and tricks to help you work better, faster, and smarter.

A Novel Example

We'll be using these sidebars to recommend graphic novels that show good examples of what we're talking about in the text. At the moment, I'll suggest that if you like *The Big Con* section you see in this book, you should head down to the store where you bought this book and ask for the finished graphic novel, published by About Comics.

Part 5, "Bring Out Your Book" is all about getting your graphic novel to the readers. You can find a publisher for your graphic novel, you can publish it yourself, you can even use the Internet to bring it to people. If you just want to stick your graphic novel in a drawer and not let anyone see it, this part won't be any good to you.

Throughout the book you can see, step-by-step, the creation of a portion of a graphic novel. Steve and I are collaborating on an eight-page section of the new graphic novel *The Big Con*, and you'll get to see those eight pages in each stage as the tale evolves from being a mere concept into being a script, and then pencil drawings, and finally inked and lettered drawings. By the time you're done with this book, you'll know that chapter inside and out.

And the book doesn't end when the drawing is done. You'll also learn how to find a publisher for your graphic novel, or even how to publish it yourself and get it into the hands of readers. (Getting the readers to actually open the book and read it once it's in their hands is up to you, although if there's enough demand we'll be glad to write *The Complete Idiot's Guide To Getting People to Open Your Graphic Novel and Start Reading It*.)

What the Book Will Not Do

There are plenty of things that this book will not and cannot do. The biggest thing is that this book cannot be a general how-to-draw book. Drawing is a huge topic and there are far too many different aspects to it to cover here. There are plenty of classes and books out there to teach you drawing, and Steve will even clue you in on some of his favorite books. The drawing parts of this book will teach you the special aspects of drawing that are unique to comics. You won't see stuff here on how to draw the human hand, but you will see things on how to make sure your characters are consistent from panel to panel (always with the same number of hands!) and how to tell the story through your drawings.

Similarly, when it comes to doing electronic production of comics, we'll be suggesting some programs, but there's no way we can teach you all about those programs. If you look around the bookstore or library, you'll see big thick books on each of these computer programs, many of them as thick as a phone book (and some no more exciting—but some are *Idiot's Guides*, full of wisdom and knowledge and cartoons).

Tools, Not Rules

We'll show you ways to create graphic novels. That doesn't mean that we'll be showing you the right way. Of course I don't mean we'll show you the wrong way, either. Creating graphic novels is a creative experience, which means that there isn't just one right way to do anything. We'll show you ways that work, usually the most common ways, and some interesting things we've tried. Don't let that limit you! Most people draw their graphic novels with pencils then go over it with pen and ink, but if you want to try doing one in crayon, go for it!

Think of this book as a toolbox. Each suggestion we make is a tool you can use if you want, but no one way is right for every creator and every project. Some suggestions will be flathead screwdrivers, good for almost every project, while others are size 15 Torx drivers, which you may never use (but which are still good to have around). People who tell you there is only one right way of doing things should be ignored, unless they're paying for the work.

Acknowledgments

The authors would like to show our appreciation to colorist extraordinaire Tom Luth for sharing his expertise on coloring. We'd also like to thank the mighty Harris Miller for handling the business end of the book, and the many fine folks at Alpha—Mikal Belicove, Jennifer Moore, Billy Fields, Susan Aufheimer, Trina Wurst, Robin Simon, and all the various other magical penguins in the great mystical Penguin Group—for their hard work in putting this book together and the patience they showed in dealing with our struggles to make this the finest book possible. Finally, we'd like to invent a delicious cruelty-free, chemical-free, calorie-free cheeseburger and live in luxury off of the patent rights. We really would.

Trademarks

All terms mentioned in this book that are known to be or are suspected of being trademarks or service marks have been appropriately capitalized. Alpha Books and Penguin Group (USA) Inc. cannot attest to the accuracy of this information. Use of a term in this book should not be regarded as affecting the validity of any trademark or service mark.

Part 1

Planning Your Novel

Graphic novels don't happen by accident. Oh, every once in a while you'll be carrying a bucket of ink, accidentally trip over a ream of paper left lying about, and find yourself facing an 88-page coming-of-age tale about a young turtle with superpowers. But you can't count on that.

In this part of the book, you'll read about the current state of graphic novels, what you can do with them, and why you would want to make one. After considering your goals, you get suggestions on figuring out what parts of the work you want to do and finding out how to locate and identify collaborators for the bits you don't want to do. And then there's the big question: What kind of graphic novel do you want to do? And what superpowers will your turtle have?

The Novel World of Graphic Novels

In This Chapter

◆ What is all this graphic novel nonsense anyway?

◆ Where did graphic novels come from?

◆ Where are graphic novels going?

The concept of *graphic novels* has taken the world by storm. Suddenly, if you read the hipster magazines, they're all talking about graphic novels. If you listen to public radio, they're interviewing the creators of graphic novels. And if you watch *The Brady Bunch*, they're talking about Jan getting hit in the nose with a football, which proves it's a rerun because if it were a new show, she'd be hit in the nose with a graphic novel!

In fact, the graphic novel is now treated as something so special, so magical, so wonderful that you'd think there must be some sort of special magic pixies who create them. That's not true. I'm Nat, I'm a graphic novel writer, and I'm here to tell you that graphic novels can be created by ordinary pixies just like you and me. This book is here to show you how.

What's a Graphic Novel? (The Short Answer)

A *graphic novel* is a comics project of substantial length that is designed to be understood as a single work.

That may sound like a simple explanation. After I tell you a bit about why people do graphic novels and where they come from, you'll see that there are actually a few twists in that explanation, so I'll answer the question "What is a graphic novel?" again, toward the end of the chapter.

Why a Graphic Novel

If you've got a story to tell, there are plenty of ways you can tell it. You can write a novel, make a movie, spin the story in a song, stage a play, make a TV show, or even dance it as a New Age cutting-edge hula. Why choose the graphic novel form?

Speaking for Yourself

A graphic novel lets you put forth a very personal vision. Many graphic novels are the work of a single person, and even those that are created by collaboration usually involve a small, tight team of people, generally no more than are in a good rock band.

The One-Man Interman

For an example of what one person can do, check out *The Interman*, a full-color action spy graphic novel, totally created and published by one person, Jeff Parker. If this tale ever gets turned into a movie, they'll need more than one person just to dice the tomatoes for the crew's salad.

If you want to tell a story visually, that's about as tight a team as you can get. In contrast, putting on a play takes about as many people as a big band. Making a TV show takes about as many people as a marching band. To make a major motion picture, you can expect to involve as many people in a band of thousands (woodwinds included). And the more people who become involved, the less likely the work will have anyone's personal vision, much less yours.

Speaking to Everyone

One of the great things about the graphic novel form is that it's very immediate. You could write a prose novel and spend paragraph after paragraph describing exactly what a certain item looks like, and still not be sure that the reader is envisioning the same thing you are.

With a graphic novel, you convey that image instantly. A clear drawing makes certain that you and reader are both seeing the same thing.

In fact, most graphic novels communicate so much by image that you can follow much of what's going on even when it's written in a foreign language. You may not understand what everyone's saying to each other, but the places, actions, and facial expressions will tell most of the tale.

Shopping for a Shop

To find a comic shop near you that might carry the graphic novels discussed here, call the Comic Shop Locator Service at 1-888-COMIC-BOOK. That actually reaches the same information as 1-888-BOOGA-BOOGA.

Going, Going, Gon

Check out any volume of the *Gon* series to see visual storytelling at its purest. These tales about a small dinosaur holding his own against the fierce animal kingdom may not be realistic, but they do follow reality in one way: Animals don't talk. There are no dialog and no sound effects within the stories, so you can read the original Japanese printings as easily as the English-language editions.

Speaking to Just One Person

Graphic novels let you bare your soul in ways that can be tough in other visual forms. Plays and movies are watched by theaters filled with people, and TV shows are watched by families together, so any emotions you choose to convey and any emotions that you bring out in your audience have to be ones that can be shared with the group. In some ways, this can limit the exploration of uncomfortable topics. If you make a movie entitled *My Cruel High School Days*, the guy watching a movie with his date will be concerned not only about how he feels about the story, but how his date might react to the emotion he's showing. If he laughs at the hero's suffering, he's afraid he'll be seen as cruel; if he cries, he's afraid he'll be seen as a wuss. The only emotions he feels free to feel are the emotions his date shares, the emotions that everyone in the theater shares.

Ah, but make *My Cruel High School Days* a graphic novel and it will have no such public audience. It may be read by hundreds of thousands of people, but they're each reading it one at a time. Now the guy can laugh or cry however he sees fit, because he's not sharing the experience. It's an intimate sharing between the creator and the reader. Just don't let his date find out about that intimacy!

Awkward but with Great Potential

Ariel Schrag has created an impressive series of expressive, emotional autobiographical graphic novels about her high school years. The amazing thing is that she started creating them while she was still in high school, so the work is fresh, honest, and not tinged by the extremes of nostalgia. The first book, *Awkward,* has some fairly crude storytelling. The second book, *Definition,* has a deceptively crude surface style that richly conveys emotions, a style that carries into *Potential* and beyond, as you can see in this example from her fourth graphic novel *Likewise.* Warning: These books do contain frank visual depiction of teenage sexuality which may make some folks uncomfortable.

The graphic novelist at work, from Likewise.

©2003, Ariel Schrag.

As Aggressive as You Want

A graphic novel need not be quiet and intimate. It can be huge. It can be explosive and dynamic. It can burst out in ways that other things don't dare to.

These days, filmmakers can do just about anything. If they need to show a bunny rabbit transforming into a Sherman tank, they can. However, that shot will eat up a half million dollars of the budget. As such, the fancy things are limited, or are set aside for movies that are about little more than special effects.

Ah, but for the graphic novelist, turning a rabbit into a tank is not only possible, but it takes up roughly the same amount of effort as showing someone drinking coffee. You may be limited by your imagination, or limited by your drawing skills, but you aren't apt to be limited in terms of how many sets you can use or how many special effects you have.

The only greater freedom is being a graphic novel writer working in collaboration with an artist. Then you can write that in one panel 50 rabbits turn into 50 different types of tanks. It takes you only 10 seconds to put that in your script, but the artist might spend hours creating the image, all the while thanking you in terms that would make a sailor blush.

As Long as You Want

The graphic novel grew out of the comic book, which grew out of the comic strip, but the graphic novel is far more free-form. You don't have to tell gags four panels at a time, or get a story wrapped up in the 22 pages of a typical-length comic book. In recent years comic books have tended to tell longer, serialized stories, but even so the tales have to be broken up into 22-page chapters. Trying to tell a long story with those limitations can be like trying to rewrite *Moby Dick* as a series of limericks.

> Call me, let's say, Ishmael
>
> My job is hunting the whale
>
> To capture his skull
>
> And his body in full …
>
> But I'm getting ahead on this tale.

Sure, it's fun to try, but it's imposing an unneeded and often damaging rhythm on the work.

A graphic novel can be 48 little pages or 480 oversized pages—whatever you need to tell the tale you want and tell it well. That can change not only what story you tell but also how you tell it. You can rush through unimportant scenes, such as where the hero eats salad. You can linger slowly on scenes that you think are vital, say, the ones in which the hero eats ice cream.

Growing the Graphic Novel

Graphic novels may have become popular overnight, but they weren't invented overnight. Graphic scientists with beakers full of words and pictures spent decades mixing and blending things to scientific perfection …

No, wait, that doesn't make any sense. But they did come from somewhere.

The Emergence of Comics

In the beginning was the newspaper comic strip. Oh, people were telling stories using *sequential art* for centuries before there were newspapers, painting them on walls and weaving them as tapestries, but the newspaper comic strip was really where it became a mass medium, a way of telling tales to thousands of folks.

Sequential Art

Comics creative legend Will Eisner has promoted the term **sequential art** to describe any series of images that are supposed to be viewed in a specific order to communicate information. It's a fancy term, but it covers the entire technique of putting images together, whether it's a series of drawings or photos or even related sculpture. The comics form is specifically sequential art made up of drawings.

Comic Books

The term "comic strip" made at least some sense at first: "comic" meant "humorous", as the early ones were humorous in nature; and "strip" referred to the strip of paper that the series of images were printed on. But **comic books** always had adventure stories in them as well as comical ones, and they were magazines and pamphlets rather than books. Might as well have called them "fragrant avocados".

The comic strip was a big hit and sold a lot of newspapers. A wise man by the name of Max Gaines realized that people might want to read all those fine Sunday funnies without having to get weighted down with news, sports, and all those other noncomics things that infest the papers. In 1934, he began putting out little full-color magazines that were nothing but newspaper comic strips, and these sold in droves. They also sold in stores and newsstands, but mostly they sold in droves.

In fact, these newfangled *comic books* were so popular that there weren't enough comic strips to fill them. So new stories were crafted to fill the demand, and the original comic book story was born. Many imitated the popular comic strips of the day but told longer stories over several pages without the daily or weekly breaks built into the comic strip.

In 1937, the comic book stepped out from behind the shadow of comic strips. Super-man not only brought the comic book its first original breakout character, but it was in a genre that wasn't stolen from anywhere else. The costumed superhero wasn't to be found in the newspaper or on the silver screen, although they would be quick to imitate what the comic book brought us. And while the ensuing years would see arguments over whether the comic book was to blame for illiteracy and juvenile delinquency, no one argued that they didn't have an effect on the culture.

The Graphic Novel Overseas

Meanwhile, in Europe the comics were taking a different direction. While both American and European adventure comic strips often ran long storylines, the European strips were being collected into book volumes. These books were kept in print, rather than the short lives of the American comic books. Generation after generation could discover the tales of Belgian hero, Tintin.

These reprint albums became more important than the original newspaper or magazine printings, and the stories were designed for the albums. This sometimes left the original appearances hard to follow, because each had only a snippet of a story. It's like picking up a prose novel you've never read before and reading two pages in the middle—you'll just find it confusing.

Comics creators in the United States would see these graphic albums and become envious. They wanted the opportunity to have their work attractively presented, to tell full tales, and to get the sort of sales and respect that the European cartoonists were getting.

Tintin Double-Double

The Tintin albums *Cigars of the Pharaoh* and *The Blue Lotus* form one two-part adventure, considered to be a turning point in the Tintin series.

"Graphic Novel" Is Coined

It took a long time for the American creators to get their wish. Although there would be individual experiments with original book-length comics stories going back to even before the invention of the comic book, these were always just individual attempts, with a book here and a book there. It was never part of a movement, never had a common name, and really never had much impact in the marketplace.

In the 1970s, the term "graphic novel" began to crop up in American comic book circles, although there are arguments between comics historians about just who it was that coined the term. And works started cropping up that looked like what we consider graphic novels, although comics historians argue about which is the first one that truly qualifies as being called a graphic novel. The moral? Don't spend time talking to comics historians. They spend most of *their* time arguing.

There is one thing that most historians agree on, and that is which graphic novel really got the ball rolling. *A Contract with God and Other Tenement Stories* was created by Will Eisner in 1978, putting Will Eisner on the cutting edge of comics. And that's very funny, but only if you know Will Eisner.

You see, Will Eisner wasn't some young creative soul full of new ideas, breaking all the rules because he didn't know any better. He was in his sixties when the book was released, and he'd been working in the comics form for over four decades. He'd been on the cutting edge back in the 1940s, when he created a comic book insert for newspapers featuring his detective

A Contract Worth Accepting

A Contract with God is still in print, and still well worth reading. It tells four tales of Jewish tenement life in 1930s New York.

superhero The Spirit. In finely crafted short stories, he was reinventing what could be done with the layout of the page and the design of the panels.

Nowadays, Will is well into his eighties. While he may not be quite on the cutting edge any more, he's still doing a fine job creating new graphic novels. And when we ask him what he's going to do when he grows up and gets over comics, he just smiles slyly.

The Slow Growth

After *A Contract with God*, graphic novels were going to be the next big thing. And for a long time, that's what they were—the next big thing, but never the current big thing. There would be a big success here and a big success there, always promising that on-going mainstream acceptance was just around the corner. Somehow, however, the form never seemed to get around that corner. What looked like a corner up ahead always proved to be someone's driveway.

The first shouts of "we made it!" came the first time a graphic novel hit *The New York Times* best-seller list. It wasn't the pure, original work that some might have hoped for. Instead, it was the graphic novel adaptation of the movie *Alien*. In the hands of the master writer Archie Goodwin and the talented artist Walter Simonson, it was probably the best adaptation of a movie that had ever been done in comics form. Publishers started putting out more graphic novels, including movie and science fiction novel adaptations, but none of them saw nearly the success of *Alien*.

Marvel Comics and DC Comics, the two major superhero comics publishers, both announced graphic novel lines. These were short works by today's standards, 48 to 64 pages. Marvel launched their line by killing off one of their characters in *The Death of Captain Marvel*. When some of the art for the book was lost in the mail, the release had to be rescheduled, leading to the unlikely headline "Death of Captain Marvel Delayed Due to Accident."

The graphic novel lines from these superhero publishers often showed more effort and more mature subject matter than the typical comic books at the time, and they were magazine size to boot. Still, people frequently saw them as merely twice as many pages as a normal comic for ten times the price. While some of these books did well in the comic book stores, neither publisher's books did well in the bookstores. In fact, they were so thin that they were often hard to find even in those bookstores that did stock them, because their spines took up almost no space on the shelf. It was like looking for a needle in a stack of bricks.

Comics publishers found more success with *miniseries*, comic books that were meant to run a fixed number of issues, rather than running on forever. Over the course of a miniseries, which could run anywhere from 2 to 20 issues, a single story would be told. Often the story from a miniseries would then be collected into a single book, and some of these collections did quite well in bookstores. Most notable among these collections were the following titles:

- *Batman: The Dark Knight Returns* **by Frank Miller.** The author delved into the future to tell the final story of The Batman. Originally published as four extra-thick issues.

- *Watchmen* **by Alan Moore and Dave Gibbons.** A 12-issue miniseries examining superheroes from a different angle.

- *ElfQuest* **by Wendy and Richard Pini.** Twenty magazine-sized issues of fine fantasy stories collected into four graphic novels.

All of these were successful not only at original release, but have been kept in print for years. Suddenly, the folks crafting the comic book stories had an excuse to take extra time making their work special, since now it could maybe keep making them money for many years to come. Comics creators like money, because it can be exchanged for action figures and Junior Mints.

The next big generally visible hit was *Maus*, Art Spiegelman spinning the true story of his father's experience as a European Jew during World War II. Originally serialized in the alternative/experimental comics magazine *Raw*, the book collection hit the book world by storm, drawing rave reviews and winning a Pulitzer Prize. Longing for both the sales and respect that *Maus* achieved, mainstream book publishers wanted in on the graphic novel craze in the worst way. And the worst way is just what they achieved, releasing mostly lackluster attempts at high art by folks with no comics experience. The anticipated graphic novel explosion was quieter than a Rice Krispy in a dry bowl.

The Title Wave

As the twentieth century faded away and the twenty-first century zoomed in to take its place, the number and popularity of graphic novels finally took off. This was the result of several different forces at work simultaneously:

- Specialty publishers like Top Shelf, Alternative Comics, and AiT/Planet Lar arose to produce more original literary graphic novels.

- Neil Gaiman's *Sandman* series became a hit in the bookstores, selling far more copies collected as graphic novels than it had sold in comic book form. This led the color comics publishers to start designing more comics with the book collections in mind. Sometimes, the individual issues made lousy reading by themselves, but they would work well as a chapter in a larger book.

Manga

In Japan, **manga** means simply "comics," no matter where they come from. In English, the term is used primarily for Japanese comics. Sometimes it's used for comics from other areas of Asia, or comics from anywhere drawn in a Japanese style.

- Lots of comics were turned into movies, whether superhero fare like *X-Men* and *Spider-Man* or more alternative works like *Ghost World* and *From Hell*. Mainstream bookstores wanted to carry graphic novels related to these films, as well as the graphic novels that might become the next Hollywood hit.

- *Manga*, Japanese comics, became popular with people who weren't reading American comics. Because Japan has a long tradition of longer comics stories, these works became most popular in book form.

- Some of the books—not all, but definitely some—were darned good.

How Big Is Big?

The graphic novel business is like the Hulk, seeming nerdish and unimportant most of the time, and then suddenly getting fiercely large and impressive. The only difference is that the Hulk gets large when you make him angry, and the graphic novel business gets big when you make it money. Oh, and the graphic novel business doesn't wear purple pants.

Graphic Novels Today: The Current Market

In 2002, American consumers (that's business talk for "human beings") spent an estimated $100 million on original graphic novels and book collections of comic books. Half of this money was spent in bookstores, while the other half was spent in comic book shops. That's just one small part of the bigger graphic novel picture, because graphic novels are shipped around the world, translated into other languages, and often generate additional money from being licensed to Hollywood. It also doesn't include the money spent on the individual issues that are later collected into book form, which in many cases adds up to more money than is spent on the collections.

Graphic Novels Next Tuesday: The Future Market

The future of the graphic novel market looks quite sunny. Graphic novels are becoming more popular even as sales of most books are shrinking. Bookstores, eager to latch onto anything that can sell, are devoting ever more space to graphic novels. Mainstream publishers also want to give the graphic novel business another try. When they do, they will come equipped with business resources and mainstream selling acumen that traditional comics publishers often lack.

As graphic novels become a standard part of pop culture, they're popping up in new and varied venues. If you haven't seen graphic novels in your local video store yet, you soon will. Then you'll start noticing them at the CD shop. Next thing you know, they'll be skulking behind the bushes, waiting to jump out at you, and there will be no way to escape ...

What's a Graphic Novel? (The Long Answer)

It's all well and good to say that graphic novels are becoming popular, but what is a graphic novel? With a name like graphic novel, you can be pretty sure that it isn't a liverwurst-filled donut, but you might also be pretty sure that it isn't something it actually is.

Not So Novel After All

The immediate assumption is that a graphic novel is a graphic form of a novel, but that's too limiting. Just as a comic book doesn't have to be a book, a graphic novel doesn't have to be a novel. A prose version of *A Contract with God*, the book that popularized the term "graphic novel," wouldn't count as a novel. It would be a book of related short stories.

Maus, on the other hand, is a single long work, but it wouldn't count as a novel either. Despite the fact that the characters are drawn as cats, mice, and other animals, the story is true, and novels are fiction.

And still, there's more to a graphic novel than being a bunch of comics in a single book. A graphic novel is still a graphic novel when it's in serial form.

If Not, Then What?

A graphic novel is a comics project of substantial length that is designed to be understood as a single work. Fiction, nonfiction—even a comics format cookbook—would count as a graphic novel.

That doesn't mean that every book of comics counts as a graphic novel. For example, *It's A Dog's Life, Snoopy*, a collection of a year's worth of the Peanuts comic strip, is not a graphic novel, because those strips weren't meant to be a single work. Nor is *The Greatest Batman Stories Ever Told*, although bookstores won't hesitate to put it in the graphic novel section.

So all questions are answered, right? Sure, if no troublemaker pops up and asks "what counts as comics?" Do you need to have traditional word balloons for speech? Does it count as comics if there's only one panel per page? What about if you use photographs rather than drawing? That's a whole 'nother can of worms, and the answer is: It doesn't matter. If there's something you want to create, do it! Let someone else worry about whether to call it a "graphic novel" or a "chocolate orangutan" or anything else!

The Least You Need to Know

◆ A graphic novel is a long comics work intended to be seen as a single unit.

◆ Graphic novels really got rolling as an artistic movement in the 1970s, and had unsteady but ongoing growth as a business success ever since.

◆ Graphic novels are an integral part of pop culture, and the future for them looks bright.

Chapter 2

What's Your Goal?

In This Chapter

- ◆ Why are you doing a graphic novel?
- ◆ How much of it should you do yourself?
- ◆ Should you make one big graphic novel or a bunch of comic books?

You want to make a graphic novel. You know that, I (Nat, the graphic novel-writing pudding-lovin' co-writer of this book) know that. Otherwise, you wouldn't have bought this book at the store, or borrowed it from the library, or stolen it from that guy on the bus. But understanding *why* you want to make a graphic novel and *what aspect* of creating a graphic novel interests you can be key in reaching your goals. You can't start to reach your goals until you know what those goals are.

In this chapter, I show you a number of things to think about in coming up with your goals. Many of these things may seem glaringly obvious. Obvious things are usually the most important.

For Money or for the Monet

The key question in setting your goals is to figure out whether your main goal is to make a living, maybe even make a killing, or whether it's to make art.

Ideally, almost everyone wants both. They want to be able to spend their days chronicling the dark pain they feel within, then spend their nights driving Ferraris and eating caviar. We'd all like to have everything, but this is a good time to separate things you'd merely like to have from those things you really want.

Money Is Far from Certain

If you look at any popular art form, you can point to a number of huge successes. In acting, for example, you can talk about Tom Cruise, Jim Carrey, Halle Berry, and other folks who make millions per movie and can pick and choose their films. Past that, you can see that there are thousands of people who aren't superstars but who make a living from acting, the sort of people you see playing waiters who serve Tom Cruise and Halle Berry. Such folks aren't stars, but they are working actors, and they may be making an okay living or just squeaking buy.

But what you don't see is that for every working actor there are plenty of would-be working actors who really are waiters. Most of the people who set out to be actors never really make a living at it.

The same thing is true of graphic novelists and the comics arts in general. There are some people who make millions doing such work, although even the top ones don't make anywhere near what the superstar actors make. Then there is a larger base of people who make an income, and may make a living, but don't make a killing. Beyond that is a very large group that wants to be making an income but isn't. This includes not only the would-be graphic novelists, but also the used-to-bes, folks whose style or efforts fell out of fashion for some reason.

And the sad truth is that the difference between the financially successful and the unsuccessful creators can't simply be chalked up to talent or quality of ideas. While being a talented creator and having good ideas will obviously help you succeed, and being able to promote yourself and your work will help immensely, luck also plays heavily into the results.

Helping Our History

A little karma can go a long way. If you want to help creators from the past who have fallen on hard times, surf over to www.actorcomicfund.org for a charity that helps such creators.

A large portion of even the folks working in the graphic novel field cannot count on it for their primary source of income. When you see Jane Graphic novelist signing autographs at a comics convention, it's easy to assume she is well-known to the world at large and generally successful. You don't see what the autographing Jane is doing the next day: signing a credit card slip for a quart of milk because she's out of cash.

Art Is a Sure Bet

If your goal is to express yourself, to get your ideas out, and to exercise your creative soul, you're almost certain to reach your goal. If your dream is to get it down on paper, then the only thing that can stop you is the fiendish paper-swiping aliens from Omicron-7.

That's the good news. The bad news is that even striving to be an artist can be a struggle. If you're not making your money from doing comics, you're likely to spend a lot of your time and energy making money from something else. Time becomes a scarce. When you're catching a few hours here, a few hours there to work on your graphic novel, you lose momentum.

Don't let that worry you too much. Many creators, particularly younger ones, manage to do amazing work in their spare hours. It becomes a bit harder as you get older, particularly as you build a family. But hey, the kids have bedtimes and you don't!

A Comic a Day

There is no better way to see the value of creative momentum than to look at some 24-hour comics, which are 24-page stories completely written and drawn in 24 consecutive hours. It's crazy, but it works. The book *24 Hour Comics* offers nine good examples of these works, edited by the experiment's inventor Scott McCloud.

Even so, working toward artistic greatness is often frustrating. Your work won't be perfect. I don't mean that it won't be perfect at first, I mean that it will *never* be perfect. Think of the best graphic novel you've ever read. I guarantee that not only isn't it perfect, but that the creator knew that it wasn't perfect, and could list a dozen things that were wrong with it quicker than you could name the handsomest five of the Seven Dwarfs.

In fact, it's worse than that. The moment you've completed the graphic novel, you won't be able to see the hundred good things you achieved from your list of 103 Good Things I Want in This Graphic Novel. Anyone who reads it will be able to see the 100 Good Things, but all you'll see are your 3 Failures.

So if you strive for art, you will achieve art. You just may not always be happy about it.

Dealing with the Difference

Years later, you'll be able to see all the good things you achieved in your graphic novel rather than all the things you failed to do. Until then, focus on the value of learning. The good thing about seeing your mistakes and weaknesses is that they give you the chance to improve. On your next graphic novel, you won't make the same mistakes. You'll find a whole different set of mistakes to make!

Counterfeiter's Truth: Money Can Be Art

There are ways to make graphic novels that are more oriented to creating art, and ways that work better for earning money, but money and art are not opposites. It's easy to look at someone's little autobiography comics and say "that's art," then look at *Superhero/Supervillain Punch-Out Volume 2* and say "that's done for money," but those two things aren't as distinct as it might at first appear.

Superhero Superart

Want a clear example that superheroes and art are not mutually exclusive? Try *Marvels* by Kurt Busiek and Alex Ross. This is a book that is grounded firmly in the Marvel superhero universe, embracing all sorts of details about the history of Spider-Man, the Fantastic Four, and the rest. Yet within that, writer Busiek spins a tale about how average people get carried along through changing times and forces beyond their control. Artist Ross's hyperrealism humanizes the superhero to a remarkable degree. You'll never wonder again whether superhero outfits ever wrinkle.

Superhero works may be commercially popular, but even when they're put out by the most disinterested hack they can't help but express something. In the hands of someone who loves superheroes or is generally inspired by the genre, superheroes can be exciting, creative, personal, and even high art. But if you want to do superheroes, you already know that.

Hero-less Hollywood Hopes

Much of the biggest money in the graphic novel business comes from licensing the story for a movie. Cut a movie deal and you get bucks from the movie company plus bucks from increased sales of your book. It's easy to look at the movies and assume that the real Hollywood money comes from making the next generic superhero. However, take a closer look and you'll notice that few of the major superhero movies are based on *new* superheroes. Everything but *Spawn*, *The Crow*, and *Mystery Men* has been based on decades-old heroes. It's too late to invent an old hero, unless you also invent a time machine.

The newer creations Hollywood snaps up are far more eclectic in nature. *Ghost World* was a slice-of-life comic, *The Road to Perdition* and *From Hell* both gritty historically inspired dramas, *Dark Town* (the source of the high-budget, low-audience *Monkeybone*) an offbeat romp of a graphic novel.

Perhaps the more surprising news is that doing comics that are primarily intended to be art can actually be quite profitable. Far too many folks spend their days trying to do work they believe is the source of the big money, turning out pale variations of existing successful work. Such works often fail to get published, much less become popular. Meanwhile, *Strangers in*

Paradise, an original romantic dramedy, has become a surprise success, and bookstores are having a hard time keeping up with the demand for *Jimmy Corrigan*, a dark, aesthetically cold but emotionally searing tale.

For Yourself or an Audience?

If you're doing a graphic novel primarily for the money, attracting a big audience is inherently part of your goal. That's one question you don't have to worry about. Go, get a sugary snack, and come back in time for the next part of this chapter.

If your goal is artistic, then the question becomes more difficult. Is your goal to tell the story? Or is it to have the story be read by someone else? Those may sound like the same thing, but they're very different. Emily Dickinson needed to write her poems, but when they were finished she'd satisfied her artistic itch and then just stuck them in a drawer. The poems were art whether anyone saw them or not. On the other hand, stand-up comedians need audiences. The true stand-up comedy art relies not on revealing what bugs you about shoelaces, but from the effect that the revelation has on the audience.

So if you do your graphic novel in a forest, and there's no one around to see it, is it *art?* That's your choice.

It's an important choice to make, because other decisions will be based on it. For example, let's say you're good at writing and creating concepts, but a poor illustrator. If your goal is expressing yourself, then you'll still want to illustrate your own work. On the other hand, having a good illustrator not only draws more readers to your work, it helps them understand the work. It does you no good to create a love scene if the readers squint at it and ask "why is that fuzzy lump proclaiming love to that strange-looking tree?"

Art _____

Art is anything you create with the intention of creating art.

Lone Hero or Superteam?

The question of whether to go it alone or to work with others is a tricky one. The common practice of publishing a new issue in a comic book series every month has really encouraged people to work collaboratively. It's hard for one person to write and do all the artwork on more than 20 pages every month, month in and month out. By having several people working on a different part of the same story, the deadline is easier to achieve. Besides, if Joe Pencilguy had to skip drawing an issue of *The Amazing Adjective*, Chris Newcomer could be brought in without the next issue seeming radically different.

Graphic novels don't have that same monthly deadline problem. This makes it far more possible for one person to do all the work. But just because it's possible doesn't mean that you have to work that way.

Working solo means that you get a pure vision on the page. This can be a wonderful thing. On the other hand, working in collaboration means that everyone can do what they're best at and avoid what they're bad at. A collaborative work can have a synergy, creating a work that is stronger than the individual contributions.

Sinister Synergies

Collaborators who think very similarly can create synergies, but pairings of people who work differently sometimes create quite well-rounded work. *The Fantastic Four, The Incredible Hulk,* and *The X-Men* were all created by the same main team. Jack Kirby is known for his broad and kinetic action pieces, while Stan Lee is known for his very human character dialog. Together, they created works that were broad, kinetic, *and* human all at once.

Knowing Thyself

Are you a collaborator? Do you play well with others, or do you find yourself constantly trying to be the boss in any situation? Worse yet, do you deal with conflict simply by shutting down your own concerns and giving in to others, silently building your resentment until you snap and find yourself running naked through the streets throwing marshmallows at police cars?

Steve Sez: Be Up Front

Type-A control freaks and passive-aggressive people can still engage in productive collaboration if they know themselves well enough to tell their collaborator about their tendencies up front. Working with an editor as intermediary and referee can help, too.

Collaborating isn't for everyone. If you're apt to drive yourself up the wall or drive your collaborators through the wall, then you probably shouldn't be driving at all. That doesn't mean that you can't get help with individual aspects of the work, but you should probably handle most of the major aspects of writing and drawing yourself. This will save your sanity and keep you from wasting perfectly good marshmallows.

Weaknesses? Moi?

When I was a kid, I just knew I could do *anything*. Riding a bike simply involved moving your legs real fast. Shooting baskets meant thrusting the ball in the right direction. Playing the piano was nothing more than pushing down on the keys. Who couldn't do these things?

Many skinned knees, missed baskets, and songs that sounded like a cat got on the keyboard taught me that things were harder than they looked. Doing graphic novels is a lot like that. Although most people don't just assume they can draw, many assume they can write good stories, or do readable lettering, or handle other aspects of graphic novel creation that they've never tried.

Don't assume that. Certainly, before you start doing a long work, try doing a very short one, a story a few pages long, and start discovering where your strengths and weaknesses lay.

Little No-No in Blunderland

The clearest example of a work that is impaired by someone not recognizing his weakness is an old newspaper comic strip by Winsor McCay. Look at any of the available collections of his *Little Nemo in Slumberland*, a classic dream series. You'll see a work that is reasonably written, amazingly drawn, gorgeously colored, and looks like it was lettered by an inept six-year-old. The randomly shaped word balloons with twisted, tilted writing don't ruin the work, but they do detract from the reading experience.

The bad news is that you will have weaknesses. The good news is that you can conquer them, at least to some degree. I've learned to ride a bike, and if you want to spend the time, you can improve on almost any of your weakness if it's important enough to you.

But you don't have to. If I spent years, I could possibly learn to draw well enough to craft a readable comic, but I'd rather spend my time writing and working with artists who are more talented than I could ever be.

Time Constraints

The more work you do yourself, the longer it takes. If you're *serializing* your graphic novel, then you'll have deadlines to meet along the way. Even if you're not serializing and don't have any deadlines, you do want to get the book done eventually, particularly if you're not getting paid until the work is complete.

By collaborating, you're doing a smaller portion of the work, and the graphic novel gets completed more quickly. Even if you're not as satisfied working with others, you will get that very real satisfaction that comes from having a work completed and released.

Collaborating doesn't always speed things up as much as you'd like. There's always a bit of time lost in finding collaborators and in communicating back and forth with them. But sometimes, collaboration can be incredibly efficient. If you're apt to spend more time figuring out what to draw than actually drawing it, hooking up with a fast writer can turn you into one speedy artist.

Serializing

Serializing means releasing your story in sections. Many graphic novels are serialized in individual comics before being collected into a single volume.

Personal Splendor

Collaborative works can still be quite personal. Consider Harvey Pekar, famed for his comics autobiography. Various artists have brought Harvey's scripts to life, ranging from *American Splendor* short stories drawn by underground master Robert Crumb to the stand-alone graphic novel *Our Cancer Year*, cowritten by Harvey's wife Joyce Brabner and drawn by Frank Stack.

Your Desires

What do you *want* to do? If you want to create a work that's all yours, then by all means do so. If you have broad ideas about what the story should be but don't want to get caught up in the details, find a writer who wants to share your vision and stick that person with the writing chores. And if you're bad at anatomy but love doing all the line work and cross-hatching, then you are an inker at heart and you should be proud of that.

This isn't to say that you will always get to do what you want, particularly if you want to make money. But look at it this way: The things you like are most likely the things you'll be good at, and the things you're good at are what you're most likely to make money at.

One Big Book or a Plethora of Pamphlets?

For some people, format is a big deal. Some dream of having a big thick real book. There's something about having a book on the shelf with your name on the spine that makes you feel like a legit author.

Other people grew up on comic book *pamphlets* and have a real love for the form. Sure, they'll be happy when a longer serialized story is collected into a book, but that's just something that comes afterward, a bonus on the tail end of the "real thing."

Going straight for the book format means a lot fewer compromises in the content, because you don't have to break it down into issue-length chapters. But if you're a procrastinator by nature, putting out a series of issues gives you deadlines that force you to get the work done. Deadlines help us get things done. Want proof? You wouldn't be holding this book in your hand right now if my editor hadn't imposed a deadline for it (a cruel and unusual one, I might add).

Pamphlet

Some comics fans use the term **pamphlet** to refer to the traditional staple-bound comic book, generally 24 to 48 pages long. Others feel the term denigrates the traditional comics printing format.

Issuing pamphlets can have other advantages as well. People read the work and give you feedback, some of which will be annoying and pointless, but some of which will be useful. There are often business advantages as well, but those I'll talk about in the more business-oriented portions of this book, all the way back in Part 5.

If you're working with a publisher, that publisher is apt to have views about what format is correct. You may have to compromise your goals, but you'll never reach them unless you have them in mind.

Don't Be a Goalie

Goals are guidelines. They can give your efforts direction and something to work toward. But goals aren't really what it's all about. Don't be so focused on your goals that you miss opportunities along the way. On your trek to the California (your goal), you still can't just drive by Abe's Alligator Petting Farm if you see it on your path. You might find that Abe's is really where you want to be. Even if you decide to keep going to California, at least you'll have learned things about petting alligators.

Steve Sez: A Philosophical Difference

The question of straying from one's goals is an area where the experiences of some writers and illustrators differ. Many artists (including me) have found that in the early days of one's career, tunnel vision is an extremely valuable trait. Writers can multitask much more effectively than artists can. Drawing comics means spending long hours at the board. For artists who work in a labor-intensive manner, even small distractions from a goal can mean big delays in ever achieving it.

The Least You Need to Know

◆ Thinking about your goals is the first step in working toward them.

◆ You can create graphic novels for commercial reasons or for artistic reasons—or, if you're lucky, both.

◆ Creating a graphic novel for the sake of creating it is different from creating a graphic novel to have people read it; both are viable goals.

◆ Collaborating has its pros and its cons. Whether you should collaborate depends on your attitude, personality, strengths, and desires.

◆ Creating a graphic novel for initial release in book form can minimize creative compromise; on the other hand, issuing the graphic novel as a series of comic book chapters can keep you motivated and build your audience.

◆ Aim for your goals, but don't miss the other opportunities that arise along the way.

Creating a Creative Team Creatively

In This Chapter

- ◆ Who makes up the creative team?
- ◆ How do you find creative teammates?
- ◆ How do you split the work and rewards?

If you want to create your graphic novel all by yourself, you'll want to skip this chapter about lining up other people to work with. Don't. I'm not saying this simply because I, Nat the writer guy, slaved over a hot laptop for hours to craft it and fill it with insight, pouring my creative soul into it. It actually might be useful. As you see all the little jobs that can be involved in creating a graphic novel, you might end up deciding that there are some small things that you'd rather leave to someone else.

Typical Titanic Team Members

There are many different ways of splitting up the work on a graphic novel. The comics field has been around long enough that certain standard categories have emerged. Even if you don't break the work up in traditional ways, knowing the names for the standard jobs can help you communicate with collaborators just what you're looking for.

Writer

When you tell someone that you write comics or graphic novels, about half the time the person you're talking to will say "oh, you put the words in the balloons?" When you start to tell them that you don't actually do that, that actually putting the words in the balloons is the job of the letterer, be prepared for a look of disinterest. In that person's eyes, you've gone from being someone who puts the words in balloons to someone who *doesn't even* put the words in balloons. It's the same disappointment that the secretary of state must get when someone realizes he's a secretary who doesn't even know shorthand.

But as a writer, I have to tell you that the writer is usually the key person in the graphic novel. Traditionally, the writer starts off the project. A writer comes up with the basic concept, and is in charge of developing the plot, the characters' attitudes and backgrounds, and coming up with the dialog that the letterer will later put in the balloons.

As you'll see in Part 2 of this book, there are a number of different ways for writers to go about this. Some projects are written with highly detailed scripts discussing everything that's in each panel. Others involve a far looser outline of the story, relying on the penciler to flesh out more of the storytelling.

Steve Sez: Writing with Pictures

Nat is correct that writing is the key part of the job, but in comics most of the content is communicated in the pictures. Stunts and gimmicks aside, no graphic novel, no matter how well written, can succeed without competent and appropriate illustration. Saying that the writer is the key person in creating a graphic novel is like saying that a man is the key component in creating a baby.

WHA...? **Layouts**

Layouts are loose sketches designating the placement of the panels and the figures within the panels of a page.

Penciler

The penciler is responsible for creating *layouts* of the page and then drawing in all the characters, settings, and objects in pencil. The penciler is considered to be the primary artist for the work, despite the fact that everything the penciler draws ends up getting covered over or erased.

Inker

An inker draws over the pencil drawing with ink. This is done because the light pencils don't reproduce very well, and besides the penciler is apt to leave all sorts of stray lines that shouldn't be reproduced. (Sometimes, the entire graphic novel shouldn't be reproduced, but that's a problem too big for an inker to fix!)

Inking is not merely tracing. The inker needs a great deal of control over pens or brushes in order to get the shape and width of line desired. Line width can be very important in creating depth on the page, and in making the figures seem lively. And where a penciler can shade things in with many shades of gray, the inker creates a work that is purely black and white. Instead of grays, the inker works in textures, *hatching*, *cross-hatching*, and *feathering* areas to create a sense of gray.

Then the inker erases all of the remaining visible pencil work, and chortles gleefully while doing so.

Hatching/ Cross-hatching/ Feathering

Hatching is drawing a pattern of thin lines to create a gray tone. When your hatch lines cross, you're **cross-hatching**. **Feathering** is hatching with lines that grow thicker as they reach areas that are supposed to look darker.

Letterer

The letterer draws all of the word balloons, thought balloons, and caption boxes, and writes the text into them. This may not sound like very special work, particularly in these days when the vast majority of the lettering is done via computer. You don't even need to have clear handwriting in order to be a good letterer.

There's more to lettering than just putting the words on the page. Letterers are often in charge of choosing where the word balloons go. Good balloon placement leads the eye naturally across the page, making it easy to follow the story. Badly placed word balloons can obscure the art and make it hard to tell who is speaking when. Imagine a scene where the Lovely Lara says "you're lying" and Villainous Vera replies "you're right!" In the hands of a bad letterer, Vera is saying Lara is right, and Lara calls her a liar for doing so!

Letterers also handle the sound effects lettering. Every *wham*, every *Ka-POW*, every *tic-tic-tic* and *EEEEEeeeeee!* has to be drawn in a way that's not only readable but looks like the sound. Signs and newspaper headlines are generally also the province of the letterer. Tattoos are generally left to the penciler.

He Can't Spell "Flag"

If you can find any of the *American Flagg!* graphic novels, you'll see examples of the art of lettering in full force. Depicting both the visual and audible noise of the cities of the future required letterer Ken Bruzenak to fill the pages with signs and effects lettering, lending the series an original and exciting look.

Steve Sez: A Balancing Act _____

An important part of the letterer's job is to make sure that none of the writer's deathless prose obscures anything important in the artist's immortal imagery. They can both make this job easier by being aware that the more space given to words, the less room there is for pictures, and vice versa. Or the letterer can letter really, really small, and if legibility begins to suffer then the publisher can arrange for the graphic novel to include a free magnifying glass or even a microscope, as needed.

Colorist

If you've ever opened a coloring book with a pile of crayons at your side, then you know the challenge that faces colorists. For color comics, they select and place the colors. Many of the modern colorists don't even bother trying to stay within the lines.

Modern coloring is done almost exclusively on computers. On a computer the colorist has thousands of different digital crayons and a wide array of special effects, include fades, glitters, and photographic backdrops. A colorist can turn an ordinary penguin standing on the snow into a glowing purple penguin standing on a picture of Winston Churchill.

Cover Artist

Some graphic novel artists are very good at storytelling, but poor at doing the sort of eye-catching cover picture that makes a reader grab the book off the store shelf and give it a look. An artist who can provide a special cover, such as a realistic painting or an energetic action shot, can help sell the book. Some readers complain when the cover artist is different from the interior artist, but they never seem to complain when prose novelists like Stephen King don't draw their own covers. Go figure.

 Paper Stock _____

Paper stock refers to the type of paper something is printed on. Different paper stocks vary in weight, color, brightness, thickness, texture, how well they hold ink, and cost.

Designer

Book designers are gaining a prominent place in the graphic novel field. The designer is responsible for the look of the parts of the book that aren't the story, such as the cover, the inside covers, perhaps a title page or table of contents. In some cases, a designer will be involved in selecting *paper stock* for the cover and interiors. A good designer helps the book appeal to likely audiences, integrating the attitude of the book into its appearance.

Editor/Proofreader/Sounding Board

Many new graphic novelists assume that an editor is someone you get saddled with when you have a publisher, an evil soul who wants to interfere with your creativity. Although there are certainly such editors (generally more incompetent than evil, although I have known a few who stink of brimstone) a good editor can make suggestions to help your graphic novel better reach the goal you set for it.

Many people don't want to work with a full editor, a title that suggests someone who gets to control the creative team. Even so, it's good to have someone with good language skills who will proofread the text. Otherwise, you're apt to end up with spelling errors—or even worse, spellling erorrs.

> **Steve Sez: Sez Who?**
>
> When you're drawing a tricky sequence, show the pencils to someone who doesn't know the story you're telling, and ask that person to tell you what is going on. Give no clues when you ask, and you'll get more useful feedback about what's clear and what isn't.

A friend whose taste you trust can make a good sounding board for your graphic novel. Your sounding board may catch stupid mistakes. ("In the first panel on this page, the girl has braids. In the second panel, the girl has a ponytail. And in the third panel, the pony has braids.") Having someone note things that don't make sense or don't feel right, or simply could be better, can be a great benefit. There's no limit to how many sounding boards you can have, and you don't have to follow every suggestion they make. A good rule of thumb: If you can't think of a reason why a suggestion is wrong, it's probably right.

> **Sounding Suspicious**
>
> Beware of sounding boards who seem more interested in suggesting good things that you can add to your story than in pointing out things that don't work. These people are exercising a desire to write, an understandable desire but one that cannot only be aggravating but can even harm your work. Trying to integrate ideas from someone else's vision can lend to a muddied graphic novel. If you want a sounding board, get a sounding board. If you want a cowriter, get a cowriter. If you want a donut, could you get me one, too?

Collaborate Uniquely, Like Others

Don't feel trapped by the standard way of working. The important thing is that you find a way that will let you put out the work you envision.

Many graphic novels have people wearing odd combinations of hats, people who get slashes in the middle of their job descriptions. I've seen such unlikely combinations as writer/colorist and letterer/editor. Using slash-folks can make your graphic novel creation go quicker/smoother.

But don't be afraid of breaking one job into several, if that will get the best results. When Sam Kieth started creating *The Maxx*, for example, he had a story to tell but wasn't confident in his dialog-writing capabilities. Sam plotted and drew the book, but brought William Messner-Loebs in to provide finished dialog, splitting the traditional writing effort. Some artists are quick at layouts and inks, but slow at the more detailed anatomical pencil rendering, so they bring in another artist to handle that stage of the art. Some comics studios have one artist who draws all the characters, another who just draws the vehicles, a third who just draws the settings, and a lazybones who just draws a paycheck.

Do what works for you. Avoid what doesn't.

Rating Goodness? Gracious!

When you search out collaborators, you're going to need to judge their abilities. If you're not used to looking at unfinished portions of comics work, you might find it hard to judge the individual components. Although part of the solution is simply to get used to seeing unfinished works, there are things you can look for to judge quality.

Good Writing

Writers should have a good understanding of how stories work. Comic book writers actually don't need to be grounded as well in English grammar as writers in other forms. After all, the plot and panel descriptions only have to be clear enough for the other members of the creative team to understand them. And dialog doesn't have to be grammatical, because people speaking are often ungrammatical. "I ain't gonna feed no ducks no donuts!" may make your old English teacher weep uncontrollably, but it's perfectly fine dialog.

Prospective writers should have a sample script. Read the script, and ask yourself the following questions:

Steve Sez: Well, Yeah, But ...

Keep in mind that poor grammar makes a poor impression on prospective publishers and distributors. If you can't write a cover letter or a paragraph of ad copy without making a mistake, you'd do well to take a couple of days to refresh your grasp of the basics.

◆ Is the story interesting?

◆ If the story uses existing characters, do they seem right? Superman acts differently from Spider-Man, and they both act differently from Reid Fleming, World's Toughest Milkman. If the character seems wrong or simply generic, that suggests the writer has a problem with characters.

◆ Can you picture the panels and pages in your mind? If you can't imagine what the panel looks like or how the page fits together, then the penciler won't be able to draw it.

◆ Can each panel's image be described with one central concept? If there's a panel where it's important that Wanda is punching Joan, Mathilda is feeding donuts to the ducks, and three suns are in the sky, there's a problem. Even if the artist puts all that in the panel, the reader will miss some of it.

◆ Does the dialog sound good when read out loud? That's a good way to catch clunky construction.

◆ Is there too much text on a single page?

◆ Are the pages stapled together with the highest-quality staples? How could you trust someone who uses second-rate staples? (This note brought to you by the Staple Advisory Board.)

Good Penciling

Penciling requires a broad range of drawing skills. You have to be a good visual storyteller, capable of communicating situation, action, and emotion clearly. You have to be good at rendering *everything*. To be a well-rounded penciler, you need a strong sense of anatomy. You need to be able to draw buildings. You need to be able to draw animals. You need to be able to draw a pizza-eating Martian driving a Studebaker, should the script call for it—and most of the best scripts do.

Proper penciling samples include several consecutive pages from a single story, and these should be in pencil form (unless you're looking for a single artist to handle both penciling and inking). General samples should include both action scenes and quieter dialog scenes, close ups and wide shots, *interiors* and *exteriors*. If the artist is looking for work in a particular genre, the samples should reflect that genre. Superhero samples should have superheroes as well as people not in costumes. Science fiction samples should have gadgets and space ships. Samples for a romance comic should have wide-eyed nurses with fiercely beating hearts.

When looking at pencil samples, ask if you can see a copy of the script the pages were done from. Some artists create samples without a script, which is less than ideal. Worse yet, some just copy a scene from an existing comic, which usually means that you're seeing the published comic's layouts rather than seeing the prospective artist's own talents.

Interiors/Exteriors

An **interior** is a shot inside a building, such as a scene of customers standing in line at the counter of a donut shop. An **exterior** is a scene not inside a building, such as a picture of the outside of the donut shop, with vicious ducks waiting to pounce on exiting customers.

WHA....?

Steve Sez: Hearts and Flowers

Gags aside, samples of a romance comic should show an ability to handle the details that drive romance stories: fashion, settings, and the nuances of facial expression and body language.

Don't Put Up with Pinups

Don't waste your time with would-be pencilers who show you just a single image per page. These folks may have had fun learning to render, but they're not showing you any story-telling capability. They don't know what they're doing.

Looking over the pencil samples, consider ...

♦ Is the drawing style attractive or interesting enough that people will want to look at it?

♦ Do the characters look consistent from panel to panel?

♦ Can you get a sense of the story just by looking at the pictures without any words?

♦ Has the artist left enough space to put in the word balloons and captions without covering over important parts of the art?

♦ Is the order of the panels clear?

♦ Does the art follow the sample script it was drawn from?

♦ Are the staples holding the pages together strong, or are they flimsy? Do you know how many people die each year from staple failures? Do ya? (If you do, please contact the Staple Advisory Board. They're quite curious about this.)

Good Inking

Proper inking samples include samples of inked pages as well as photocopies of the original pencils that were inked. That way, you can tell how well the inker captured the look of the work being inked. You don't want an inker casting aside what the penciler drew. Good inkers can sometimes save lousy pencils, but at this stage of the game you shouldn't be planning to have lousy pencils.

When looking at inking samples, ask yourself the following questions:

♦ Is it clear whether the pages were inked for color or for black-and-white publication? Pages meant for color should have plenty of open areas and little cross-hatching, while pages meant for black and white publication should have more solid blacks and shading. You definitely want to see samples that reflect how you're going to print.

♦ Do the foreground characters or the most important items in the panel clearly stand out?

♦ Do the pages look attractive?

♦ Are the panel borders clean and sharp?

♦ Are the staples holding the samples together certified to meet OSHA standards for purity? Many foreign-made staples contain up to 17 percent rat hairs.

Have anyone you consider a good inking candidate try inking a photocopied page of the penciler's pencils so you can see if the two artists' styles mesh. New inkers will probably do a sample page for free, particularly because they can then add this page to their samples. Established inkers may well ask to be paid for the samples, which is a fair request and worth doing if you want an established inker. Delusional inkers will want to be given a porcelain fish and a tube of toothpaste.

Good Lettering

Lettering samples should include examples of both standard balloon lettering and sound-effect lettering. Look at the balloons, too. If possible, you want to see an actual lettered page, so you can check balloon placement.

Top-notch letterers can also design new typefaces for special needs, so that your slavering beasts speak with dripping words, your robots talk digitally, and your crumperneous qualifackers speak crumperneously.

Don't Do Handwriting Analysis

Never judge letterers by their usual handwriting. I've had some of the best hand letterers in the business write down their addresses and phone numbers so I could call them later, but I never did reach them, because I couldn't read what they wrote down.

Good Coloring

A top-notch colorist will not only know how to use all sorts of fancy digital special effects but will also have the wisdom not to use them all. Lesser colorists create many garish, showy pages that interfere with the storytelling. Good colorists often choose a very limited pallet, and use the special effects when they will have a special effect.

Color printing is a lot more complex than black-and-white printing. Your project's colorist should have a good understanding of the printing process and the effect that his color choices and placement will have.

Make sure you get to see the color samples printed out, rather than seeing them on the computer screen. Someone who learned to color images for websites or videogames won't know about the complexities of the printing process. Use a colorist who doesn't have an understanding of printing and concepts like *trapping* and you're apt to get a fuzzy, smeary gap-filled mess. That's fine, of course, if your graphic novel is *Sherlock Holmes and the Strange Case of the Fuzzy, Smeary, Gap-Filled Mess*.

Trapping

Trapping is the technique of making color areas slightly larger than they ideally need to be, so that no gaps are left if printing plates don't quite line up. This is an example of the printing knowledge colorists need.

Working Well Together

In addition to artistic talent, you should make sure that your collaborators are talented in the art of cooperation. Your collaborators have to be willing and able to communicate with you. This means more than just sharing a language, it means sharing an understanding of creative goals. If you're an artist concerned with visual theme, invocation of tropes, and other sub-tleties, and you've found a writer who's more concerned with having vast explosions and busty babes in the work, then you're apt to create a graphic novel full of compromises that satisfy no one. There's something to be said for having somewhat different views, but if you cannot understand where each other is coming from, it won't work.

Flake Detection

Beware of any collaborator who promises samples but doesn't deliver, or who claims to have done published work without being credited in that work, or whose work looks like it was traced from someone else's.

Don't mistake someone's background for that person's ability to understand you. Differences in age, background, and social circles can actually bring a richness to a work. As long as you can understand each other, you should be fine.

Creative Crew, Where Are You?

It is easy to find enthusiastic collaborators. It is more difficult to find talented ones. Harder still is finding ones who will actually get the work done, but even that isn't impossible.

You can find new folks who are not yet established in several ways. If you live in a major metro-politan area, there are probably a number of talented folks working on breaking in locally. Often, the folks at the local comic shops will know where they are. To cast your net wider, check out the numerous websites like www.talkaboutcomics.com and www.digitalwebbing. com, where struggling writers and artists hang out, often trying to find collaborators. These folks often have websites with samples of their work, so you can quickly check out whether they're another Will Eisner or simply a Won't Eisner.

My favorite source for new talent, however, is the major national comic book conventions (see Appendix B). Because representatives from various publishers are there, new creators show up in droves looking for work. It's easy to spot the artists carrying around their portfo-lios. Hang around the place where a major publisher is looking at art samples and you'll get a chance to scope out a lot of artists. Writers are a little harder to track down, since they don't actually show their wares at the convention. The larger conventions often have talks about breaking into comics. Those panels are good for the information and for the people you can meet in the audience.

Digital Webbing Presents and *Writer's Bloc* are just two examples of anthology comics pub-lished by groups of unknown creators trying to generate experience, exposure, and feedback. The talent in such books are generally eager to expand into larger and more prestigious work.

If you're looking for established professionals to work with, your best bet is to meet them at conventions or reach out to them via the web. Most folks in comics these days are reachable by e-mail. Use your comic shop as a reference library to figure out who you want to work with, then reach out and see if they're interested. If you're not established, you're apt to hear "no thank you" repeatedly unless you offer to pay them for their services. Which segues us into our next topic …

The Benefits of Paying People

If your graphic novel is intended to be a money-generating venture, you really should consider paying your collaborators a page rate for the pages they turn in. Paying a page rate keeps you in control of the project. It encourages others to follow your vision, to meet deadlines, and to not simply drop out of the project when they get bored.

Paying people also allows you to get a higher grade of collaborator. Experienced working artists aren't likely to drop what they're doing to work on your labor of love. They need to be doing labors of paying rent, paying the cable bill, the alimony bill, the whiskey surcharge tax, and other such monthly realities of the professional comics creator.

 Steve Sez: On the Clock _____

Speaking *very, very* generally, 10 hours is a fair estimate of how long it takes an artist to turn a blank sheet of paper into an inked page of comics. If you've written a 24-page story, a typical artist might need to spend 240 hours at the board drawing it. That's the equivalent of six 40-hour workweeks. A hundred-page story? That's six months at a full-time job. Keep those sorts of numbers in mind when figuring out what the artist's contribution is worth.

Paying folks also allows you to give them a smaller amount of control over the rights to the work. This can be important when it comes to finding a publisher or cutting a deal to have your *Tales of the Dark and Ooky* turned into a movie, a TV show, or a mouthwash.

About the only downside to paying people money is that it costs money. For a long graphic novel, it can cost *lots* of money. If you have a publisher in place paying a page rate, of course that can be split among the creative team. But even if you're packaging a full graphic novel to show around, or if you have a publisher but are being paid only royalties (additional money for every copy sold over a certain number), paying is worth considering. After all, people like money.

Doing Right with Rights

From a creative standpoint, you're creating a graphic novel to be shared with the world. From a business standpoint, you're creating a bundle of *intellectual property rights*, legal control that you can license to publishers and other people who want to use aspects of your graphic novel. Someone who wants to make a movie out of *Dexter the Donut-Eating Duck* or put out a series of socks with Dexter has to license the rights. The question of who owns *Dexter* becomes about something more than who has to buy him donuts.

If your graphic novel is for a corporate-owned character, the corporation will probably require that it hold all the copyright and trademark to your work. Even if you're doing an original work, larger publishers may want to hold on to the copyright (which covers the content of the novel) and trademarks (which cover the title and perhaps the character names and likenesses).

Intellectual Property

WHA...?

Intellectual property refers to the ownership of concepts, ideas, and expressions, things that can't be held or touched. This category includes items like copyrights, trademarks, and patents. Graphic novels rarely involve patents, unless you've found a new way to print panels on individually wrapped cheese slices.

Lawyers! Oh No!

The rights and payment agreements should be put in a contract, for everyone's sake. There are various books that offer sample creative contracts, but you may want to get a lawyer to work out the details. Remember, your lawyer is your friend. It's other people's lawyers who are the enemy.

Generally speaking, unless one member of the creative team is paying the others, the copyright will be split between the writer and penciler. Sometimes the writer and penciler share the copyright to the whole work, which means that either one can license out publishing rights and other rights to the work. That can create sticky situations down the road, in which the writer may license the publishing rights to one company and the artist may license it to another. However, most publishers won't want the rights unless they can get exclusive rights. It's hard enough for a publisher to sell *Dexter* when competing with all the other graphic novels out there. So a publisher doesn't want to compete with someone else's printing of *Dexter!*

Alternatively, writers sometimes claim the copyright in the script they wrote, while artists claim copyright in the art, often splitting the copyright between penciler and inker. This may make it possible for the writer to sell certain movie rights or do a prose version of the graphic novel without the artist's cooperation, or for the artist to turn his or her panels into posters and T-shirts. There are legal questions about this method that no one has answered yet, so working this way opens up a big can of worms. Of course, a can of worms would be handy for feeding Dexter, if not for his donut addiction.

Doling Out Dollars

When it comes to paying the creative team, one of the first things you need to decide is what share of the money everyone gets paid. This is different from the way the rights are split up. The division of the rights says who gets to make the deal, not who gets to keep the money.

If you're dealing with just a page rate or just a royalty/profit sharing deal, then you'll probably want to divide all the money based on percentages. Usually this depends on the specific amount of time that each creative task generally takes, so a writer might get 20 percent of the creator's income, the penciler 40 percent, the inker 15 percent, the colorist 15 percent, the letterer 5 percent, and the cover artist 5 percent. Ducks that serve as models get nothing. Never, ever pay a duck; they'll just lose it all at the racetrack.

Many graphic novel deals involve an advance payment from the publisher, plus a royalty. In those cases, the letterer and colorist might get all of their payments from the advance. The writer and penciler might split a slightly smaller part of the advance, but they share the royalties. Again, the poor duck gets nothing.

Money for movie, TV, and product licenses is usually split evenly between the writer and the penciler. This is an attempt to weigh in how much they each contributed to a creation. Of course, if you ask the writer, the writer really contributed 80 percent of the concept. The artist also contributed 80 percent. A 50/50 split is the best solution, unless you can convince some sucker to pay you an extra 60 percent.

Of course, all of this is just what other people do. You should do what works for you. To convince qualified and experienced people, you may need to give them bigger cuts of the various moneys, especially if you can't afford to pay them up front. And if you really want to win them over, tell them they get to keep the duck!

The Least You Need to Know

- There are plenty of creative folks looking to create graphic novels with other creative folks.

- Be picky: Review samples carefully and look for signs of flakiness before choosing to work with someone.

- If you're trying to get people to work toward your vision, you'll have more luck if you can pay them.

- You should work out details of how rights and moneys will be split before asking anyone to do much work on your graphic novel.

Chapter 4

What's It All About?

In This Chapter

- ◆ What genre is your graphic novel?
- ◆ What's it *really* about?
- ◆ How do you build in that concept?

So you're going to do a graphic novel. Now the question is, which graphic novel are you going to do? You could do *Maus*, which means that you'd sell a lot of copies and win a Pulitzer Prize. Of course, you'd be sued by Art Spiegelman, who already did *Maus*. No, you'll have to have to do a new graphic novel. But what is it *about?*

Genres Are Generally Germaine

Genre is rarely a question people give much thought to. Some people are just naturally drawn to creating, say, Eskimo romance graphic novels, because they loved reading *Love Among the Igloos* and *Frozen Kisses*. To them what a graphic novel should be is the things they like to read. But your favorite genre may not be the best way to say what you really want to say.

Don't Be Drawn Away

If you're an artist, you might think that determining what the graphic novel is about is a topic just for the writers, and that this chapter should appear later in the book where we talk about writing. You have to involve yourself in the big picture of what the graphic novel is about, or you'll find yourself drawing *The Secrets of Maintaining Automatic Transmissions.*

The Thousand-Pound Superhero Gorilla

Superheroes are a genre that was invented for American comics. The superhero in a graphic novel is the guy who shows up to a formal ball in a glittering purple tux—gaudy and distracting from the somewhat embarrassed crowd around him, but still a lot of fun. Even the comic pamphlets have been moving away from telling the basic hero-meets-villain, hero-punches-villain, hero-wins story, and when done in graphic novel form that becomes even more true.

Verisimilitude

The state of something feeling true within an established context. A teenager getting superpowers from a radioactive penguin bite is not realistic, but since it works in the superhero context, it has **verisimilitude.**

The superhero is inherently an unrealistic form. Some graphic novelists do a lot with that unreality, veering off into silliness or abstract work. Others try to handle what superheroes would be like if they were real, looking at the ramifications of their presence and their actions, working hard at *verisimilitude.* Still others simply embrace the superhero as existing in a world with superhero rules, telling tales purely in the superhero tradition. There is much to be said for the basic morality play of the dastardly villain being brought down by a hero with nothing but pluck, drive, dedication, and a lifetime supply of Super Soldier Serum.

A Big Creamy Slice O' Life

Slice of life graphic novels are about mundane topics in realistic settings. These are generally very human tales about emotions and reactions. A story about a woman getting fired because she's drinking on the job, that's a slice of life. A tale about the trading card collector who finally finds the last card needed to complete a set, that's a slice of life. The story of a man whose bus is always so late that it makes him late for work, that's a slice of life as well, unless the man becomes so angry that he turns into the superhero Anti-Late Bus Man.

A Good, Fake Life

It's a Good Life If You Don't Weaken is an interesting slice of life graphic novel by Seth about a man searching for an obscure magazine cartoonist. It's an artfully faked autobiography, a story that is not factual but is emotionally true.

Many people assume that slice of life graphic novels are trite, downbeat, and boring. Sometimes these people are wrong, but only sometimes.

Auto-By-You

Autobiographical graphic novels are true tales about you and the things that you've done. Most of these are the nonfictional version of slice of life graphic novel, but they don't have to be. If you've done anything in your life that isn't mundane, that can make a great source of information. Write about your days in the Americorps, or about the time you were kidnapped, or even about the day you were bitten by that radioactive penguin.

Steve Sez: Making It Visual

If you are telling a slice of life or autobiographical story, you'll want to make a special effort to provide a visual experience for the reader. Pay careful attention to the small things your characters do, and find the details of costume and setting that will bring the story to life. Your fifth grade humiliation story just won't work as well as it ought to unless you get the embarrassing haircut right.

You don't have to be the star of your own autobiographical graphic novel. Consider *A Fax from Sarajevo*, Joe Kubert's tale about getting faxes from a former publisher. The heart of the story is in the contents of the faxes, about the publisher's struggles in a war zone.

Burglars, Killers, and Other Fine Folk

Tales of charming detectives chasing fiendish criminals, or, more stylishly, charming criminals eluding fiendish detectives, are mainstays in the graphic novel field. The new century has proven a prime time for crime.

The fashions in crime comics tend to follow the fashions in novels and movies, focusing either on stylish private detectives or on groups of enthusiastic-but-not-fully-competent criminals, in the *Pulp Fiction* tradition. The cop, popular on television, has failed to get much play in graphic novels.

Graphic History

It's easy to choose to set your novel in the present day. Everyone loves the present day, mainly because they like the presents. "Happy present day!" they shout, confused by the concept. But you shouldn't feel stuck with that.

History provides a lot of options. A historical graphic novel can delve into the drama of a specific historical event. On the other hand, you can explore the nature of the time and the nature of humanity by using a fiction story set in a key period in the past.

The good thing about working on historical graphic novels is that you have the vast richness of history to pull things from. The downside is that you really should know the period you're writing about, and that means research!

Ten Gallon Graphics

Rio? Bravo!

Doug Wildey's *Rio* graphic novels showcase the work of an impressive artist at the end of his long career.

Westerns filled with cowboys, ranchers, schoolmarms, and shootouts sound like they should be part of the historical genre. Some Westerns do qualify. The graphic novel Westerns come from the tradition of movie, TV, and novel Westerns, which means that they are often divorced from any real version of the Old West. In many ways, the Western form is just as artificial as superheroes.

Future Robots of America

Most science fiction graphic novels come from one of two traditions. There are numerous tales set in heavily governed futures, filled with media saturation and focusing on fun-loving nonconformists. *American Flagg!*, *Channel X*, and the *Transmetro-politan* series all fit into this format. The other is space opera, the tales of travelers, explorers, and warriors on spacecraft. Actually, they're usually *in* spacecraft. Riding on the outside is discouraged in space.

WHA...?

Hard SF

Hard SF stands for science fiction grounded in actual science, dealing with the repercussions of technological advances and real physical laws.

Literary science fiction offers a far wider range of material, ranging from *hard SF* tales to sociological explorations. Although you can find examples of these things in English language graphic novels, they are, sadly, the exception rather than the rule.

Fans Love Fantastic Fantasy

Wizards and warlords, barbarians and thieves, elves, dwarves, and orcs—they all like fantasy graphic novels. The trick to fantasy is coming up with a realm that is clearly not our world, yet is internally consistent and has something to interest the human reader.

No Bones About It

Jeff Smith's *Bone* series starts as a deceptively lighthearted tale about three humorous beings on the run who find themselves in a strange land. By the end, it's an epic tale of war, power, and stupid, stupid rat creatures.

Drafting a Military Novel

To some, serving in the military is a long stretch of tedium punctuated by moments of grueling dehumanization. For others, it's marked by excitement and danger. Either is an interesting base for human drama, or feline drama if you prefer drawing cat soldiers.

Most military fiction fits into the history category. Most stories are set not just in war in general, but in a specific war. That's not a rule. If you're writing something, you can write about being a soldier in peacetime. You can even invent your own present-day war.

Lovey-Dovey Love

People love love, and that's made romance quite a genre. You can set it during a war, you can set it in a castle, you can put it in outer space, but if you have two hearts tugging at one another you have a romance. Unless the winner goes on to tug at the kidneys, in which case you have organ wrestling.

Remember that romance, as a genre, doesn't always have to fit the narrow strictures of romantic comedy. It need not always be about love found despite obstacles. It can be about love sought, love lost, love fading, love lasting, and the most tragic of all: love not being enough.

Eek! Horror!

Horror definitely has a place in graphic novels. There is plenty of room for things that jump out and bite you, that invade your body and your soul, that eat your ferret without spitting out the fur.

Although the graphic novelist can easily do complex gruesome things that outdo any screen horror, most graphic novel horror has more of an intellectual bent. Movies have a much easier time creating that moment that makes you jump out of your seat, but a graphic novel's intellectual horror can chill you to the bone.

And All the Rest

Spy stories, sports stories, erotic tales, pirates, school tales—there is nothing that prose novels or movies do that graphic novels cannot. Well, perhaps not musicals. But even that's been tried!

And in fact, you don't even have to stick with stories. Some graphic novels are essays, talking about a topic with visual examples or told by a drawn narrator. *How to Get Peanut Butter Out of Your Automatic Transmission* would be a graphic novel, if it showed the

Genre Confusion

You don't have to limit yourself to one genre. There are graphic novels that are horror Westerns, science fiction romances, and military fantasy tales. In fact, choosing two genres and trying to fit a story to them is a great imagination starter. Superhero autobiography, anyone?

process using a series of pictures. Take a look at *Understanding Comics,* Scott McCloud's graphic novel that explains how sequential art storytelling works.

Just remember that you don't have to create a graphic novel that's a particular genre or fills a particular set of rules. A genre can be a comfortable thing and great for marketing, but if your story doesn't fit any known genre, that's great, too!

Make a Theme-Filled Cupcake

If someone asks what your story is about, and you answer "it's a Western," then you haven't answered the question. That would be like a sculptor saying "my sculpture is about a stone cut into a shape." The genre is the context in which things happen, but it's not the heart of the story.

The theme is the heart of the matter. What makes a Western interesting is not merely that it's set in the Old West. If it was, you could just have page after page of cowboys, Native Americans, railroad barons, and morticians just standing around doing nothing. That's probably what the Old West was like on hot days anyway.

Steve Sez: Making It Visual, Redux

Always look for ways to express the story's theme visually. For example, reinforce a story about the allure of dangerous things via a candlelit scene with moths circling the flame. I'll go into more detail about this sort of thinking later on, when I've liberated this book from its oppression under the hated Gertler regime.

Emotional Exploration

Emotional themes are great to explore, because we all have emotions. At least, I assume we all do. There may be people who don't have emotions, but they're probably not reading graphic novels. Even if they do, they won't like what you create because liking is an emotional response, so ignore them.

What makes emotions work is that simple conflict can lead to complex situations. "The cowboy loves the schoolmarm" expresses a simple emotion, but it has inherent complications. If he marries the schoolmarm and stays in town with her, then he's not out riding the range. He's losing his freedom, he's having to change himself. And she knows he would have to change to be with her, and isn't sure that she would love the changed man. Besides, she thinks his horse is smelly.

Having an emotional theme doesn't mean that people are just standing around emoting. The things that happen in the story should all either reflect or have an impact on the emotional situation. The cowboy faces down the evil rancher fearlessly, because he knows if he dies he will at least be spared the decision. The schoolmarm rides off in search of the wounded cowboy, and in riding fast and far learns to understand the feeling of freedom that the cowboy loves. The horse, tired of being smelly, takes a bath.

> **Theme Check**
>
> A good way to check if you have a grasp on your theme is to see if the same concerns would work in a different setting. The same concern the cowboy has for leaving the open range is the concern that the tennis player has about being in love while being on the circuit, or the time traveler has for those he leaves at home while going to ancient Egypt.

Existential Exposition

You can explore other aspects of the world that go beyond human emotion. The rise of humanity, the fate of nations, the delicate balance of ecology, the conflict between science and religion, the tendency of things to fall apart, the effect of censorship, and the importance of pizza are all themes that could be explored.

Don't worry if confronting such a topic head-on seems too blunt. A large abstract theme can often be handled by allegory. That means that instead of telling a story about God's relationship with man, for example, you tell a story about an inventor and the robot aardvark he invented.

 Been There, Done That

Tales of the Beanworld is an ecological fable. Larry Marder created a fantasy world with a simple ecology, and explored what happens to the world and its inhabitants when changes or outside intrusions occur.

Action Action Action

Action is actually a legitimate theme. It may not be the deepest, most meaningful theme, but life isn't solely deep and meaningful. The fight, the chase, the hunt, can all be gloriously kinetic. If you think about Indiana Jones movies or the more recent James Bond films, adventure is at their core. Oh, they may sprinkle them with morality lessons like "we must respect the mysteries of life" or "faith is better than misplaced self-confidence" or "if you're going to take over the world, don't tell your plans to the man inches away from the giant shredder." Those are mostly window dressing. The core of the story is the physical struggle against nigh-impossible odds.

Hilarity Ensues

Comedy can be a tool, or it can be a goal. *Satire* is the art of using comedy to comment on the real world. A satirical work might have a straight-talking janitor become a congressman, contrasting him with the confusing politics of the more realistic congressmen. Satire makes you laugh to make you look at the world differently.

But straight comedy makes you laugh to make you laugh. Silly, goofy, funny stuff doesn't need an excuse. We could all use a laugh in this silly world of ours. Unless you're ready to pump laughing gas into everyone's house, comedy is the best way to spread that joy.

Mix 'n' Match with Care

You can have multiple themes in a single graphic novel, but stick with one main one. Minor themes can be used when they won't interfere with the main one. You don't want to end up with an action comedy that is hilarious for the first two thirds then turns into a bloody, heart-wrenching gun battle, for example. The action kills the comedy while the comedy leaves it hard to take the action seriously.

The Concept of Concept

You have a genre, you have a theme you want to explore. Now you need a story, a tale to tell within that genre that explores that theme. You're not going to start off with a full plot, but there are two key items that drive most stories: the situation and the complication.

The situation is usually simply the position your lead character or characters are in. The complication is something that makes the situation an uncomfortable one, forcing action or a decision. If you want to describe your graphic novel, you can probably do it by mentioning the situation followed by the complication with a big *but* in between.

Think about these examples:

◆ An inventor makes a robot aardvark *but* the robot aardvark starts doing things the inventor didn't plan.

◆ Gloria inherits a million dollars *but* the money is buried in the middle of a minefield.

◆ Tony's getting married *but* his girlfriend from 20 years before suddenly shows up.

◆ Little Bobbie is taking cupcakes for the class at school *but* she has one cupcake less than she should.

◆ The star warrior has retired to The Planet of the Donuts, *but* the space pirates are coming to steal this year's donut harvest.

◆ Jill has moved to Las Vegas, *but* small-town life has left her ill-prepared for the big city.

When the story is done, there will probably be more than one complication, but one will generally get your story going. So you have the base of your story *but* there is still a lot more work to do!

As a practice, think about some of your favorite graphic novels and movies, and see if you can name the basic situation and key complication. This practice identifying *buts* will make you a better butter!

The Least You Need to Know

- The genre is the category of setting of the tale.
- The theme is the point of the story
- Most stories are built from a situation and a complication.

Part 2

The Writer's Art

Writing graphic novels is like building a watch. No one sees all that delicate work you've hidden inside, they just see the smooth-looking surface. If you do it right, people will think it was easy, because the details of your work are invisible. And if you do it wrong, everyone will laugh when it's thirty o'clock.

This part of the book has tips on how to tell an interesting story filled with interesting people doing interesting things. The secrets of writing effective dialog and conveying your vision to an artist are unveiled. You even learn why the exclamation point is so popular!

Chapter 5

Who, Why, and Huh? Interesting People and Events

In This Chapter

◆ Who are these people?

◆ What do they want?

◆ What develops?

It's time to turn your vague, fuzzy concept for a graphic novel into a less vague, still somewhat fuzzy concept. Once you set up who your characters are, where they are, and what the heart of the story is, then your work is done. Well, not really done. Not even nearly done. But if you think of your graphic novel as a toy airplane, you've now created the big red rubber band that will make it move.

Who Are These Characters?

People are going to be at the heart of your graphic novel, unless you're doing a graphic novel about vampire turtles, in which case vampire turtles will be at the heart (and throat) of the work. These characters are what your story will rise and fall on. Readers will pay attention to boring things happening to interesting people long after they've turned away from interesting things happening to boring people.

Awesome and Average Abilities

It's easy to see superheroes in terms of abilities. Lady Power has the ability to fly, read minds, and has eye-beams that can turn anything into a large veal patty. But even the less super among us have a list of abilities. I can write, do crossword puzzles, drive a car, and say "I do not speak Spanish" in Spanish. Steve can draw, perform CPR, and convince editors that deadlines aren't really deadlines.

The Following People

Characters don't always come first. You can generate your graphic novel starting with anything that gets your imagination going. In this book you'll see portions of our graphic novel *The Big Con*, set in a comic book convention. I started with that setting, and that led to the type of characters. A scene, a snip of dialog, a title, a single drawing—anything can provide a spark.

What your characters *can* do tells you the limits of what they will do. Some abilities come naturally, such as the abilities to run, breathe, or turn things into veal patties. Other abilities will suggest certain attitudes or histories. A character who can fly a plane, for example, may have a thrill-seeking attitude, or may be an Air Force veteran, or the child of a renegade sky-writer who was driven out of the business for purposeful misspelling.

WHA...?

Character Identification

Character identification is created when your character has aspects that get readers picturing themselves in the character's place. This can be something as blatant as making an eleven-year-old boy the hero in a book aimed at eleven-year-old boys. It can also involve putting the character in a common emotional situation, such as lusting from afar or having a lousy day.

Attitude? No Problem!

Characters should have attitudes, ways of looking at life and facing situations. They can be happy, grumpy, or bashful. (Sleepy, dopey, and sneezy are conditions, not attitudes, and Doc is merely a dwarf.) Attitudes make the characters human, and help with *character identification*.

In reality, most people have varying attitudes depending on their situation. The world's strongest woman might be confident, proud, even obnoxious when it comes to facing physical challenges, but uncertain, self-effacing, and yet still obnoxious when dealing with affairs of the heart. A father may be loving around his children, and yet cold-hearted to the rest of the world. A hypnotist's assistant may be polite and demure, yet become belligerent whenever someone says "paprika." This doesn't mean that people are inconsistent. Every Tom, Dick, and Englebert has some picture of his place in the world, and his attitude at any given moment shows how what he is doing relates to that place.

Perhaps the most important aspect of attitude is desire. What does your character, whether *protagonist* or *antagonist*, want? Everything anyone does is driven by a desire. We seek love, money, peace, sex, salvation, children, food, relief, warmth, safety, pleasure, knowledge, respect, and a complete set of Snoopy books. Most of us want most of these things, in differing amounts and at different times.

A Road Paved with Attitude

The Road to Perdition, written by Max Allan Collins and drawn by Richard Piers Rayner, tells the tale of a mob hit man. When the situation changes, his attitude toward the mob changes, yet still reflects his core belief system.

Protagonist/Antagonist

A **protagonist** is the character our story focuses on, the one facing the main challenge of the tale and whom the reader is likely to root for. **Antagonists** are people who stand in the way of the protagonist. An antagonist doesn't have to be a villain. If Aaron and Eli both want to be the world champion cat juggler, and Aaron is your protagonist, then Eli is an antagonist even though he's no more evil than Aaron.

Remember, villains are people, too, and few are villains in their own mind. People do bad things with good motives. Many of the worst things in history have been done in the name of the greater good. The villain who steals pizzas to feed the hungry or to protest the power of the International Mozzarella Cartel is far more interesting than a thief who just wants a pie. If your villain earns the reader's respect, the interaction between hero and villain will be fascinating.

Have Strength in Weaknesses

Weaknesses are aspects of the character that will cause problems for them or unintended problems for others around them. These are not the opposite of abilities—the inability to fly is not a weakness unless you're a bird. Weaknesses include such things as a short temper, distraction, addiction, social ineptness, tics and spasms, cowardice, an undue belief in your own abilities, allergies, and letting love or lust overrule logic. We all have weaknesses, and we wouldn't be the same without them.

Weaknesses put limits on your heroes, often giving them something to struggle against. In many adventure tales weaknesses are simple physical things that the hero must confront (Indiana Jones faces the snakes he fears) or avoid (Superman avoids Kryptonite). In human-interest stories, weaknesses are often the center of the plot. We each have things in our character that could destroy us, given the right conditions. A *tragedy* is a story in which those elements overtake us, while in *life-affirming stories* we pull away from near destruction, making it through the crisis.

Putting the Stories in Histories

Few graphic novels start with a character being born. Characters have histories that are shaped by their abilities, attitudes, and weaknesses. Histories also shape abilities, attitudes, and weaknesses. What size family is the character from? What's the character's religion? Race? Educational background? Has the character fallen in love, and if so, what happened? What jobs are on your character's resumé?

A character whose history you know is a character you know. With the history and attitudes down, you'll be able to answer such questions as *What's the character's favorite movie? Favorite meal?* and *What's a character likely to do upon winning a lifetime supply of macaroni products?* You'll still have trouble with any question that begins "if the character leaves the station on a train traveling at 75 miles per hour …"

Great Hollywood Names

Character names can suggest so much about them, so be careful of relying on generic names. Before you name one of your characters Bob Smith (or, worse yet, name all of your characters Bob Smith), delve into more interesting names. My favorite source for interesting names is the credits at the end of the movies. Fast forward past the actors' names and you're apt to find a multitude of memorable monikers. Mix a best boy's first name with a key grip's last name and violà! you have a character name.

Revealing Characters You Never Vealed

Your character The Amazing Clive may be full of interesting aspects. He may be a master juggler, secretly afraid of invisible tigers, who served five years in Sing Sing for cold-bloodedly killing a six-pack of beer. But if he stands around ironing socks for the entire graphic novel, then the only interesting thing revealed about The Amazing Clive is that he irons socks. That's barely interesting, and certainly not amazing.

You could have The Amazing Clive talking about himself whilst ironing the socks, and that could be a cute idea for a four-page story, but it'd make a lousy graphic novel. No, we need to learn about him in context. It's far better to be *shown* what makes the character interesting than to be told it.

You Look Like Yourself

The physical appearance of a character, including face, clothes, and stance, is a vital way of revealing character attributes. People can look rich, poor, kind, mean, smart, stupid, stylish, clueless, attentive, befuddled, and so on. Most of this is in the hands of the artists, and will be covered in the art-oriented chapters of the book.

Steve Sez: Worth a Thousand ...

Graphic novel writers sometimes send magazine photos or movie stills to their collaborators. "She should have a jacket like this, but worn out, with patches." "He has this sort of amused expression." You can refer you artist to movies, too. "The produce department manager is a big, swaggering guy who compresses his upper lip like Humphrey Bogart and walks like John Wayne."

Some visual ways of showing character may seem like stereotyping, since you'll be saying that people who look mean actually are mean. However, there is some legitimacy in that. While most of us are born with a certain appearance, over the years our attitudes and beliefs give us facial expressions that change the way we look. We earn our faces.

Of course, even that has plenty of exceptions. Characters who aren't what they appear to be, while harder to depict, are interesting for that very aspect. The man who looks like a kindly grandpa but is really planning to blow up the bank makes a tough villain, and the cruel-looking lass with a heart of gold will face interesting problems.

"He Chose What?!?"

You can tell a story without any characters making decisions, but perhaps you shouldn't. Consider this: An earthquake causes a rockslide that sets off sparks. The sparks set the brush in the canyon ablaze. However, the rocks also block the narrow path that the stream takes out of the canyon. The blocked stream causes the canyon to flood, extinguishing the blaze. A story has occurred, and no one has made a decision. You could, with some effort, make a hundred-page story like that, but it would be almost impossible to make it interesting.

Steve Sez: Belaboring the Visual Thing

Do it with pictures. It's better to show the protagonist pocketing the dollar, and perhaps his expression, (guilty? sly? cheerfully whistling?) than to use dialogue or a caption announcing "he decided to keep the dollar." On the other hand, having the character say "I gave the dollar back" while showing him keep it cleverly uses two story details to communicate a third—that he's a liar.

Most of your readers will be human, and humans are interested in human-style decisions. Great stories turn on decisions made. This doesn't mean that lovely Mabel has to spend page after page mulling over "should I go and rescue the prince, or should I stay home and get some ironing done?" When she rushes off to rescue the prince or performs any other voluntary action, a decision has been made. Even if she just stands around doing nothing while knowing that the prince is being thrown into the Pit of Impressive Depth, that inaction is a decision as well.

Interesting decisions are ones that have major effects or that reveal interesting aspects of character. When someone decides to lie to a child, to keep hope alive, to finally ask Sarah out, to sing on the subway, to keep the dollar bill instead of handing it back to the person who dropped it, or to not have a drink today, a bit of that person's character is revealed.

Why Should Anyone Care?

If your graphic novel is just a bunch of characters who aren't doing things, experiencing things, and causing things to happen, you don't have a story. You have a phone book.

You could use huge paper and do a one-page graphic novel and never worry about whether the reader will want to turn the page. For the more common, multipage sort of graphic novel, however, you'll need the reader to keep turning the page. It's not good enough to tell interesting information; the reader has to want to know what happens next.

Conflict: Picking a Fight

A *conflict* is simply when there are two things working against one another. Sometimes this occurs on a very physical level, as when the Fabulous Meatball Guy fights the many-tendrilled Spaghetti Monster. It can happen on an emotional level, when Bo Thompson and Roderick Rutherford III are both competing for the love of the Spaghetti Monster. It can even happen internally, as the Spaghetti Monster is torn between her love for Bo and her knowledge that Roderick could help her in the battle against the Fabulous Meatball Guy.

The thing that makes conflict interesting is not the resolution, the result of the conflict. Oh, the reader will hang on until the result is clear, but the interesting part is how the result is achieved. In traditional genre works, we know that the good guy will beat the bad guy and the Monster will pick true love over wealth and revenge. In fact, the reader will sometimes be very disappointed by works where the expected result doesn't happen. Let your conflict be resolved, but not too quickly or easily.

Change Isn't Just Nickels and Dimes

Characters that are going through changes are interesting. The reader may want to know what the character will be like at the end of the change, or simply what the fallout of the change will be. The changes can be external, like when the small-town gal moves to the big city. They can be physical, like when the small-town gal turns into a big city. Or they can be emotional, like falling in love, falling out of love, finding or losing religion, going insane, going sane.

Changes cause other changes. The physical changes of puberty bring complex emotional changes. The emotional changes of falling in love lead to the external changes of marriage, family, and dinner parties.

While some changes are instantaneous, many are gradual, and these are a writer's delight. Once the change begins, readers will want to see what it leads to. When a caterpillar enters its cocoon, everyone will want to stick around to see it emerge as a beautiful alligator.

A Perfect Effect Has No Defect

People start turning into chocolate bunnies. That's an eye-catching sentence, but it can be made even more interesting by extending it just a little further. "People start turning into chocolate bunnies, and then …"

It's that "and then …" that turns a concept into a story. What happens? What's the effect of this choco-bunny transformation? Rioting in the streets? Hopping in the streets? Perpetual Easter? If you can take a cause and create an interesting but logical effect, people want to read it. *Mystery*, a popular form, is merely the revelation of effect before the cause.

And the effect can serve as the cause for the next part of the plot. Perpetual Easter causes a shortage of egg dye, driving the prices through the roof and making Hortense Cheswick, heir to the Eastwick Easter Egg Enhancement Enterprise, a wealthy woman. And that effect draws suitors, both human and chocolate bunnies, to her. And so on.

Miracle Movie

I'm going to cheat here and recommend a movie rather than a graphic novel. *Miracle Mile* has a great plot that all flows from a single cause: Anthony Edwards receives an important phone call to a wrong number.

Ideally, you want to start with a situation and a single cause, and have everything else that happens in your plot arise directly or indirectly from that cause. If in the middle of the story, you suddenly need to have anvils fall from the sky and squish the bunnies, then you should rethink your plot. New plot elements that come out of left field feel like cheating, and the later in the story they appear, the worse the reader will react.

Example Characters: *The Big Con*

While writing this book, Steve and I are also working on the graphic novel *The Big Con*. The spark for this graphic novel was my wanting to do a tale set at a large comic book convention. I've spent a lot of time at these conventions, and there are a lot of interesting people having interesting experiences there. So I decided to build the novel as a series of short stories, all set at a single convention. I made up a list of characters whose stories I might tell. This included …

- ◆ The enthusiastic comics fan who spent almost all his money just getting to the convention, and now has less than $10 to make it through the four days of the show.

- ◆ The comics dealer who has thousands of old comics to sell in the show, but has to keep an eye out for shoplifters.

- ◆ The comics writer who finds herself without people to hang out with during the convention, and is feeling lonely in the midst of a crowd of very similar people.

- ◆ Two contestants in the convention's costume contest, who fall in love.

- ◆ An older comics artist who is surrounded by fans who love the work he did in the 1960s and 1970s. He needs a job, but the comics editors at the convention don't think he can interest the current audience.

- ◆ A group of movie actors at the convention to promote the latest installment of their series, but who are uncomfortable being surrounded by their fans.

As you can see, each character has a conflict, a challenge, or a change during the course of this convention.

The Least You Need to Know

- Interesting characters make interesting stories.

- Characters can be made interesting by giving them interesting abilities, attitudes, weaknesses, and histories.

- Characters reveal themselves through their statements, decisions, and appearance.

- To keep your readers interested, give your characters conflicts and put them through changes.

- The resolution of a conflict is not as interesting as how that resolution is reached.

- Introducing new, important elements of the story late in the tale makes the story seem forced. You should have a continuous chain of events set off by one cause.

Chapter 6

What, Where, When, and Whatchamacallit?

In This Chapter

- ◆ Plotting your story
- ◆ Adding complications
- ◆ What develops?

It's time to turn your scanty little concept into the robust plot that will carry you through the rest of the work. Your plot is your story, just in a very cheap form that no one would pay to read.

You're Nowhere Without a Place

Choosing a locale for your story gets it ready to be detailed. A story about a cop chasing after a bank robber in New York is very different from one in Los Angeles, and even more so if it's in Hong Kong, the middle of Kansas, or even if he's a space cop from Uranus. And if it makes a difference in the writing of the graphic novel, it makes an even bigger difference in the art.

Real Places Are Where It's Really At

The advantage of using a real location is that you get a built-in richness. Real places have their own cultures, institutions, street names, and sports teams. All this rich material will actually help you in your writing. When faced with the question of where the thief will hide or where the young couple will go on a date, you'll have your answers. If they're in Pasadena, California, for example, they can go to the movies in the Paseo Colorado mall. Suddenly, you know that if they have small talk to make, they can mention that they're on the street that the Rose Parade goes down, or they can take a look at the most beautiful city hall in the nation. If it's a winter night, it will be chilly, but not snowy. Knowing this makes your work rich.

Steve Sez: Home Is Where the Art Is

There's a lot to be said for setting a story in a place you know well. If a writer's story takes place in her home town of Pittsburgh, she can spend an afternoon out with a camera, shooting photo references of buildings and settings. This will make it much easier for her artist, who lives in Buenos Aires, to illustrate her tale of love and desperation on the banks of the Monongahela.

The Only Right Place

The Sandwalk Adventures explains evolution by focusing on follicle mites who live on the body of Charles Darwin and think he's a god. Cartoonist/biologist Dr. Jay Hosler researched Darwin's home carefully, and that gave him much of the rich detail of this bouncy, happy work, including the title.

The down side, of course, is that you have to know your stuff about the place. If you don't know where to go to the movies in Pasadena and you set the story there anyway, it will cost you. You won't get any of the richness of the place. People who have been to Pasadena will know you've got it wrong the moment you have someone say "y'all done shoveling that snow yet?"

Check out the travel books at your bookstore or library to find books focusing on most states and most nations, giving you details of those places. For less touristy info, go to the websites for the local newspapers. And if you can talk to someone who's actually from the area, you'll be much better off.

Made-Up Places: Fake Estate

Real places have their advantages, but so do made-up places, or places that simply go unnamed. You can create a place that has certain important attributes that you can't quite find in the real world. Need an island kingdom with a strong high-tech center and wild monkeys? That's the tropical isle of Goodnamus! You can't get it wrong because there's no source to get right.

One time when you really might want to use a fictional place is when your story is built around the local government. If you create a crooked police force, a drunken mayor, and a paranoid dog catcher, attributing it to a real place may make it seem like you're writing about specific people. Dark depictions of real people can bring about lawsuits. Lawsuits are bad.

Really Fictional Places

When writing fantasy or science fiction, you could need a city that's not on this Earth. Make it feel real by basing it on a real city. Basing a spaceport on New York City would be very different than one based on Las Vegas. The home of your elves could be based on ancient Rome, or it could be based on a small Iowa town to very different effect.

When creating a city or town, ask yourself questions about it. What industries are in the town? What's the government like? Are there different neighborhoods? Does everyone get along? Are there sports teams? Is it an older city with brick buildings, or a newer steel-and-concrete place? Are big sandwiches called "subs", "hoagies", "grinders", or "Charles Sebastian McShane, with extra cheese"?

Time for Time

When does your story take place? People usually have a vague answer for this, and often vague is fine. Most things you see take place in a vague form of today. They don't say the exact year, but the characters seem to listen to music from the past couple years.

Still, being precise can often help. Even if you're dealing with a "vaguely today" setting, you should at least know the season. Some people try to set things in the next year, so that it will be fresh when it comes out. Of course, that proves a mistake when the characters aren't all wearing the giant purple bunny ears that became required under the Congressional Purple Bunny Ear Act just before the graphic novel was printed. It's often better to set the story slightly in the past.

Your Days Are Numbered

You may never mention the actual year or even the day of the week in your graphic novel. It's still good to know the date things are taking place. For tales that take place over a period of time, pick dates for everything that happens. By tracking your story against the calendar, you'll know when weekends and holidays fall, and even know when people age.

Steve Sez: That Grass Sure Is Greener

It's easier for writers to get away with being vague about when a story is set than it is for artists. A writer can tell an artist "Gretchen climbs out of the car and steps onto the city sidewalk." This could take place in 1920, 1950, or the day after tomorrow. Unless the artist is working in a style that's deliberately fanciful or obscure, readers will note basic details like the make of the car, the buildings, and Gretchen's clothing and hairstyle, and then form their own ideas about when a story takes place. An artist who doesn't want to confuse the audience should either pick a year and try to keep things consistent, or quickly make it clear to the reader that this story is set in its own world with its own rules.

If you're delving into history, being precise can be necessary. The Old West covers a number of years, and the crowdedness of the cities, the status of the railroads, and the availability of certain firearms all varied during that time. If you mix up your times, the Old West fanatics will glare severely at you.

If you're setting a story substantially in the future, the year is not as important as the situation. What has become of humanity? What wars have occurred? What is the state of technology? Have the potatoes finally conquered? Understand the world and the society, and you'll be ready to have things happen in it.

Paperize It

At this point, you should be ready to start putting things down on paper. This isn't to keep you from forgetting something, nor is it time to start showing your plot to other folks. The very act of writing out what you're doing forces you to make sure it's clear in your mind. In writing down your plot, you're likely to discover problems, like the fact that your hero is both an Air Force veteran and attending kindergarten. Or you'll discover new opportunities for your story that you hadn't noticed before, like how your hero being in kindergarten means that the vehicle he hot-wires for the chase scene will probably be a school bus, which will look real cool.

Writing down the plot doesn't mean that you have to answer every question. In fact, writing down the questions will make it clear to you just what you have yet to answer. Consider this rough plot for our example story from *The Big Con:*

> Setting: A recent year, say 2003, early summer. A big fictional comics/multimedia convention, as big as the Chicago or San Diego comics conventions. It's at a big convention center in Seattle. (A fictional one? Does Seattle have a convention center?)

Characters: Four of the stars from some popular science fiction film series. They're at the convention to promote the next installment.

Story: They have to get to the auditorium for their panel at the convention. It's on the other side of the convention hall from where they are, and if they just try to walk across the crowded convention hall, they're going to be swarmed with fans wanting autographs, attention, whatever, and as celebrities they're sick and tired of everyone wanting a piece of them. They've gotten cynical about people's interest in their fame. There's probably a back route that is usually used to get people in. It's closed off. (Why?). So they borrow some costumes from people there for the costume contest, costumes based on the movies they star in. Full-body costumes, so no one can see the celebrities in them. (Who arranges this? Con security? Someone from the movie company?) And then, crossing the floor, they see how people really react to the costumes, and realize that folks really love the movies they make. This makes them realize that not everyone who acts like a fan is trying to take advantage of their celebrity. The actors know the joy that they have brought to their fans, and feel joy in sharing it with them.

That's not very detailed, but it gives me something to go on. It also shows me where I have problems, like the fact that I have four actors and with this level of detail, they're all the same. I also see where I can start adding some basic details, like choosing a name for the movies they're in. That name will help me envision the film, the costumes, what the fans are like, and so forth.

Plot-Checkin' Fricassee

With that written down, we can check to make sure the key elements are there. Do we know the goal of the characters? Yes, they are on a quest, seeking to find the other side of the convention hall! Why are the characters on the quest? Because they are scheduled to be there to promote their movie.

Does the quest have obstacles? Of course. The cast has an internal conflict, because crossing the hall involves dealing with the masses of people, which they don't want to deal with. Then there are external obstacles, the fans themselves, who could prove to be real physical obstacles.

These conflicts are a cause that leads to a decision, the decision to wear the costumes. That decision has effects, the fans reacting to the people in costume. That effect causes other effects, the actors having emotional reactions to the fans' reactions.

Notice that the quest has become unimportant. We still need the quest, we need to have the actors trying to cross the convention hall, but the important thing about the story is not whether they make it. It's the journey that matters, not what happens when they arrive.

Sometimes whether the protagonist achieves a goal is important, but sometimes it's like a roller-coaster ride. It's not important where the roller-coaster is going, because we know it's going back to the starting point. It's the rises and falls and the near vomiting along the way that make the roller-coaster interesting.

Pile On the Problems

We've got a short little tale here, and that's fine if you want a short story. For a novel, however, your characters have to go through a lot. It's not enough to say *Charlie wanted to be a world-famous donut baker, so he baked some very good donuts and everyone loved them and he achieved his goal.* The lack of complications may be good for Charlie, but it's lousy for the reader.

Looking at the convention story, there are a lot of complications that can be added. Many of them come from adding needed detail—just how do the fans show their love for the films? Other complications come from adding new situational elements that take places before or after the existing plot. Here are some possibilities that come to my mind:

- The fans in costume don't want to lend the actors their costumes, because they fear the actors won't return them in time for the costume contest.

- Some people on the convention floor find out that the actors are traveling in costume, and start bugging the costume wearers for photographs.

- It's hard to see through the eye holes of some of the costumes, causing some of the actors to run into things, trip, or knock stuff over.

- Some fans want photographs with the folks in costumes.

- Fans dressed for the costume contest assume that our protagonists made their own costumes, and want to know details.

- One of the actors is dressed in a villain costume, and a little girl attacks the actor because she hates the villain.

- No one told the auditorium security that the actors would be arriving in costume, and security tries to keep these costumed folks out.

- After being transformed with joy, the actors return the costumes to their owners. The joy is soured somewhat when one of the owners says he's going to make a lot of money auctioning off this celebrity-worn costume.

WHA...?

Climax/Denouement

The **climax** is an intense point toward the end of the story where the main conflict is resolved, such as the hero fighting the villain. The **denouement** (pronounced *DAY-noo-mwa*) is anything that takes place after the climax, such as the hero picking up a reward check from the National Council Against Villainy.

If this story was going to be a full graphic novel in itself, I'd probably use all these features and more. Since this is supposed to be just an eight-page portion of a larger work, however, there's not room for everything. By having this list of possibilities, I can pick and choose what I think will make the most interesting story.

Combinations and Permutations

If you watch a soap opera long enough, you'll see the writers try to combine every possible pair of characters into a couple. On *Throbbing Hearts University*, the dean's wife will have affairs with all the professors, the staff, the students, the town dog catcher, and so on. Who knows, she might even have an affair with the dean himself.

That's not a great way to build a coherent story, but it's a great way to think about plotting. When you're stuck on what should happen, look at each pair of characters. How do these characters relate to each other? What effect do they have on each other? Can you do something interesting with them? Taking two otherwise unlinked characters and having them fall in love, or in hate, or start a pizza delivery service together can move things forward. Build relationships, and remember that *relationship* doesn't just mean romance; it's any kind of regular dealings between people. The neighbors who throw garbage on each other's lawn have a relationship, even if they never actually see each other.

When you have a relationship established between two characters, it's time to look at all the other characters and see what effect that relationship has on them. How does Jane's husband feel about her starting a pizza delivery service with her old math teacher? Is he happy? Jealous? Hopeful? Scornful? Gassy? If the reaction would add something to the story, go with it!

Are there characters that aren't part of the plot for a while? Their lives haven't stopped just because the reader doesn't see them. The things they do when the reader isn't watching, whether that's drinking a cup of coffee or raising a family, can be important when they come back.

Steve Sez: Artistic Limitations

Each artist has strengths and weaknesses. You don't have to take them into account when you plot your story, but if you're working with an artist who has a knack for drawing attractive women but is terrible at young kids, keep that in mind when deciding whether your hero should hide in a harem or in a nursery.

Take Out the Garbage!

Now's the time to get rid of anything that doesn't work. If you have a conflict that doesn't make sense, strike it out. If Mrs. McWallaby just sits around for the whole plot doing nothing, you don't need her.

Plot points that don't address the theme of the story and don't move the story toward its ending are pointless points. Remove them now.

You might find yourself removing points that seemed very important once upon a time. You would not believe how often the very concept that inspired the whole story ends up being unnecessary.

The Least You Need to Know

◆ Using a real place adds richness to your story, but don't use a place that you don't know anything about.

◆ Stories set in the past should be set in a specific time period.

◆ For stories set in the future, have a clear idea of how society and technology have advanced.

◆ Writing down your plot will help clarify what you have and what you still need to invent.

◆ Considering every combination of your characters and thinking about how they relate to one another can generate more plot complications.

◆ Get rid of anything that doesn't help your story.

Chapter 7

Planning the Panels

In This Chapter

◆ Break your plot into pages

◆ Shatter your page into panels

◆ Describe your panels for the artist

Now that you've got a basic plot for your story worked out, it's time to start building a script, working out in more detail where everything goes. Even if you're drawing the graphic novel yourself, you need some form of script or at least a more detailed plot to work out the pacing. Otherwise, you'd be like the artist who tried to paint *The Last Supper* without sketching it out first, with the four apostles taking up most the picture and everyone else scrunched down at the right end, piled up as if a game of musical chairs were in progress.

Pacing to the Pages

First, figure out what happens on each page. Consider the key elements of your plot and figure out how many pages each takes. There's no simple rule for how many pages something will take, because pacing is a style choice. If your plot has a despondent man jumping off of a bridge, you could do that in a single panel, with motion lines showing him coming off the bridge and a thought balloon saying "goodbye, cruel world." Or you could do the same thing over six pages, as the man approaches the edge of the bridge, trembling, looks out over the water, sees the whole world around him, pulls out the photo of his recently deceased wife, steels up his courage, steps out, and plummets into the water.

If you have a plot written out, you could just break that into sections, marking where each page begins. Or you could write out a new, simple version of the plot just for the page breakdown. For example, take a look at the picture of the breakdown of the sample chapter from *The Big Con.*

A little bit of The Big Con, *chopped into chunks.*

> Page 1: Establishing shot. The fans take off their costume as the cast discusses what's going on.
> Page 2: The cast puts on the costumes. Derrick gets the head villain outfit.
> Page 3: They stride into the convention hall. Someone tries to take their photo.
> Page 4: SPLASH: Derrick pushes the photographer away. Inset shot, Terry noting that the photos should be okay.
> Page 5: They pose for a couple photos, exchange banter with dealers.
> Page 6: Derrick is attacked by a six year old dressed as the character he plays. Yeo shows him how to really attack the bad guy
> Page 7: A pile of photos that people took with the characters. The cast reaches their destination.
> Page 8: Derrick admits that he has come to see the fans differently, as something more than just people looking to profit off of him. He returns the costume to the lending fan, who mentions to his pal just how much they can now sell their costumes for on eBay.

Serialized Subsections

If your graphic novel is going to be serialized in magazine form, break your plot up into individual installments. That way, you make sure that each chapter starts and ends with something interesting. Then you'll break the first chapter into pages, and probably write that script before breaking down chapter two.

Notice that you can't follow the full plot from the page breakdown. I don't explain details like who Derrick and Yeo are. This breakdown isn't meant to be shared with others, so put down only the level of detail you'll need.

Not everything even needs to be broken into individual pages. If you have one element of the plot that takes up several pages, putting down *Pages 10–12: Myrna and Leroy discuss the spaghetti dilemma* is perfectly fine. Don't fret over getting everything exact. When it comes time to write the script, you may find that Myrna and Leroy need an extra half page of spaghetti discussion, or that you can sum it up in just two pages.

Script Style: Every Which Way but Wrong

The next step is to decide what your comic book script is going to look like. If you've seen several play scripts, you know that they all look alike. Movie scripts all look alike, too.

But graphic novel scripts from different writers are like snowflakes; no two look exactly the same. Now you may think that's because graphic novel writers are like flakes themselves, but that's not the case. Graphic novel scripts are different because they don't have to be the same.

A movie script is designed so that actors, camera operators, sound engineers, costume folks, set decorators, and all the other people involved in production can quickly locate the information they need. A graphic novel script, on the other hand, is more of a personal letter from the writer to the penciler. The letterer needs to be able to get some information from it, but beyond that the script can use any technique that gets the writer's vision into the penciler's brain.

Full-of-Possibilities Script

The various script styles do fall into certain general categories. The most commonly used style is a full script. A full script has a written description of each panel, each of the individual pictures that make up a graphic novel page.

If you take a look at the sample script in Chapter 9, you'll see that the script is broken down into pages. Each panel on that page is numbered; then there's a description of the picture in that panel. Following that is a list of all of the dialog, thought balloons, captions, and special effects lettering that go in that panel. The captions and dialog are usually numbered for the letterer's convenience.

Laying Out the Information

Some graphic novel writers don't type, they draw scripts. As you can see in the following image, a layout script (sometimes called a drawn script) is really just a quickly drawn comic book.

Layout scripts are popular with graphic novelists who both write and draw the work themselves. They're also popular with writers who have experience as artists, even when writing for someone else to draw from. As you can see from the example, however, you don't have to be a good artist to draw a layout script. As long as you make it clear who is in each panel so that the artist can follow what's going on, you should be fine.

A One-Time Layout

Every writer should write at least one short story using a layout script. Drawing out the script teaches you the limits of what can be done in each panel.

Some writers use layout scripts expecting artists to follow their layouts, placing each panel and each character on the page exactly where the writer designates. Others want the artist to use the script as merely a rough description, letting the artists choose the camera angles and panel sizes, so long as they keep the right characters, actions, and facial expressions. Let your artist know which of these tacks you're taking.

A layout script page.

Plots to Make You Plotz

Some graphic novels aren't fully scripted before landing in the artist's hands. Instead, the writer writes a reasonably tight version of the plot. This plot doesn't describe most of the panels and doesn't have most of the dialog. Instead, the writer describes the action that is happening. For example:

> Page 6: Dmitri lies on the ground, stunned. As the penguins gather around, Loretta stands over him and explains that if he hopes to ever see her again, he'd best return the penguins and get her a real gift. This takes several panels, over which she actually grows angrier. As she storms off, she yells, "Penguins? They're just pigeons with a better paint job!"

Page 7–8: The penguins work themselves under Dmitri, carrying his dazed form above their heads. As they carry him up the ramp into the back of the van, they exchange various remarks about Loretta's uncouth nature and how Dmitri can do better than her.

Many plots will have more detail than that, but some will actually have less. The penciler figures out where the page breaks and the panel breaks occur, and draws the story. Then the writer gets the story back and figures out what Dmitri, Loretta, and the penguins are actually saying. Some pencilers love this method because it gives them freedom and more control over the storytelling. Some feel that it forces them to do much of the writer's job. Artists working from loose plots became popular at Marvel Comics in the 1960s, when an overburdened writer/editor Stan Lee was teamed with folks like Jack Kirby and Steve Ditko, artists with good writing instincts. Now this style of collaboration is sometimes called *Marvel style*, and fans debate whether Kirby and Ditko should get writing credit on their work from that period.

So which script style is the right one? That depends on the writer, the artist, and the project. A graphic novel involves a lot of work, and folks should not be working in a method that they're not comfortable with. Talk to your artist until you come to a decision. If you're drawing the work yourself, go in the corner and mumble to yourself until you decide.

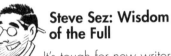

Steve Sez: Wisdom of the Full

It's tough for new writers to know how many panels a Marvel-style scene will need, leading to horribly overcrowded pages. Convert a few of your longer Marvel-style pages to full-script to see if you're asking for too much.

Breaking the Page Window Is a Pane

Unless you're writing plot-first, you'll need to break the contents of each page into panels. A panel is a tricky thing, full of possibilities and limitations.

The dialog in the panel may cover 20 seconds, but the picture itself is a snapshot, a second in time. In one panel, Loretta cannot pick up a penguin, turn, and throw it at Dmitri. That may sound like one activity but it's three separate actions taking place in three separate moments.

You could show that in three panels, one with the penguin being picked up, one with Loretta turning, and one with the penguin being flung. That would work, but if you could do that same thing in fewer panels, your plot would move forward more quickly. Readers are smart enough that they don't need to see every moment, and can assume what happens in between. If in one panel the penguin is picked up and the next has Loretta with her arm outstretched and the penguin hurtling toward Dmitri, the reader knows that she turned. In fact, you could rely on implication even more, with Loretta picking up the penguin in one panel, a look at Dmitri talking in the next, and then Dmitri is suddenly hit in the face with the penguin in the third.

Another limitation is that you can have only one important visual concept in each panel. If you can't tell the reader what's going on in one single short phrase, the panel won't work. "Dmitri watches Loretta pick up a penguin" works. "Dmitri doesn't see Loretta pick up a penguin" also works. But you cannot count on the reader getting "because Dmitri is winding his watch, he doesn't see Loretta pick up a penguin." You really get to show only one action. Everything else in the panel—other characters, furniture, penguins—is merely context.

A Longshot That Works

In *Longshot Comics*, Shane Simmons fits 160 panels on each page by drawing each character as a single dot. While no one is impressed by Shane's art, many are impressed by how his dialog and placement keeps these identical-looking characters distinguishable.

So you need to break what happens on the page into a series of individual visual moments. You can have as little as a single panel on a page, or you can actually have dozens of panels on a page, particularly if it's a series of single-character shots with little dialog.

Use the Rhythm Method

It's useful to start by picturing every page as being made up of the same number of panels. The number of panels varies from project to project, depending on the art style and the size of the pages—just think of how many typical panels of two people walking will fit on a single page. With that in mind, you can then consider how to vary the number of panels on each page. If your default panel count is six, then a page with just headshots of penguins talking might have 10 panels. On the other hand, a big action shot of penguins parachuting off of an aircraft might take up two thirds of a page, leaving space for two normal panels.

You might never have a page with the actual default number of panels on it. Still, by using that number as a base, you keep a certain rhythm through the entire story. Pages with fewer panels mean pages that read quickly, even though the large panels may each take a bit longer to read. This emphasizes the action as big, explosive moments. The smaller panels that make up a higher panel-count page capture a lot of small moments adding up to a tense flow of activity, while the page as a whole takes longer to read. Keeping the rhythm helps the reader pay attention to the storytelling, rather than being distracted by randomly sized panels.

I lean toward using a default of five or seven panels per page, with the odd number keeping me from assuming that the default page is three rows of two panels apiece. Because *The Big Con* will be published on smaller paper than most graphic novels, I've written the sample chapter around a default of four panels per page. That works for me.

Panel Planning

You could make a graphic novel with varying size pages, so one page is very small and the next is very large. It would, however, be expensive to print and difficult to read.

Barring that, you have to keep an eye on how much you're putting on a page. If you have a panel that needs to be larger than normal, either to emphasize the image or to fit in all the dialog, then you have one of two choices: Either make other panels smaller than normal, or put fewer panels on the page.

The good news is that as the writer, you don't have to come up with the final panel placement. The penciler has to make those decisions. But even if you don't make up *the* panel layout, you should have *a* panel layout in mind. Otherwise, you might ask for the impossible, and most artist don't like to do the impossible.

For example, let's say you write a four-panel page. Panel one is a normal-sized picture of Loretta talking. Panel two is an extra-tall panel of penguins climbing a rope up the side of a building. Panel three is a standard-sized shot of Loretta gasping as she looks out the window. Panel four is a wide shot through the window of the sun setting over the city, with a penguin dangling from a rope in front of it.

✒ Writers Draw Rectangles

If you have a specific panel arrangement in mind, don't describe it in words. Draw a little panel diagram on the script, just like the ones in the layout example. Artists understand pictures.

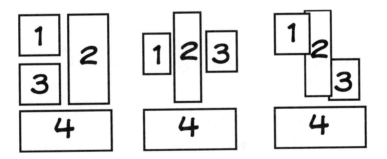

Possible layouts.

That page sounds fine until the artist has to place the panels. Look at the diagram of possible layouts to see the problem. Once you put down the short panel one and the tall panel two, where do you put panel three? If you put it below the first panel, some readers will read the panels in the wrong order, as the vertical gutters (the spaces between the panels) lead their eyes straight from panel one to panel three. Some graphic novelists would try using arrows to lead the reader from panel to panel. In things read to order what them telling instructions need shouldn't readers! (Read that sentence backward.)

Putting three panels in a row gives you wasted space and an odd-looking design. There's nothing inherently wrong with wasted space and an odd-looking design, but they should be there for some reason besides a writer being too lazy to plan.

Set Your Scene

Now that you have the panels in mind, you have to describe them to the artist. If you're drawing the graphic novel yourself, then a quick sketch or a brief sentence may be enough. If someone else is penciling the book, however, you're about to face one of the biggest challenges in writing comics: instilling an image in the brain of an artist.

What's Going On?

I said earlier that you should be able to describe what the panel is telling the reader in a single simple sentence, such as "The penguins carry the pizza out of the restaurant." Don't just think that sentence; type it. Make it the first full sentence of your panel description.

You don't have to end the panel description there. You can add more detail after that, talking about how the penguins are struggling to keep the pizza aloft, how the waitress is looking bewildered at the exiting food, that there are smell lines emanating from the pizza box, whatever.

Who's Going On?

Some writers and artists work out what the main characters look like before the script is written. If that hasn't been done, make a list of the key characters and what they look like as a separate section before the start of your script. That way, your artist can focus on designing those characters before getting into the flow of the script.

Whenever you introduce a new character in the script, even if it's someone minor, give that character a name and type it in all capital letters. "There's another penguin, BOB, who's a happy little chap with a New York Yankee's hat and a scarf." That capitalization makes it easier for the letterer—seeing that a line of dialog is coming from Bob, the letterer can find where it says BOB in the description and know which penguin is supposed to be speaking.

> **Watch Your Language**
>
> Avoid terms that your artist might not know. One writer wrote that his character had on a *catsuit*, a type of leotard. The artist, unfamiliar with the term, drew the character wearing a cat costume. This made for an unusual scene.

When describing a character, keep focused on the impact the character has rather than the details of appearance. If you write "CHUCK has short hair, reflective sunglasses, and a worn leather jacket," you may get someone who looks like an aviator or someone who looks like a street corner drug dealer. If you write "CHUCK looks like a street corner drug dealer" or, better yet, "CHUCK is a street corner drug dealer and looks it," you'll get a character that looks the part.

You can still mention the leather jacket and the reflective glasses, if you want. Putting the important stuff first shows the penciler it's important. If you need to rush and leave the unimportant stuff off altogether, that's okay, it's unimportant.

Where's Going On?

For the first panel of your graphic novel, and any other place where the characters change location, you'll have to describe where the scene is taking place. Remember, locations are more than just places where things happen. Locations create the mood for the scene, and tell you things about the characters that inhabit it. When describing a location, include the following:

- **A name for the place.** This way, you can later set a scene "back in Loretta's living room," rather than "that same room we were in back in the first three panels of page 34."

- **A description of the place in terms of its effect.** This can include the effect it has on the characters, or the effect it has on the reader in what it says about the situation. The living room might be "cluttered, showing that Loretta is too busy to clean up," or it could be "a cozy, romantic environment for our characters to fall in love in," or "stark, empty, and cold, looking bereft of human touches, much like Loretta's soul," or even "stark, empty, and cold, a perfect environment for penguins."

- **The details.** Describe the style of furniture, the size of the TV, the Moxy Früvous poster on the wall, the titles of all the books on the bookshelves, and so on.

The same rule that applies to character descriptions applies here: The most important part is the description of the effect. If you skip the effect and give the same details about a room to two different artists, you'll get two different rooms. One might seem like a friendly, happy young person's living room while the other seems dilapidated, with the exact same furnishings. On the other hand, if you skip the details and just tell two good artists "it looks like a room where penguins would feel comfortable," you'll get two different-looking rooms, but they both will serve the needs of the story. The penguins will be comfortable.

When describing a setting, describe the whole setting, not just the part you see in that first panel. The penciler will figure out what the whole room looks like before picking an angle to draw it from. If the living room first appears on page 1, and on page 23 the penguins sit on a beanbag chair in that room, mention the beanbag chair on page 1.

What Impact?

Don't be afraid to explain to the artist what emotional impact you want from the entire panel or the sequence of panels. You may think it's obvious that the penguin juggling three other penguins should look silly, but the penciler may assume he should look heroic, or come across as a showoff, or be the sexiest thing the penguin-lovin' reader has ever seen.

Letting your artist know how the art should feel and what the reader should experience makes it more likely that the art will feel right and that the reader will experience what you planned. This makes it more likely that your graphic novel will be popular, making it more likely that you'll sell millions of copies and probably win back the love of your prom date.

Reading Replete with Research

If you have specific looks, clothes, furniture, vehicles, buildings, or other items in mind, you can do better than describe them. Give the artist a picture. To an artist, a picture is worth far more than a thousand words.

Cut pictures from magazines. If your graphic novel is set in an interesting location or time, you can probably find entire books of photos or drawings about that setting. Send the book to your artist, and you'll be able to say "he's riding a camel like the one on page 37 past a mosque like the one on page 49."

The Internet offers a plethora of pictures, and not just the kind you're not allowed to view at work. Surf over to http://images.google.com and you'll find a search engine that's surprisingly good at locating the pictures you need. Then you can print the picture out, or just send your artist a link to the relevant web page.

Talk to your artist. Some artists have scads of reference photos of interesting things. Other artists have oodles of reference. And some have oodles of scads of reference.

Be a Remote-Control Cameraman

Graphic novel writers frequently request a camera angle for a particular panel. Obviously, there is no real camera involved. The *camera angle* is simply the position from which the reader is seeing the described scene. The term comes from the movies, where cameras are actually used. Besides, calling something the pencil-and-paper angle just wouldn't make sense.

The movie folks have given names to aspects of their camera angles, and we graphic novelists feel free to rip them off:

◆ **Wide shot.** A shot that shows an entire area, whether it's a city block or an entire room.

◆ **Medium shot.** Shows an entire person or persons or something of a medium size, such as a car. The penguins standing in front of the pinball machine, trying to reach the buttons, would best be covered by a medium shot.

◆ **Close.** A shot that shows most of something, but not everything. For example, a panel that is "close on Bob the penguin" will show him from the top of his Yankees cap down to his shiny wrestling champ belt buckle, but won't include his fuzzy bunny slippers.

◆ **Close-up.** Shows the important part of something. You'll get Bob's Yankees cap and possibly his scarf, but not much below that.

◆ **Extreme close-up.** Shows a very small section of a person or item. You could call for "an extreme close-up of Bob's happy, shining eyes."

In addition to calling the distance, you can describe where the view is from and what it's looking toward. "A wide shot, looking through the window toward the street corner, crowded with traffic." If a panel des-cription gets complex, you may want to sketch that panel, even if you're not doing a layout script.

When you're describing where things appear in view, use the terms *foreground* (things that are closest to the camera), *background* (things furthest from the camera), and *midground* (things between the foreground and background). You don't need to put things in all three areas in every shot. You can have a facial close-up without any other items in the panel, a foreground against an empty background. You can just have a string of marching penguins in the distance, a midground with no foreground, no background, and no flying Chihuahuas.

Establishing Shot

An **establishing shot** is a wide shot that opens a scene, usually showing an entire room, building, or outdoor area to give the reader a good sense of where the scene occurs.

Angles That Work Angelically

Remember that panels don't exist in isolation. You can create cinematic effects over a series of panels, based on how your nonexistent camera operator moves the nonexistent camera.

Zooming involves moving the camera directly toward (*zooming in*) or away from (*zooming out*) what you're looking at. You can start with a shot that's close on Bob, talking. Zoom out to the next panel which is a mid shot of the penguins forming a penguin pyramid, with Bob on the top. Zoom out even further to a wide shot, showing that the pyramid is on the wing of a biplane.

Where zooming out is great for revelations, zooming in builds the intensity. Moving from a distant shot of a conversation to a close-up makes that conversation ever more important.

Keeping the camera angle the same makes it easier to pay attention to the actions in the individual panels. That sort of repetitive shot is particularly good in humorous situations.

Read through some graphic novels, paying attention to how the camera angles are used. Not only will you see a lot of interesting possibilities, you'll also get to spend time reading graphic novels while pretending you're getting something useful done. How great is that?

How Loose Is Too Loose, Lautrec?

So now you know how to call the camera angle and how to fill your panel with detailed descriptions of people and places and items. But writing like that is like driving with your feet—just because you know how to do it doesn't mean that you should.

Some writers script quite loosely, averaging only two sentences per panel description. Others describe everything, calling every camera angle, the placement of every item in the frame, and describing characters not only in terms of their appearance but also how they move, what songs they like, and all sorts of details of varying importance. Alan Moore, the writer behind *Watchmen*, *From Hell*, and *The League of Extraordinary Gentlemen*, has written seven single-spaced typewritten pages to describe a single panel. That's maniacal, but in his case it works.

The right density is whatever works for you and your artist. A rule of thumb is to be specific about whatever you have a particular vision of. If you have a certain outfit in mind for a character, describe it. If you have a vision of a keen way to use camera angles, state those camera angles and explain why you're using them. But don't fill in details and call camera angles just because you think you're supposed to. Any artist worth working with will have an artistic vision to handle what your vision lacks.

The Least You Need to Know

- There are many different styles and formats for writing comics, all of them right in certain circumstances.

- Picture the page in your own mind to make sure that you aren't asking for impossible drawings or camera angles.

- Picking a default number of panels per page will help you build a good rhythm for your script.

- The key information for the reader in each panel should fit in one short, clear sentence.

- Describing the effect that a character, object, or setting has is more important than describing the appearance.

- Describe in detail only those things that you have a particular vision for.

Delicious Dialog

In This Chapter

◆ Write people that sound like people

◆ Use or avoid captions

◆ Make the text fit

A graphic novel doesn't need text. You could make a graphic novel in which no one speaks, and you wouldn't be the first. But just because you can do something doesn't mean that you should, as anyone who has tried jalapeño ice cream will tell you.

Properly handled text is not a distraction from pictures. It's a companion to the pictures, an integrated part of telling the story. People who insist that the words or the pictures are more important are like those who argue that red is more important than blue in making purple.

Dallying with Dialog

Most of the text in graphic novels comes spilling out of characters' mouths. Conversations, monologues, mutterings, and coughs all have their place in telling a story.

Dialog is the Achilles' heel of many new graphic novel writers. They produce scripts with so much dialog it leaves no room for art, or not enough dialog where it's needed to make matters clearer, or simply clumsy dialog that makes it hard to believe in the characters. Most of the things that make for good comics dialog also make for good dialog for prose writing or movie scripts.

"Sounds Like Someone!"

Dialog carries information. While half of that information is in what the person is saying, the other half is in *how* they say it. Someone talking into a cell phone saying "Hey, that looks like a purple aardvark coming around the corner!" is saying the same thing as the person who says "A quadruped has come into view on the corner, switching on to this street. It's violet in hue. Otherwise, it matches the description of *orycertops capensis.* Correct, an aardvark." But the way they're speaking suggests so much more about who they are, who they might be talking to, and why.

Steve Sez: Stay Out of My Room!

Tiny pictures are a lot harder to draw, and important story details can become illegible if the pictures are too small. You'll make everyone's life a lot easier if you leave your artists enough room to do their job.

Eschewing Exclamations

Some writers end most dialog sentences with exclamation points! This tradition comes from the early days of comics, when printers would sometimes mistake periods for stray dots and remove them! You don't need to follow this tradition!

The first trick to making dialog that sounds real is to listen to people. Really listen, not just to what they say but how they say it. What sort of words do they use? How do they use them? What impression do they create? What do they emphasize with their inflections? What accents do they have? What slang do they use? Listen to many different people, loud folks, quiet folks, old folks, kids, people for whom English is a second language. People don't speak like textbooks. If you think you're having trouble noticing the details, tape what people say and then type it out. Even just writing down, word for word, the messages people leave on your answering machine will help.

The second trick to writing dialog is ignoring a lot of what you learned in the first trick. Nobody wants to read genuinely realistic dialog. Real people hem and haw, talk in partial sentences, fragments, and phrases, and generally speak inefficiently. A little bit of these things is good for establishing the character or emphasizing moments of indecision of confusion. But try to, ummm, y'know. Too much, it becomes a painful in the … Just don't.

This is especially true for accents. Don't try to creatively spell every word a character speaks to reflect a strong accent. Yerr readerr vill kvickly tire uv tryink to dezypher ebery verd.

Brevity: The Soul of Fit

Keep your dialog short unless it needs to be otherwise. Dialog takes up space. The more it uses, the more you either have to lengthen your entire work or make the art smaller and thus have less impact.

Some writers have maximums that they keep in mind. They might limit themselves to 17 words per *word balloon*, the individual bubble that holds one speaker's words. Their limit could be 30 words for a typical-sized panel, no more than 60 words on a page. There is no exact set of magic numbers. Look through a graphic novel with a graphic style similar to what yours will have. If you can find some word balloons that look too big or pages that look too crowded with text, start counting words and see what your own personal limits are.

The toughest dialog to keep short is when someone is explaining something, giving a lot of information for the reader to absorb. Consider the case where a character says, "My father was a great inventor. He was working for a big car company, and he invented this spring-powered car. The only problem was that the car could only be driven on winding roads." It may be an important revelation, but it's far too long. Let's see what we can do to shorten it:

- **Lose unimportant details.** Is it really important who Dad was working for when he invented the car?

- **Become less formal.** Some characters can speak with slang, dropping formal words and relying on "it" and "that" instead of longer terms.

- **Break it into two balloons.** This doesn't actually save space, but two shorter balloons are less daunting and easier to integrate into the art.

"Dad? *Great* inventor. Invented this spring-powered car."

"Problem was, it could only be driven on winding roads."

That's shorter.

But the best way to keep the dialog short is to show, rather than tell. You could have a panel of Althea saying "for my birthday, Bob got me a fancy new watch covered with diamonds," or you could just show the watch on her wrist, with "Bob got it for my birthday!"

Balloon Physics

You can use word balloons for visual impact. In my graphic novel *The Factor*, I had one series of panels where a character describes his demeaning job. As the description became longer, the balloons became bigger, leaving the character smaller in the remaining available space. Another time, as you see in the sample picture, I placed a boring man's word balloon behind his girlfriend, to show that he was still talking but that she wasn't paying attention.

The boring boyfriend is based on me.

(Art drawn by and copyright by Janine Johnston.)

Interesting Interchanges

Most characters aren't the crazy person on the bus, jabbering away into the empty air (that's me). When they talk they're talking to someone, having a conversation of some sort. Conversations can be great things, full of dramatic revelations and conflict, or simply be a way of demonstrating character.

In real life, conversations go back and forth a lot, often with two people overlapping each other, interrupting each other's sentences, and getting in a lot of short bursts of words. You can do any of that in a graphic novel, but be careful when doing a lot of it at once. Placing the word balloons becomes difficult when you have two characters each talking more than twice in a single panel. The balloons tend to end up getting placed between the two characters, so suddenly they have a great audible relationship but visually they're separated from each other.

Make your conversations more interesting by putting information into each statement whenever possible. In real life, conversations often flow with one person saying little more than "oh really?" "uh-huh," and "what did she say?" all of which may coax more information out of the first speaker but add no information themselves. When Althea tells Bob "I've built a perpetual motion machine out of marbles, mousetraps, and uncooked rotelli pasta," he can say "really? how?" and add no information. Or he could say "I don't believe you," "doesn't that violate the third law of thermodynamics?" or simply "again?" each of which adds a different type of information.

Read your conversations out loud. If they sound stiff, formal, or unreal to you, then the reader will probably have the same reaction. I often work out conversations aloud *before* typing them up to avoid that stiffness. That's why you see me talking to myself on the bus.

Put your conversation in an interesting setting. There's an instinct to stop everything, putting characters into chairs to do nothing but chat. That's not a wrong thing to do, particularly in drama. But if you take the same conversation and stage it during a bike ride, or at a boxing match, or at the zoo, it becomes more interesting. At the very least, there are more interesting pictures, and the context usually adds something to the conversation. To add a lot more, put it on a bike ride to a boxing match at the zoo.

Here's a Thought

The *thought balloon* is a special form of word balloon, used to show the thoughts of one of the characters. The thought balloon has a series of circles pointing to the thinker, rather than the pointy pointer used by word balloons. Some letterers make the thought balloon outline bumpy rather than smooth.

Writers use thought balloons far less frequently than they did in the past. There's been a drive to make comics more cinematic, to make them more like movies. Some writers believe that because you can't hear what people are thinking in the movies, you shouldn't "hear" it in comics either. And for some projects, that's the right way to go. But not always.

The thought balloon is a tool in the writer's toolbox, and shouldn't be thrown away just because it can be misused. These days, some graphic novelists spend pages showing what a thought balloon could capture in a single panel. Others add an unnecessary character for the main character to spill out all his thoughts to. But prose authors don't hesitate to tell you what a character is thinking, because it's useful stuff to know. And Shakespeare, unable to use thought balloons in his play, relied on the far more artificial *soliloquy*, where a character just speaks all of his thoughts out loud when no one is looking. Let's face it, if Hamlet were spouting his soliloquy on the back of the bus, he'd seem like just another crazy person. Which, come to think of it, he was.

Thought balloons are great for expressing emotions and for summing up situations. "Three o'clock already? If I don't get the purple aardvark back to the zoo before the boxing match, Ms. Alverado will fire me for sure!"—give that thought balloon to a panicking character in the very first panel of your story and the reader starts out with a lot of information. Of course, if we never see that character again the reader will be merely confused.

For naturalistic thought balloons, avoid full sentences. Some people use words more in their thoughts than others do, but people don't constantly think in full sentences. You could have someone saying "should I go out with Vincent or Jacques? Vincent's a very kind and upright fellow, but on the other hand, Jacques has a physical attractiveness that is hard to beat," but for a thought balloon you'd be better off with "Vincent or Jacques? Vincent: sweet … Jacques: yummy!"

Of course, you don't need to be naturalistic. Being stylized in comics is fine, as long as you're doing it on purpose. Remember, the great musicals weren't great because they reflected how people naturally break into song and dance. They were great because they painted an unnatural world in an unnatural but exciting way.

Captions Courageous

Use of *captions*, narrative text generally placed in rectangles and not associated with a specific on-panel character, has also fallen off a lot because of the quest for cinematic storytelling. Mostly this has left two types of captions, the settings caption and first person narration.

A *settings caption* is a brief caption telling you where or when the scene takes place, such as "The following Tuesday:" or "Edwards Air Force Base. 3:17 A.M." With *first person narration* a character in the story tells you some of what is going on, such as "I'd been sitting all day in my office, drinking peppermint-flavored discount beer and reading *The Complete Idiot's Guide to Being a Hardboiled Detective*, when this redheaded dame walked in."

A type of caption that has faded away is the omniscient *third person narration*, where some unnamed, unseen narrator is telling you everything that's going, whether any of the characters know it or not. "Thrung the Unruly descended the stairs slowly, uncertain of where the vicious purple aardvark lurked." Yes, this sort of narration is often used to give information that should be visible in the panel, making it redundant, but even then it usually adds bits of information and can make a work seem richer. It does make the work take longer to read, which sounds bad but can be good, particularly when it comes to people feeling like they got their money's worth.

Between First and Third Person

Second person narration speaks of the reader as a character, telling you what "you" are doing. The only obvious comics example of this is the classic EC Comics eight-pager "Master Race."

But the third person narration doesn't have to describe what's currently going on. You can talk about interesting related information. While Althea chases after the purple aardvark, your narration could be explaining how she spent her teen years training as a sprinter, but never being good enough to make the varsity track team. Or you could explain how aardvarks are members of the anteater family, a misnamed group because they subsist primarily on termites. Narration that informs the reader about subtleties of what is going on or remains calm during hectic events can be powerful.

Sounds Effective

Sound effects like "WHAM," "tic-tic-tic," and "fuh-*woosh*" are a very special part of graphic novel text. As with captions and thought balloons, sound effects are optional. They should be part of your toolbox, but not a tool you have to use in every project.

Some objects have standard sounds, like *bang*, *boom*, or *vroom*. Feel free to use those—they're cliché but they work. But you don't have to stick to those, and you'll sometimes have to come up with a sound for something that doesn't have a standard. To come up with a sound for something, do your best possible vocal imitation of the sound. The effort of making the sound will help you put that sounds into letters.

The right sound effect spelling will get you only so far. Most of the impact of a sound effect comes not from what it sounds like, but from what it looks like. You'll have to rely on the letterer to see to it that your *whffft* is a delicate little sound and your *kBooooom* shakes the world.

Mark Your Words

Once you've figured out what your characters and captions are saying, you have to share that information with the folks who will be reading your script, especially your letterer. Time for typing!

First thing after the panel description should be the sound effect, if the panel has one. Type *SFX:* followed by a tab followed by the sound effect.

Next type any noncaption, nondialog text that the letterer should put in, such as newspaper headlines or signs. If it's flat lettering that the reader has to be able to read, it's the letterer's job rather than the penciler's. Type *HEADLINE:* or *SIGN:* or whatever, followed by a tab, followed by the words on the item.

Each caption and word balloon on a page is numbered in the order in which they should be read. As you can see in the sample script in Chapter 9, each line of dialog in the panel should have its number and the name of the speaker, while captions should have a number and the word *CAPTION*. After that, of course, you type the actual words that go in the word balloon or the caption.

Most graphic novels keep the comic book tradition of using ALL CAPITAL LETTERS for their dialog (and some even for their panel descriptions), but some use upper- and lowercase. Your typing should match that style. I like to set my word processor font to a handwriting-style font for writing dialog. Since this font is similar to what will be used on the page, this helps me see what the lettering will look like on the page, and makes it easier to see when I have too much text.

> **Keep It Cheap** _____
>
> Some programs designed for word-processing screenplays now include options to help you format graphic novel scripts. Unless you're already using them to write screenplays, save your money. You don't need them.

Typing Type Types and Blatant Balloons

Writers emphasize certain words in the text for different reasons, either to focus reader attention on important words or reflect the way the character speaks. For simple emphasis, either underline or italicize the words you want emphasized. Don't emphasize too many individual words, because *after* a *while* the *emphasis* starts *losing its effect* and the *changing lettering style* just *becomes annoying*.

If you have any special requests for the lettering in a word balloon, put it in parenthesis before the balloon. That way, you can request "(Small lettering, large balloon) WOW" to make the speaker seem quietly overwhelmed, or "(extra large)EEEK! BUNNIES!" for a shout. You can even ask for a special typeface, like asking for a robotic font for a mechanical voice.

You also use the parenthesis to request special types of balloons. Inside the parenthesis is where you'd request a thought balloon. You can also request a *burst*, a spiked balloon used to indicate a shout. There is also the *electric balloon* (also known as a *radio balloon*), which is used to show sounds coming from speakers, radios, telephones, and haunted talking coffee pots.

Occasionally, you'll want a word balloon for someone who isn't actually pictured in the panel. If it's the first word balloon in the panel, you can have it coming from someone in the prior panel, as long as that prior panel is either right above or just to the left of the current panel. You'd mark that with "(from previous panel)." Similarly, the last balloon in a panel can come from a character in the panel immediately to the right or below this panel, and would be marked "(from next panel)."

Otherwise, the reader will just have to imagine the person who is speaking. You can specify a word balloon with its pointy bit (called the tail) pointing to someone unseen outside the panel by indicating where it's coming from, such as "(from off-panel left)." You can even have a balloon with no tail, which is good when you have a panel with a lot of people speaking and it doesn't matter who is actually saying the words. For example, in a press conference scene you might have "(from off-panel; no tail)*SENATOR*, IS IT TRUE THAT YOUR SON IS IN *LOVE* WITH AN *AARDVARK*?"—It's not important which reporter is asking the question, merely that it is being asked.

That Dashed Double Dash ...

When you want to break up a single sentence between two word balloons, finish one word balloon by typing two hyphens--

--then start the text of the next word balloon with another two hyphens, as you see here.

Any English teacher, if he or she is worth his or her salt or pepper, will tell you that writing a double dash like that is wrong, that what's needed is a wider single dash, something called an em dash. That's true. You're seeing an odd language evolution in action. Old typewriters didn't have an em dash, and the standard in the prose publishing world was that writers would type a double dash wherever they wanted an em dash.

Comic book letterers didn't come from the typesetting world, however, and when they saw a double dash, they figured the writer wanted a double dash. Now some letterers will put in the double dash and some will put in the em dash, but the double dash has been used enough over the years that it's a standard part of comics punctuation. With all-capital lettering and the abuse of double dashes and exclamation points, is it any wonder that comics make some English teachers cringe?

Don't break a sentence with the three periods that make up an ellipsis …

… then pick up the second half of the sentence with another ellipsis, like you see here. An ellipsis goes at the end of a word balloon when someone trails off without finishing the sentence. It's used at the start of a word balloon when we start hearing someone in midsentence, or when a person is finishing a sentence someone else started. And it's used in the middle of a sentence in a word balloon to indicate a particularly long pause. In fact, one of its coolest uses is when there is just an ellipsis in a word balloon, used when a character is trying to respond to a statement but can't think of anything. The character's speech is just a big, blatant pause.

For some characters, that lack of response is the smartest thing they say in the whole story.

The Least You Need to Know

- Keep dialog brief.
- Every statement should add information, either via what it says or what it implies about the speaker.
- Narrative captions, thought balloons, and sound effects should be part of your toolbox.
- Number all the captions and word balloons.
- Speak your dialog out loud to determine whether it sounds natural.

Chapter 9

A Bit of *The Big Con:* Script

Here is the actual script for a chapter of the graphic novel *The Big Con*. You can see Steve's pencil-drawn version of this script in Chapter 17, and the final inked and lettered version in Chapter 20.

The Big Con
Chapter: "Con Cognito"
by Nat Gertler
nat@aboutcomics.com
(805) 499-███
Script for 8 pages

Characters: We have three stars of the new movie *Galaxy Beyond III*.
DERRICK is haughty, ruggedly handsome action star, 45, impatient, polo shirt and pleated pants. He carries himself proudly.
TERRY is a slim, sexy, intelligent 29 year old, sophisticated make-up, sunglasses, silk blouse and tight jeans.
YEO is a short, playful, happy Chinese man, bouncy and energetic, a gymnast/martial artist/clown, a bit of AN elf. He's got a t-shirt with a picture of his own smiling face.

GENE is a studio publicity guy, a shorter black man in his 40s, looking very precise and controlled; clean haircut, dark shirt with two silver pens in the pocket perfectly upright, creased dark pants, a leather organizer on a strap over his shoulder.

Other characters are introduced as needed.

Key design items: Three costumes, all of characters from the *Galaxy Beyond* film series:
LORD ZATAN: basically a convex shape of brushed steel. Think of it as a verical tube that's been constricted at points so it's widest at the base, narrows into a curve up to the neck, and flairs to the top of the head... kind of an art deco chess queen. Add arms, mean-looking triangular red eye lenses, and any further flairs you want. Most of the costume comes off in two parts – the head slips down over the lower part, which is held on by shoulder straps.
THE MONK is a shimmery, tech version of a monk's robe, with a hood that actually covers the top half of the face.
WARRIOR BOT is basically body armor, with a head piece basically the shape of a UFO disc. The armor needs to be very flexible at the joints, as Yeo will be wearing it and moving in ways that require a lack of restriction.

PAGE ONE

(1)

ESTABLISHING SHOT: exterior, day. A big, modern convention center, shiny, angular, and broad.

1 CAPTION:	SATURDAY, 2 PM
2 CAPTION:	THE STARS OF THE MOVIE *GALAXY BEYOND III* FACE A PROBLEM.
3 DERRICK:	(FROM NEXT PANEL) WITH ALL OF THE COPS BACK THERE, SHOULDN'T THE BACK ENTRANCE BE *SAFE?*

(2)

LARGE. DAVE is explaining to TERRY, YEO, and DERRICK, most directly toward Derrick. They're standing in a small conference room in the convention center, with a dias and chairs set up. Behind them in the room, three fans are taking off their costumes – this shouldn't be the focus of the panel, but it should be there. It's the LORD ZATAN, MONK, and WARRIOR BOT costumes described earlier. The guys inside are all in their early twenties, dressed in t-shirts, a bit disheveled from having been in the costumes. When we see them more clearly, their friendly looking, a bit geeky.

4 GENE:	(FROM NEXT PANEL) THEY SAY EVERYTHING'S CLEARED UP BACK THERE, BUT WHY RISK IT?
5 GENE:	WITH THESE DISGUISES, YOU CAN REACH THE AUDITORIUM UNRECOGNIZED.
6 YEO:	BUT THIS IS A *PUBLICITY* APPEARANCE. DON'T WE *WANT* TO BE SEEN?

(3)

Close on Terry (patient) and Derrick (less so) explaining to Yeo. I see this as being Terry's head on the left, Derrick's on the right, and short Yeo only having the upper half of his head in panel, his eyes paying attention to Terry.

7 TERRY:	AH, THE IGNORANCE OF THE NEWBIE. YEO, *NONE* OF US STARS FROM THE TWO RELEASED FILMS CAN WALK IN A CROWD.
8 DERRICK:	TERRY'S RIGHT. EVEN IN *NORMAL* PUBLIC, IT'S ALL "SIGN THIS FOR EBAY" AND "MAKE ME FAMOUS" AND "I'LL KISS YOU NOW AND SUE YOU LATER" --

PAGE TWO

(1)

Derrick throws up his hands in disgust while Gene points a finger at him, lecturing

1 DERRICK: --AND HERE IN THIS *GEEKFEST*, IT WOULD BE...

2 GENE: WATCH IT! THESE COMICS FANS AREN'T *GEEKS*, THEY'RE THE
               FOLKS WHO BUY TICKETS TO YOUR MOVIES.

(2)

Gene gestures toward the fans, ALF, BERT, and CHARLIE, who are happily bringing over the Monk, Warrior Bot, and Lord Zatan costumes, repectively.

3 GENE: AND *THESE THREE* FANS ARE HELPFULLY LENDING YOU THE
               WONDERFUL COSTUMES THEY'D MADE FOR TONIGHT'S
               COSTUME CONTEST!

4 BERT: GLAD TO HELP.

(3)

Derrick holds the head of the Lord Zatan outfit in his hands, staring it in the eyes, perturbed.

5 DERRICK: I'VE GOT TO BE *LORD ZATAN*? YOU COULDN'T GET US *HERO*
               COSTUMES?

(4)

Gene is holding up the Monk's robe while Terry sticks her arms in the sleeve.

6 GENE: IT'S A *DISGUISE*, DERRICK. YOU KNOW YOUR *GENROY-7* OUTFIT
               IN THE FILM DOESN'T HIDE YOUR FACE.

7 TERRY: (THOUGHT) LIKE *HE'D* HAVE TAKEN THE HERO ROLE IF IT MEANT
               HIS PRETTY FACE WOULD BE HIDDEN?

PAGE THREE

(1)

Terry is pulling up the hood of her Monk robe, while Derrick and Yeo, now in the body of their outfits, are just starting to lower their heads on. Derrick is looking up into the head, Yeo grinning wickedly.

1 DERRICK: OH, THIS WILL MESS UP MY HAIR.

2 YEO: ...OR MAYBE IT'LL MESS UP YOUR *MIIIIIIND!*

(2)

Same angle as panel (1), only now the hood and heads are in place. (This should help cement in the reader's head the link between the characters and the costumes)

3 TERRY: LET'S GO!

(3)

The three stars, in costume, area heading into the convention sales floor, through double-doors with a WELCOME TO COMICARAMA SEATTLE banner above it (it need not be fully readable.) LORD ZATAN inherently walks stiffly, since there's really no movement to the costume; the MONK has grace. Yeo, in his Warrior BOT outfit, has gotten into being in a costume and is doing a bouncy, crouching, monkey-type lope.

          NO COPY

(4)

The three stars are now in the convention hall, where a camera-carrying WIFE is pointing toward them while her t-shirt-and-backpacked HUSBAND heads toward them. Typical large comics convention dealers. We don't need to see much scope, but what we see should look busy (sketchy is fine).

4 WIFE: WHAT GREAT OUTFITS!

5 WIFE: LET'S GET A SHOT OF YOU WITH THEM!

PAGE FOUR

(1)

FULL PAGE: Lord Zatan shoves Husband away with one arm, sending him staggering. (Steve: we might get some energy out of tilting this shot; it's one of the few actiony moments in this tale.)

1 ZATAN: (BURST, LARGE) HEY, *NO PHOTOS!*

(2)

INSET, lower right. Close up on The Monk, a cocked smile on the visible lower half of her face.

2 TERRY: DERRI... UMMM...

3 TERRY: LAWD *ZATAN*, THEY-ALL JUS' WANT PITCHERS OF OAH CAWSTOOMS!

Gertler/The Big Con—"Con Cognito"/ p. 6

PAGE FIVE

(1)

Lord Zatan puts his arm around husband's shoulder, while the Monk poses to one side and Warrior Bot squats in front.

1 ZATAN:	OH, RIGHT...
2 ZATAN:	SURE, WHY NOT?

(2)

Wife snaps photo, while beside her an overweight but pretty and happy-looking woman dressed as a FAIRY waves her wand in the air, excited.

SFX:	(CAMERA) KLIK
3 FAIRY:	ME NEXT!

(3)

The three of them walk past a chubby comics DEALER behind his longbox-covered table. Zatan is in front, the Monk behind him, and the Bot crouched in a monkeywalk behind her, top of his head about at the top of the longboxes.

4 DEALER:	HEY, ZATAN, I GIVE *TWENTY PERCENT OFF* TO ALL FORCES OF *EVIL!*

(4)

The Bot hooks his fingers over the top of the longboxes and is peering over them to face the dealer, who is playing along.

5 BOT:	YOU KNOW, THE DEALERSSSS WHO *SSSURVIVE* ALL OFFER LORD ZATAN *FORTY* PERSSSENT OFF!
6 DEALER:	I WOULDN'T GIVE MY OWN EVIL *MOTHER* FORTY PERCENT OFF ON A *SATURDAY.*
	NOW ON A *SUNDAY...*
7 KID:	(BURST FROM OFF-PANEL LOWER RIGHT; IT CAN COVER UP THE END OF THE WORD "SUNDAY" IN THE PREVIOUS BALLOON) HI-*YAAAA!*

PAGE SIX

(1)

Close on A KID, a five year old boy in a space hero costume, whacking Lord Zatan repeatedly in the middle of his back with a plastic, high-tech version of a battleaxe. His costume is a Galaxy Beyond outfit, Derrick's character's costume. The kid is in high-sugar mode, screaming and is wielding the battleaxe in an overhead fashion.

SFX:	THWANG THWANG THWANG
1 KID:	(BURST) TAKE *THAT*, LORD ZATAN!!!
2 ZATAN:	(THOUGHT; STEVE, DEPENDING ON HOW YOU FRAME THIS SHOT, ZATAN'S HEAD MIGHT BE OFF-PANEL. THAT'S FINE, JUST POINT THE BALLOON TOWARD WHERE HIS HEAD IS.) WHAT NOW?

(2)

The Bot is loping up to the scene of the attack, while the Monk looks on amused.

3 BOT:	HEY, KID, DON'T ATTACK LORD ZATAN THAT WAY!

(3)

The Bot has wrapped his arms around the kid and his hands are encircled around the kid's hands on the shaft of the axe, showing him how to hold it sideways. Think of someone showing a kid how to swing a baseball bat, and you've got it.

4 BOT:	YOU GOTTA SWING *SIDEWAYS* TO CUT THROUGH HIM.
5 BOT:	OTHERWISE, YOUR LASERAXE WILL JUST BOUNCE RIGHT OFF HIS CURVED ARMOR!

(4)

Close up on the Bot and the Kid, who has turned to face him.

6 KID:	THANKS! I WAN' BE THE *BEST* GALACTIC WARRIOR, JUST LIKE *GENROY-SEVEN!*
7 BOT:	YOU EVEN *LOOK* A LITTLE LIKE DERRICK GREY
8 KID:	*WHO?*

PAGE SEVEN

(1)

Most of this page is just a pile of scattered, overlapping photos taken while the cast were in the convention hall. Using some white-bordered prints (even though those are out of style) should convey this. The pictures can include (though we need not see all of these, use your layout judgment):

> Bot's hands holding the Kid up so that he can whack Zatan on the top of the head.
> A sexy woman in a cat outfit (ears, tail) leaning seductively against the expressionless form of Lord Zatan
> The Monk squatting to talk with a wheelchair-bound female with palsy
> All three posing with two muscular guys in tight black shirts with white lettering: BAD GUYS RULE
> Lord Zatan posing with another Lord Zatan, this one in a weak, home-made costume covered in tinfoil. They're facing each other in mock battle.
> A pair of women in oversized Japanese schoolgirl uniforms holding Bot aloft horizontally.

1 CAPTION: THE STARS JOURNEYED ACROSS THE CONVENTION FLOOR
                             UNIDENTIFIED, BUT NOT WITHOUT INTERRUPTION.

(2)

The three stars head out an exit into a hallway where Gene is waiting.

2 GENE: FINALLY! WE'VE GOT A LITTLE ROOM OVER HERE FOR YOU TO
                        CHANGE IN. YOUR TALK STARTS IN TWO MINUTES.

3 ZATAN: SORRY, BUT *THAT WAS* _FUN_!

Gertler/The Big Con—"Con Cognito"/ p. 9

PAGE EIGHT

(1)

Gene holds open a door. A somewhat sweaty Derrick is removing the Zatan head as he heads toward it.

1 DERRICK: I MEAN, IT WASN'T ANYTHING ABOUT "CELEBRITY".

(2)

Derrick and Terry talk. Derrick has his arms around the costume head. Terry, hood now off, is gesturing vaguely toward Alf, Bert, and Charlie in the background (although they need not all be visible.)

2 TERRY: I KNOW, IT'S JUST LIKE THESE GUYS HERE AND THOSE FOLKS OUT THERE, THEY ALL JUST WANT TO HAVE FUN IN THE *GALACTIC BEYOND* WORLD.

3 DERRICK: MAKES ME A LITTLE PROUDER TO HAVE HELPED BUILD THAT WORLD.

(3)

A grateful Derrick hands the Zatan head back to Charlie, who looks thrilled.

4 DERRICK: HEY, THANKS A LOT FOR THE LOAN.

5 CHARLIE: ARE YOU KIDDING?

6 CHARLIE: DO YOU KNOW HOW MUCH I CAN GET FOR A *LORD ZATAN* COSTUME WORN BY **THE** *DERRICK GREY*?

(4)

Derrick looks at Terry and Yeo painfully. Terry is rolling her eyes, and Yeo just shrugs.

7 CHARLIE: (CONTINUED FROM PREVIOUS PANEL) I'LL EBAY IT OFF A PIECE AT A TIME!!

-END-

Part 3

Putting It in Pencil

The first stage of drawing a graphic novel is usually done in pencil. This way, you can draw construction lines that help you shape your drawing but can be erased later. You can also correct mistakes easily when you draw in pencil. That's not so easy to do when you draw in ink, blood, or rhubarb pie filling.

In the following chapters, you learn to design characters and settings. You get tips on turning the script into well laid-out pages made up of stylish, well-rendered panels.

Chapter 10

Designing Your Characters

In This Chapter

◆ Reading the script

◆ Creating your characters' faces and physiques

◆ Deciding what they're wearing

◆ Designing fantastic characters

This is Steve writing, now. That means you've reached the drawing part of the book. Without characters, there is no story. You're here to tell a story, and you want to do it with pictures. That means you have to figure out what your characters look like. Your goal is to come up with interesting and distinctive character designs that fit your story. Sharpen your pencils. I'm going to design some characters from *The Big Con* and you should try along with me.

Reading Is Fundamental

Before you start designing, you need to know some things about the characters. Read the whole script carefully, paying attention to anything that might tell you what the characters look like and what sort of things they need to do. Take notes, mark important story points with a highlighting pen and jot down any questions you have for the writer. You want lots of information about the characters. Where is it?

Sometimes the writer puts a good, thorough description right up front. That way, you know what the writer wants and expects you to deliver. Nat does that in his descriptions of Derrick, Terry, Yeo, and Gene.

Dramatis Perwhatsis?

As you read a script for the first time, write down the name of each new character as you come to it. As you progress through the script, take short notes about each character.

Nat Sez: Keep Unimportant Characters Unimportant

Your background characters needn't be bland, but if you give FIRST MAN ON STAIRS a face like a god and a body like a California governor, readers will be confused when he remains just a man on the stairs.

For minor characters, you'll often find their description in the panel in which they first appear. On Page 3, panel 4, the script says "a camera-carrying WIFE is pointing toward them [our heroes] while her T-shirt-and-backpacked HUSBAND heads toward them." Nat didn't have to go into much detail, because he knows I'm familiar with comic book conventions. If this had been a rodeo clown convention, Nat might just as well have mentioned her Stetson and his rubber nose.

Sometimes you'll need to figure things out for yourself. Nat doesn't specify what sort of footwear Terry is wearing, and in this script, he didn't need to. But suppose that on the next to last page of the story, she stumbles on the stairs and loses a shoe. You'd want to remember that scene when deciding whether to dress her in mules or mid-calf, lace-up boots.

And sometimes, you get no clues at all. When this happens with a minor character, it probably means that it doesn't matter what FIRST MAN ON STAIRS or WOMAN IN OFFICE looks like. When it happens with a major character, it probably means that the writer forgot that comic books have pictures. When in doubt, or even if you think you might be in doubt but aren't sure, ask.

Start at the Head

Usually by the time I've finished reading a script, I've got some notion of what the characters look like, and I sometimes supplement that by flipping through some magazine photos or my old sketchbooks, looking for the right type of people to "cast" as my leads. Anywhere you can find people to look at, you can find inspiration. Then I start sketching simple, cartoony little head doodles, trying to find one that seems right for the character. Doodles shouldn't be complete drawings. Just scribble down shapes and ideas. You're brainstorming on paper.

Head doodles like these don't have to be tight or detailed.

The Basics of Basic Shapes

Any drawing is built out of basic shapes. Make those shapes distinctive. Don't worry about features like eyes or noses yet. For now you're just building a rough structure out of simple forms like spheres and cubes. I gave Derrick a boxy head with a big jaw—something that the reader will associate with the sort of action hero he portrays. Terry has an elegant oval head, the delicacy of which should contrast nicely with Derrick's rugged features. And Yeo's head is nearly spherical, which I hope will emphasize his clownish qualities, like a face drawn on a toy balloon.

We need distinct rough structures to build consistent and recognizable heads.

Over the course of an entire graphic novel, you're likely to draw these people from a variety of angles and distances, in bright light and deep shadow, and wearing all sorts of odd outfits. If you give them distinctive head shapes, readers will have no problem keeping track of who's who.

Finding the Right Features

Unless your graphic novel is a going to be a romance between a pair of department store mannequins, you'll want to flesh out those heads a bit. This is where things really get fun, which is great if you like fun.

Some graphic novel artists just pick a real person to base each character on. "The hero will look like my fifth grade teacher, but without the beard, and the villain will look like Harry Houdini." That's fine, but be careful with this approach. Don't make those likenesses so close they distract the reader or get you sued. A similar and safer approach is a bit like playing with Mr. Potato Head. Pick one real person and base your rough structure on the shape of his head. Then think about some other people: your friends and family, celebrities, the plumber. Try borrowing parts from each. Take your best friend's eyes and eyebrows, your mailman's nose and Elvis Presley's mouth. Now put them back, apologize, and make a drawing of someone with that set of features.

There's a huge range of options for every part of the head. Start asking yourself questions about the following features:

- ◆ **Hair.** Long, short, or missing? Straight, wavy, kinky, curly? What color? What sort of style? Any facial hair? Mustache? Beard?

- ◆ **Skin.** Smooth or wrinkled? Clear or scarred? Clean or dirty? Any tattoos, freckles, or birthmarks?

- ◆ **Eyebrows.** Bushy or sparse? Straight or arched? Broad or narrow?

- ◆ **Eyes.** What color? Close-set or far apart? Wide or narrow? Full lashes or thin? Prominent eyelids? Bags or circles underneath? Crow's feet?

- ◆ **Nose.** Long or short? Pointed or flat? Does it curl up or down? Do the nostrils flare?

- ◆ **Mouth.** How broad? What are the teeth like? Are the lips full or thin? How do they curve?

- ◆ **Chin.** Prominent or recessed? Sharp or rounded? Any cleft? Stubble?

Your Pals in Palomar

Palomar, by Gilbert Hernandez, is a graphic novel that follows the entire lives of dozens of characters in a small South American village. Hernandez's careful choice of distinctive features helps readers keep track of who's who, even as age and hard living take their considerable toll.

Your choices are restricted by the story you're telling, of course. Nat notes that Yeo is Chinese. To make that clear to readers, you wouldn't design his face with round, Western eyes or a long pointed nose.

I tried different combinations of facial features on Yeo's basic spherical head shape.

Body Building

Now it's time to lower your sights and think about what sorts of bodies your characters have. Clothes can do an awful lot to change the apparent shape of a body, so design your characters at first as naked mannequins. You needn't get too explicit here, unless you're working for a very specific audience.

Once again, scour the script and notes for clues and requirements. And again, it's a good idea to keep real people in mind when you begin doodling.

In my body doodles, I tried out different builds for our three leads.

Body doodles don't require much detail. Keep loose and look for interesting proportions.

Look for something that fits the character and will be easy to recognize, even if you draw it in silhouette.

Start with what the writer asks for: tall, short, slender, chunky, pear-shaped, tiny waisted, whatever. Then move into the specifics. If the character is fat, is one part particularly heavy? If Joe Action is described as "muscular," does he look like a wiry runner or a beefy weight-lifter? Remember what that character does throughout the story. If someone asks Sarah Sidekick to get something from a high shelf, make her tall enough so that request makes sense. Does she have to crawl through a narrow ventilation duct without getting stuck? Design her so that crawl would be plausible.

Even if the script calls for everyone to be of average build, we still want to find traits that make our characters distinctive. Try exaggerating a single body part. Give one character small hands. Another could have a longish neck. Maybe one is slightly bowlegged. Build one out of hard angles and another out of flowing curves. Start with the incredible variety of real life and exaggerate from there.

Dressing for Success

In real life, we judge people by their clothes all the time, so it's no surprise that we do the same in graphic novels. Often these judgments are simple. Policemen, soldiers, and nurses have uniforms that make them instantly identifiable. The same goes for the gear that utility workers and scuba divers wear. Some clothes scream "*wealthy!*" Others label the wearer as poor. And yet others label their owners as being "with stupid."

When you dress your characters, keep the following things in mind:

- **Why did your character put on this outfit?** People choose clothes for a reason. The CEO of a multinational corporation wears expensive dark suits that make him look serious and powerful. A rebellious teen dresses to freak out her parents. A movie star who doesn't want to be recognized in public dresses down to conceal his identity. A homeowner cleaning out her attic puts on comfortable clothes that she doesn't mind getting dirty. A character in 1940 might put on a fedora because he wants to fit in. His grandson in 2005 could wear the same hat as a way to stand out in a crowd.

- **What do you want the reader to learn about the character?** The scene is your hero-ine at home, putting on a bikini. She thinks: "I better wear this today while I still can. Summer's almost over!" That tells us one thing about her. In the next panel we see she's wearing it at a funeral. Alarmed mourners are glancing sideways at her while she sings reverently from a hymnal. That tells us something very different. When you show an aging bachelor smiling in the mirror as he buttons up a purple leisure suit, you aren't just telling the reader that he likes the color purple.

◆ **How often do you have to draw it?** Before your warrior chieftain puts on a tunic covered in elaborate beadwork, or you dress your wealthy hostess in a spectacularly decorated kimono, make sure you'll be comfortable drawing those details over and over again. Suppose they take an extra 10 minutes to pencil and ink. That isn't bad if you have to draw an outfit only once, but if it appears in 200 panels. That adds more than *30 hours* to your workload. Is there something you can draw faster to get the same effect? Can you use a computer to repeat the pattern for you without calling attention to the shortcut?

In the sketches for Terry's outfit, I tried to find a look that was sharp and attractive, but comfortable. She's doesn't want to attract a lot of attention, so I avoided anything flashy. And I don't want to draw those flowers over and over, so I nixed the floral print.

Some sketches for Terry's outfit.

Your Work, It's Fantastic!

All this is fine if your graphic novel takes place here and now, or in the recognizable past, or in a foreign culture. But what if it's set in the future, or on another planet, or in some impossible magical world? Odd and fantastic characters and costumes are a spectacular opportunity for a graphic novel illustrator to cut loose and use imagination. But there are still important factors to consider when you invent aliens and monsters and robots and design their weird wardrobes.

Your designs should serve the needs of the story. If I were drawing a serious adventure story with Lord Zatan, I'd want to make him as threatening and impressive as possible. Since this story is a comedy about an actor forced to wear a Lord Zatan costume, I'm going to design it to look a little goofy.

Relate your design to something real. Choose something familiar: If your robot hauls away trash from space stations, try to evoke a garbage truck in your design. Or if it consumes and digests the trash, you could give it piglike aspects. Does that ogre do a policeman's job? Try caricaturing a policeman, then push the distortions further to bring out the ogre. Dress him in an outfit that resembles a beat cop's uniform. Maybe he's got a helmet like a British Bobby, or a bit of armor that looks like a badge.

Make it functional. In the real world, vehicles have power sources. Houses are built to protect their occupants from intruders and the elements. People and animals need to be able to move, to eat, and to respond to stimuli. The same goes for your Martian tripod walkers, your underwater condominiums, and your Four-throated Menace from the Planet Fruvous. They have to seem functional. A story casts a very fragile spell over its readers. When the dragon swoops down out of the sky to attack your heroine, you want your readers to worry about how she's going to escape. That's a hard feeling to sustain if they're wondering instead how wings that small could possibly keep a 2-ton dragon aloft.

Be prepared to do it over and over again. As with real-world outfits, you may need to draw your fantastic creatures over and over. Does the bug-eyed Slampyak really need eight tentacles *and* four sets of pincers?

When you're making things up, *anything* can be a source of inspiration. Need an interesting pattern for armor? Look at the skin of a pineapple. Can't come up with a good instrument for a Venusian musician to play? Flip through a book of art deco perfume bottles. Are your mutant freaks insufficiently freaky? Study your own reflection in the back of a spoon and apply those distortions to your mutant's proportions.

I based these sketches of Yeo's Warrior Bot armor on some insects I read about in a magazine. The script says that Yeo has to be able to move around in it, and I want it to be both cool and silly.

Sketching ideas for Yeo's Warrior Bot armor.

Put It All Together

Not everyone makes *model sheets*. If you're working on a project all by yourself, you might be able to keep track of most of the details in your head, flipping back through previous pages now and then to see if the heroine's jeans have a back pocket, or to confirm which ankle has the tattoo. But if different artists are drawing different chapters, or if the inker is unsure if that squig-
gle is a necklace or just a stray pencil mark, a model
sheet will help keep things consistent. As the pages
pile up, even solo artists can find it difficult to keep
track of dozens and dozens of character details. With
a model sheet, the energy that takes can be applied
elsewhere.

This model sheet of Yeo shows him from several
angles, in both his ordinary clothes and the Warrior
Bot armor. I also included a few close-ups of tricky
armor details.

Model Sheet

WHA...?

A **model sheet** is a
drawing or set of draw-
ings of a character, prop, or setting used as reference to help
keep a consistent look. Model
sheets are particularly important
when more than one artist draws
the same character.

The Yeo model sheet.

The Least You Need to Know

◆ Read the script carefully for information about what your characters should look like.

◆ Design them so they're easy to recognize.

◆ Use real people as a starting point.

◆ Make your fantastic designs seem functional.

◆ Avoid complicated designs for things you'll have to draw over and over.

◆ Make model sheets to help keep characters consistent.

11

Places, Things, and Other Dead Nouns

In This Chapter

◆ Figure out what the story requires

◆ Design settings and props

◆ Make settings and props recognizable

You know who your characters are. Now it's time to flesh out their world. Can you imagine Colonel Mustard without a candlestick to do it with or a study to do it in? Unless you intend to tell stories about the inhabitants of a cloudy, unspecified void, you're going to need settings and props.

Read That Script Again

Find out what the writer is asking for. Are there specific objects you're going to need to design? Where is this story set? What sort of place is it? What do your readers need to know about the settings? Can you travel there yourself and deduct the expense as "research?"

How Important?

Some settings only appear in the story for a panel or two. Others might be explored in exhaustive detail for dozens of pages. And if you're telling a serialized story, you may find that the dentist's office you dismissed as unimportant in the first issue has become much more significant in the third. If you're collaborating, talk to the writer and make sure that you'll need to draw the place only once. If you're working solo, talk to yourself. Most cartoonists do.

"Unimportant" doesn't mean that a setting should be eliminated, just that it doesn't need to be distinctive. If the scene is set in a dentist's office, your reader needs to know that, or the reader's going to wonder what that man is doing inside that woman's mouth. In an unimportant scene, a *tag* or two are often enough to let the reader know where things are taking place.

You can tag a scene for general information. A striped pole behind the villain says he's at a barber shop. Or you can tag a scene specifically. Knock the pole on its side or put a distinctive carved eagle on top. Then, whenever we see it, we know we're at that particular barber shop.

Tags are an important storytelling tool. On a crowded page, you may have several different scenes. If you don't have room to include an establishing shot of Tex's arrival at a grocery store, arrange the panel so that we're looking at Tex holding a basket, framed by a hand at a cash register. Later, when he's been arrested for shoplifting, you might just show him behind bars rather than draw an entire prison.

All at Once

I broke character design away from setting to make things easier to digest, but when taking character notes, you can (and should) take set and prop notes at the same time.

Tag

WHA...?

A **tag** is a visual element included to make a person, place, or thing readily identifiable.

An unconventional convention center. I tagged the convention center with triangular window patterns and an unusual flagpole.

If You're Sticking Around

Simple tags are enough for settings you'll visit only briefly. For longer, more important scenes, you'll want to work things out more carefully. Read the script, looking for information about the settings. If the writer followed our suggestions in Chapter 7 of this book, his or her script will include establishing shots of the important scenes, the details that the story requires, and descriptions of the place in terms of its effect. If such details are missing, talk to the writer and work these matters out.

You can design a scene carefully before starting a scene, or you can just build the scene around your establishing shot. The rule of thumb is that the longer the scene, the more important it is to plan the space in advance. The following sections start off with questions you should ask yourself about the settings.

Gerhard: The Hard Way

Gerhard (no last name) was the background artist for Cerebus, a series of graphic novels. The characters often stayed in the same small area for hundreds of pages, so he built paper models of his sets to help him visualize the space and keep his backgrounds consistent.

What Needs to Happen Here?

Let the events in a scene tell you what a setting needs. If Cowboy Gus is inside eating lunch when he sees a twister approaching, put a window where someone at the table could see it. And if he has to close the window, don't make it a single, fixed pane of glass.

How Big?

One of the dirty secrets of the graphic novelist is that you can cheat a bit when depicting space. It's common to give a room a 10-foot ceiling in your establishing shot, then draw a bird's-eye view of the room from 20 feet up. But clearly communicating the size of spaces is still important. Show a king's grandeur by giving him a big throne room. Lost orphans look more lost in a wilderness full of giant oaks than they would among scrub pines. If Timmy's fallen down a well, show that it's too deep for him to just reach up and pull himself out. And if he has to climb up a well shaft by bracing his legs on either side, keep the shaft narrow enough for him to do this. Don't make it so narrow that Lassie has to squeeze down the well, pull Timmy up by his collar, and give him the dog-language talking to about the danger of wells that the boy so obviously needs.

What's the Feel?

Some stories require only the basic facts of a setting. It might be enough to know that Bob is at the auto body shop when his car grows a face and begins complaining like a sick hospital patient. Other stories need more than that. In another story, a social worker is concerned about a mechanic who takes his young children to work. Emphasize the darkness, dirt, and danger when designing that setting, filling it with sharp tools, exposed wiring, and heavy objects, balanced precariously. A story about an older mechanic confused by modern ways might be set in a shop that's unusually clean, and dominated by diagnostic computers instead of the wrenches and hoses he expects.

Even a real city will vary in feeling from one story to another. The films *Breakfast at Tiffany's* and *Serpico* both take place in Manhattan, but they're very different settings.

Believable or Correct?

How accurate should your depiction of a setting be? Depends on the story. Some stories allow, or even *require*, bizarre distortions of reality. A police station in a nightmarish horror story is going to be quite different from one in a realistic detective mystery or a screwball talking-animal comedy. There's no right answer to how accurate you need to be, but as a rule of thumb, when you want to emphasize the reality of a story, keep your setting accurate. When you want to emphasize mood, distort as necessary.

Is This Going to Ruin My Life?

Your time is valuable. Avoid set designs that take hours and hours to draw if you'll have to draw them repeatedly. If there's no way around a complicated design, tag it with an easily drawn detail so that you can just use that instead of redrawing the whole setting every time. An elaborately decorated temple, for instance, could be tagged with a distinctive statue.

You can also use clever page and panel design as a way to eliminate time-consuming detail from a scene. Once you've established a scene, increase the stylization a bit. Show the whole barber shop in panel one. In panel two eliminate everything but the barber and his chair.

Getting Real

Getting a realistic scene right takes time. (A fantastic setting can be time-consuming, too, but no one is going to quibble about the accuracy of your twenty-third-century kitchen.) The writer can say "It's a summer evening in 1904. We're in a Czech army barracks," then go on to tell you what the characters are doing. But what did a Czech army barracks look like then? Are there bunk beds? Are the walls plastered or wooden? Are there gaslight fixtures or electric lights? What did light bulbs look like in 1904? Could a soldier put girly pictures on the wall near his bed? What would a girly picture look like back then? What kind of rifle would a soldier have and where would it be stored? Why is the z silent?

In an ideal world, the writer has done all of this research for you and has included stacks of reference with the script. In a less-ideal-but-still-good world, the writer assumes that everyone knows about Czech army barracks and didn't think to send this material to you, so a quick phone call may help. Otherwise, it's time to take off the beret and put on pince-nez. You're about to become a researcher.

Plenty of resources are available to you. Sometimes the real thing is out there for you to visit and sketch or photograph. (It's a good idea to get permission first, particularly if you're shooting photos.) Ask your librarian. Look for appropriate websites. For historical subjects, there may be a museum in your area that has a picture archive, period artifacts, or even complete reconstructed rooms. Find a movie set in the right time and place. If all else fails, draw the stuff you're sure about, and choose compositions and lighting that "just happen" to cover up everything else. This can be surprisingly effective.

My Years on The Ice

For *Whiteout* and its sequel, two graphic novels I illustrated that were set in Antarctica, I read books and magazine articles, found photos and journals on the web, watched videotaped documentaries, and e-mailed questions to some people who had lived there.

Making Stuff Up

Your setting might be imaginary. That doesn't mean you get to slack off. As a general rule, fantasy requires more detailed settings, because you have to introduce your readers to an unfamiliar world. And since you can't assume their familiarity with its workings, you'll need to draw in a more literal style. You can draw a modern office expressionistically, showing only oddly illuminated workers and computer screens floating in darkness, and the reader will know that it's a room drawn stylishly, and won't be surprised when someone picks up a monitor and tosses it out the window. In a science fiction story, those floating screens might be holographic projections in an empty room without any furniture. As you might have guessed, we have a few tips for making your imaginary settings and props believable.

Make It Clear

If your Victorian mad scientist has built a gunpowder cannon 40 feet tall, put it in a context that makes its size unmistakable. If there are normal-sized doors and windows in the wall 35 feet below the cannon's mouth, that's a good clue. And choose angles that make its size obvious. Don't draw the cannon huge in the foreground of your panel with its builder far behind. That could just be exaggerated perspective. Put the builder in the front, with the cannon looming up behind him, or show them from an angle that puts the size in emphasis.

Make It Consistent

You're setting up a world with its own rules. Follow those rules or lose the reader. Santa's elves need elf-sized tables and chairs. The mermaid bedchamber should be made out of materials that one could scrounge from the sea. If they don't have fire, they shouldn't have anything that they'd need fire to build.

Make It Familiar

Even the most fantastic scenes should have familiar or recognizable aspects. A tavern in a space station can still resemble a typical tavern. Make it dark and smoky. Put in a long bar with a mirror in the back. Add lots of small tables and neon lights advertising something. Your readers will recognize the space as a bar, even though the place is full of aliens sipping blue ooze from long tubes. Any imaginary place you create should have some familiar counterpart, but it doesn't have to be a perfect match.

You can create a lot of interesting effects by combining unlikely elements. A future courtroom might evoke a modern game show or a medieval torturer's dungeon. A gnome family's toy-making workshop could resemble a modern cubicle office or an automotive assembly line. An alien spaceship could evoke a submarine or a cruise liner.

To evoke something, identify the elements that tag a place as what it is. A church has plenty of seating looking up at a dais. It probably has stained glass or otherwise decorative windows, and it uses high vertical spaces to encourage a feeling of reverence for some higher power. A library has tall shelves full of books, computers, places for people to sit and read, and perhaps someone saying "shh." A bedroom is designed around a place to lie down. A living room might have furniture that one could lie on, but is clearly designed for people to interact.

Getting Your Props

All of what I've said about settings applies to props as well. In the movies and on stage, an object is considered set dressing unless someone handles it. Then it's a prop.

Research your authentic props, and design the imaginary ones, according to the rules I gave for settings. Mickey Mutant has only one tiny eye in the middle of his enormous head. His rifle still needs a carrying strap, a trigger, and some place to load ammunition, but design it so that the scope is set off well to one side, or he won't be able to sight a target while bracing the stock against his shoulder. And if he has weird hands, the trigger assembly should reflect that, too.

Sometimes a prop needs only to be identifiable. A student's notebook can be recognized by its spiral binding. But if everyone is hunting for one particular notebook that contains the atomic bomb plans or the list of the Colonel's seven herbs and spices, find a good, unmistakable tag. Rip one corner in a way the reader can't miss, or put an upside-down sticker on the cover.

Nat Sez: Prop Yourself Up

Steve's tip on character props is just as important for writers. Interaction with a prop can indicate thought processes and emotion in a visual way. That nicotine inhaler not only shows that the character is quitting smoking, it also can be tapped on a table in boredom, squeezed in a hand to show tension, sucked to show contemplation, and flung at the cat to show frustration.

Many characters have props that are utterly identified with them. Friar Tuck carried a wooden staff. Linus carried a blanket. Madame DeFarge had her knitting needles. Sherlock Holmes smoked a pipe. Harriet the Spy always had a notebook. There's Captain Queeg's metal exercise balls, John Henry's hammer, Paul Bunyan's axe. Groucho's cigar. The right prop can help fix a character in the reader's mind.

Some props become so iconic they're almost characters themselves: Think of King Arthur's Excalibur or Captain America's shield. Others are the center of their stories, like The Maltese Falcon or The Glass Menagerie or Cinderella's slipper or The One Ring. If you've got an object like this, find a tag to make it unique. Give the Stuttering Sword an oddly shaped blade. The Haunted Handbag can look like a distorted human head, its clasp holding the mouth closed. Grandma's Grimoire needs a big gold bookmark and delicate metal latticework on the binding.

No Sheet, Sherlock

As I said in Chapter 10, a model sheet is a drawing or set of drawings used to keep a character, prop, or setting consistent. You won't need to create model sheets for most props or settings. Unless it's really special, you'll probably design it right on the page, and your first clear shot of it will serve as the model. It is a good idea, however, to make a photocopy of that page and keep it with your model sheets, so that four months later, when you have to draw the Pirate's Magic Chum Bucket again, you won't have to remember what page it was on. For important settings, your establishing shot might not include all the necessary details. Make an overhead diagram. It doesn't need to be a real drawing. A simple plan of the space and its major features is enough.

Use a diagram like this to plan a complicated scene.

Don't settle for the easy way out when designing props and settings. Creating a believable world for your characters takes time and effort, but a well-thought out environment will make your stories far more real to you and your readers.

The Least You Need to Know

- Use tags to make settings and objects recognizable.

- Research your realistic scenes and props.

- Fantastic settings must be clear and consistent and should evoke something familiar.

- A good prop makes a character more memorable.

- Map out your most important settings.

Decrypt the Script

In This Chapter

- ◆ Analyze the script
- ◆ Find visual themes
- ◆ Choose a style

You've thought about the characters and their environment. Now it's time to start thinking about their story and how best to tell it to your readers. There's a lot more to good visual storytelling than just drawing what the writer asks for, but the writer's script is where it all begins.

Different Sorts of Scripts

As Nat discussed in Chapter 7, there are as many different approaches to script-writing as there are scriptwriters. Some writers know in advance who their artist will be, and can tailor their material to play to that artist's strengths. Others work in more of a vacuum, with no idea who'll be tapped to bring their ideas to life.

The script might be dense, every panel described in exhaustive detail, with long paragraphs specifying everything from camera angles, to the body language of incidental characters in the background, to the exact size and shape of every panel. Or it might be a half dozen sentences handwritten on a bar napkin, with an under-lined exhortation to "make it rock." I've seen both in the past year. Regardless, almost every script offers opportunities for a diligent illustrator to explore the possibilities of the medium.

Read Like a Writer

Once again, I'm sending you back to the script. At this point, you're probably wondering if you know the story better than the writer. Good. You should know it better. Once you put pencil to paper, you are the storyteller. Collaborating on a graphic novel can be a little like playing "telephone." The writer tells the artist, the artist tells the reader. (Actually, the artist tells the printer, who then tells the reader, but I'm trying to convince you of your godlike power, and such minor details will often fall by the wayside at times like this.)

When you read the script this time, keep one big question in mind: What is this story about? You're looking for a theme, a central idea that unifies the story. The writer doubtless has ideas about what that would be. The script may even say so in bold type in the first paragraph. If so, avert your eyes and skip to the second. You want to approach this with as unspoiled an attitude as possible.

Themes are generally universal. Sometimes they can be boiled down to maxims. "Love conquers all." "No man is an island." "As a man soweth, so shall he reap." That sort of thing. Other times they aren't quite so tidy. "The sacrifices of motherhood." "Law versus justice." Think back to eleventh grade. If you were like most budding cartoonists, you ignored your English teacher's lecture on great themes in literature and filled your notebooks with ball-point sketches of tanks, horses, or that hottie in the next row. Take a moment to offer a silent apology to that teacher, because she was trying to teach you some pretty useful stuff, and if you'd learned it, we could skip ahead to the part where Atomicus saves Tokyo from a giant metal insect.

So what's your story about? In Chapter 4, Nat gave the example of the cowboy/schoolmarm romance. What are some themes we might find in a story like that?

- The conflict between freedom and attachment.
- The end of frontier life as civilization encroaches.
- The battle of the sexes. (Men want A, Women want B, and ain't that difference grand?)
- The struggles of women in a world run by men.
- The dangerous thrills of adventure.

The possibilities are endless. Take notes, and make a list of options worth developing. (And again, this needn't be its own step. You'll probably do this while jotting down notes for other parts of the job. You might even skip the formal process and do this entirely by instinct. But "do everything at once," and "just follow your instincts" aren't very helpful lessons, so I'm breaking up the tasks here to make them easier to explain.)

Did your writer specify a theme, or make his or her intentions absolutely clear? If so, great. You know what's going to drive this story. Your list of other possibilities can still come in handy. If the story seems to have too many possible themes, or worse, none whatsoever, the ball is in your court, and you have to make a choice.

Pick a Theme

Suppose it's a big story, and the subplots don't seem to have much to do with the main story, or with each other. It all just seems sort of random. You aren't sure if the writer knows where the narrative is going, and your questions are getting waved off with "Just draw what I wrote!" You can still take steps to unify the story and make what's there have more impact.

You can glean some of a writer's unstated intentions by looking at the script's most dramatic moments. Where do you think the reader is most likely to gasp, weep, or shudder? Once you find that, go through the story for other scenes that could amplify that idea or feeling or look at it another way.

Here's an example: If the best line in the story is delivered by Victoria when she shoots the wicked law professor who smothered her dachshund, that's a revenge moment. And if we know that Victoria's taking revenge for the death of her dog, why not go to the earlier scene, when she sees her neighbor out walking his Pekinese. In the script, it just says that she asks him for the time while he checks the leash. But suppose you draw it so that the neighbor and the dog are having a great time together. He's laughing, delighted by Fido's antics, and Fido's up on his hind legs, wagging his tail. Show the reader how Victoria is shattered by this moment of doggy bliss, and you've managed to intensify the reader's understanding of her loss with a single panel.

Are there other scenes you can develop this way? Think of every aspect of the pet/owner relationship. Is it sort of parental? Look for scenes with parents and their children. Exploitative? An underling "fetching" coffee for the boss. You want to *gently* nudge the story toward a crucial central idea. When you illustrate a graphic novel, you're constantly making decisions. A good, unifying idea gives you a firm basis for making them.

Using the Theme

You've got a good grasp of what the writer is trying to say. (Or, alas, you've made that decision on your own.) Now you get to apply that idea to everything else you do.

Let's look at the script at hand. In *The Big Con*, the main characters are minor celebrities. They're accustomed to standing out in a crowd and enjoying a certain amount of admiration from the public. Now they're in an environment where their status, the thing that makes them special, is a liability. To cope with this situation, they have to voluntarily lower their own status. They can't be celebrities anymore. They have to pretend to be their own fans, geeks in goofy outfits. Eventually, they learn an important lesson. They can use their position to make people happy, and that doing so is rewarding, even if some people will exploit them. So what's it all about? I say it's this: The pluses and minuses of celebrity.

Whenever I have to make a storytelling decision, I'm going to take *The Big Con*'s central idea—the pluses and minuses of celebrity—into account. Here are a few typical questions, with my answers:

- ◆ When drawing the characters, how much should I exaggerate their features, expressions, and gestures?

  I'm going to need more exaggeration than I usually use. The indignity of their situation as trapped celebrities is a big part of the story, so I'm going to push the faces a bit to emphasize moments of humiliation. I won't caricature their features much though, because I want them to have some dignity to lose.

- ◆ Does this story need realistic light and shadow? Should you eliminate all the shading and draw with a clean line? Or should you use heavy areas of shadow?

  Convention center lighting tends toward the fluorescent and bland, so leaving the shading out isn't all that far from drawing "realistically." Eliminating all the shading, though, would impart an elegant quality I'd rather avoid, particularly since these celebrities are stuck among the unwashed masses. Heavy chiaroscuro wouldn't be appropriate for the setting, either, as it would create a sense of physical danger that isn't what I'm going for. The concern here is loss of status, not life or limb.

- ◆ Should the pictures be noticeably attractive or should they just communicate the bare facts?

  This story leans more toward the bare facts. I'm not trying to show my readers wonder or beauty. The beautiful people here are being brought down to earth.

◆ Do you want to use perspective to create a consistent illusion of three-dimensional space, or would you rather use a flatter, more symbolic approach?

I'll need a sense of real space. Flat-looking art is often funnier, but it wouldn't make it clear how far they need to travel in these ridiculous outfits.

◆ Do you want characters that are fully constructed in three dimensions, or should they be mostly flat designs (like, say, the characters in South Park or Dick Tracy?)

Definitely three dimensional. I want the reader to compare Derrick is in his "Lord Zatan" costume, with Yeo in his Bot outfit. Derrick is awkward and humiliated in the outfit and, by extension, in his position as a celebrity among his fans, whereas Yeo is perfectly comfortable in each. I need solid-looking figures with a sense of mass to show that.

◆ Is the story better served by backgrounds full of lots of precise detail, or by a few basic indications of where things are taking place?

This is going to need some detail. The convention isn't just where things happen to be happening, it's the engine that's driving the story.

◆ Will you have any trouble drawing in the style that you think would be right for the story? Should you hire an assistant to help out with the parts you can't handle?

Nope and nope. This one is right up my alley.

◆ Should I use a simple grid layout or a more complex or organic approach?

The script calls for overlapping, snapshot-style panels on page 7. That suggests to me that a grid would be a good idea for the rest of the story, because it would help that page, with its different sense of time, to stand out.

◆ Time is always a consideration. Can you draw the story in an appropriate style in the time allotted, or do you need to find a faster way?

No comment.

> **Caricature**
>
> **Caricature** is the expressive distortion of faces and features. This can be done for laughs or to highlight some aspects of the subject's personality.

You Can't Always Get What You Want

Some answers will trump all the others. For instance, your limitations as an artist might always be a factor. Few artists are good at more than a couple of styles. If the only drawing you do is flat and designy, you'll have to either work that way, or try another style and risk producing something that isn't as polished as your other work.

Other times your decision is made for you by external concerns. Budget is a big one. Suppose the most important scenes in your story call for a room to be suddenly lit by a blue light. If you can afford to print in only black and white, you'll just have to find some other way to get your point across. One solution would be to use a distinctive style of rendering on the blue light scenes. Or you could compose the panels in such a way that it'll be hard for your readers to miss the comparison. Either way, save that rendering or composition for the blue light specials.

A Digression About Original Art Size

Another limitation you might run into is the size your book will be printed. If you're self-publishing, that's your call. But if you aren't the one paying the printer, it's a safe bet that someone else will be telling you how big the book will be. If the published work is going to be 3 by 5 inches, you'll either have to limit yourself to very few panels per page, or draw really small. And if you're drawing small, design your pictures so that your readers won't have to squint at them to figure out what you drew. Not to mention that your writer may have given the characters a lot of dialogue, which also has to fit into your panels.

Not that print size limits the size of your original art. Wanna draw that page 6 feet wide and 9 feet tall? Go for it, but be aware of how much detail you'll lose when it's shrunk to 6 by 9 inches. And don't be surprised if the publisher asks you to scan it, because the company's scanner isn't big enough.

How big to draw your original art? That's a personal choice. On a smaller original, there isn't as much space that needs to be filled, so you can finish more quickly. But many artists find it difficult to produce good drawings below a certain size. It can be hard to judge proportions, and mistakes are magnified. If you're making a 4-inch figure drawing and the head's a quarter of an inch too big, that's no big deal. On a 1-inch drawing, that quarter inch will make your figure look like the first arrival of an alien invasion. Also, without room to swing your arm a bit as you work, your drawings can get stiff and diagrammatic.

Keep It Clean

Small pictures are much more easily understood by readers if they're simple. Save the complex arrangements, amusing little background jokes, and intricate rendering for bigger pictures.

Working large can be fun. Errors are easily recognized and corrected. You've got room to move your hand and arm, and the pictures don't feel so cramped together. There are downsides to this, too. It can take longer to fill all that empty space. Not everyone has a large enough table to work big. Big sheets of paper cost more. You'll have to spend more on ink and brushes or pens. Big finished art can be a pain to ship or to scan, and, if you live in a small space, difficult to store.

So what's the right size? Many artists find that working *one up*, one and a half times the printed size (150 percent), is a good proportion. It's big enough to see what you're doing, but not so big that it hurts your productivity or takes over your apartment, and it's standard at most American publishers. For art that reproduces at 6 by 9 inches, working 141 percent larger gives you original art with a *live area* of 10 inches by 15 inches. That fits well on an 11- by 17-inch sheet of paper, which is a standard size available from art supply stores. It's easy to find express shipper boxes that can hold pages that size, and most professional photocopier shops can handle 11 by 17 without difficulty. When you want to see how an 11-by-17 page will reproduce when shrunk down, reduce it on a copier to 65 percent of its original size.

> WHA...?
>
> **Live Area**
> The **live area** is the section of your original page that the printer will definitely reproduce. There'll be more on this in Chapter 13.

The Strength to Resist Your Strengths

Every artist is better at some things than others. We all want to put our best foot forward. But there are times when playing to your strengths is a bad idea. Suppose Joe Cheesecake loves drawing glamorous women and he's terrific at it. Unfortunately, he's drawing a story about the difficult lives of the women who work in a feed truck assembly plant and their long struggle to organize a union. It'd be hard to take the story seriously if the women are all depicted as slender and gorgeous, radiating health and vitality. The reader would wonder if their lives are really that bad. And if the women all have that "come hither" look that Joe draws so masterfully, the big scene with the abusive boss is going to read very, very different from what the writer intended. If Joe is going to illustrate the feed-truck women's story, he's going to have to suppress his interest in drawing lovely ladies. Either that or he's going to subvert the meaning of the story he's telling.

Another example: Years ago at school, a classmate of mine was adapting a scene from *A Christmas Carol* into comics form. He had a knack for horror art, and though he wasn't trying to do so, he drew Scrooge as a hateful, monstrous ruin of a man. Our teacher observed that no one would ever believe that a Scrooge like that was capable of redemption, and that Scrooge's reform at the end would feel false. The artist needed to change his emphasis from Scrooge's ugly face to his even uglier behavior.

A drawing style can undermine a story, too. Excessive rendering can stop a story cold by drawing a reader's attention to the wrong aspects of a panel. A style that carefully describes subtle effects of light on various materials is great for a story with some quiet pauses. The action stops, the CEO puts down his drink, and we look at the glass and its reflection in the dark polished wood of his desk. That's a good moment. On the other hand, if we're in the middle of a screwball comedy sequence, where he's hiding under the desk while a jealous chimpanzee tears up the office, that reflection, no matter how well drawn, is going to be a distraction.

Think of it this way: Sometimes a graphic novelist should tell the story as if he or she's telling a joke: "A man enters a bar. He goes up to the bartender and says …" Other times, the approach required is more like that of a novelist: "A man in his late fifties, with flinty gray eyes and hard, thin lips, pushed open the fireproof doors to the bar at the top of the Bayview Hyatt in San Diego. He worked his way through a maze of hideous polyester nest chairs and approached the bartender. The bartender was a recent hire and his apron was damp with spilled Zima and flop sweat …"

The Big Book of Stylists

The *Big Book of Losers*, one of several Big Books published by Paradox Press (a division of DC Comics), contains dozens of short comics stories, each illustrated by a different artist. Aside from being fun, these books are a useful catalog of drawing styles.

Motifs

You can also unify your story with a well-chosen visual motif. The idea of the motif comes from opera. Different parts of the story are assigned musical themes, and when they appear in the story, their themes are worked into the larger melody. When the warrior's magic word of destiny is first discussed, we hear a bit of the sword theme. When he actually gets his hands on the sword, the theme becomes the main melody.

The movie *The Sixth Sense* used this technique, but with color instead of music. The movie was filmed almost entirely in neutrals—grays and browns. But whenever emotions were heightened and something horrible was about to happen, the filmmakers would bring a vivid, primary red into the screen. As the film progresses, the mere presence of a red balloon or sweater on the screen is enough to get audiences nervous.

A couple of years earlier, I used a similar strategy in *Whiteout*. I worked a square grid pattern into scenes where the lead character was feeling helplessness or rage. I tried to associate the grid with the character's feelings, so that even when she was too frozen to emote, we'd have a sense of what she felt.

My grid motif. Note the less-than-subtle arrow pointing right at the grid in the first panel.

Repeated Shots and Imagery

Repetition doesn't have to be dull. Put two similar things near each other and they invite comparison. Say you're illustrating a redemption story, and the hero seems to spend a lot of time on the phone. That could be visually dull. But what if every time he's on the phone, you use a similar camera angle and change the picture to emphasize a change in his status? The progression could work something like this:

◆ He's counting pennies with his baby daughter's empty milk bottle and several empty liquor bottles on the flyblown table in front of him.

◆ The table is clean and he's circling a help wanted ad.

◆ Now the table is a cluttered office desk. He's being handed an overflowing bundle of papers. There's a picture of a nine year old in braces and a baseball cap.

◆ Now it's a handsome oak desk, clearly that of an executive. He's opening an expensive leather briefcase. Next to the picture of the nine year old, there's a framed photo of an 18-year-old woman graduating college in cap and gown.

◆ He's at the same desk, looking nervous and sweating, holding a newspaper with his non-phone hand. The headline reads "Insider Trading Scandal." The desk is cluttered with file folders and an overflowing Shreddy 9000.

That simple image of him at the phone becomes a sort of milestone to check his progress, and gives rhythm and shape to the story, almost the way a chorus does for a song. Look for ways to reinforce your story's theme with repeated imagery.

Harm Reduction

Creative differences happen. There may be times in a collaboration when you resolutely disagree with the point your writer is making. It might be a political difference, or a disagreement over some important thing a character does or says. It could even be an aesthetic difference. "How could you saddle a great story with such a lame ending?"

> **Nat Sez: Please Ask Questions**
>
> If there's something in the script you don't understand, then there's no way you can make the reader understand it. I'd much rather explain a confusing part once for an artist than 1,000 times for fans.

Is It Just a Misunderstanding?

Tell the writer your concerns. Perhaps the writer left something out. The scene in which Atomicus exterminates the Squirrelmen of Neptune wouldn't come across as a flat-out endorsement of genocide if the writer hadn't forgotten he'd cut the part where we learn that the Squirrelmen are actually robots. Maybe that line that evokes Stalin was an accident. If something seems right out of left field, perhaps it's because the story is being serialized. Your objections might be answered in a subsequent issue.

Work It Out

Make your case. Be diplomatic but be clear about what you think the problems are. Sometimes e-mail is better for this than the phone. You can take the time to express your argument more clearly, and it'll take some of the edge off any anger that might be simmering.

Be positive, not disparaging. Tell your writer "the climax in the ballroom just doesn't rise to the level of the rest of the book." Don't say "the ballroom scene is a reeking puddle of sewage. Why did you write this? Did someone crack open your skull and stick a spoon in your living brain?" Look for some compromise that you can both agree on. Bring in an editor or some other third party to mediate. If you're on the losing side, just do the best job you can.

Surrender, but Subvert

No compromise is possible. The writer has made it clear that your opinion is worthless: Draw it or quit. The story ends with Private Parker gleefully clubbing baby harp seals with a shovel, saying, "This is a hoot!" You can deemphasize the "gleeful" part by backlighting him so that we can't read his expression. Or you can establish a big cook fire several pages earlier, so that there "just happens" to be lots of smoke that obscures the whole seal-clubbing scene.

Cut Your Losses

If you aren't bound by a contract, you can withdraw from the project. The earlier you do this, the better, because it's unfair to everyone else involved to leave them scrambling for a new illustrator at the last minute. Even if you have a contract, it's worth asking if the publisher would consider letting you out of it. The publisher will want an artist who can commit to telling the story rather than one whose art will undercut it, as flawed as that story may be.

The Least You Need to Know

- Unify the story with a central idea.
- Keep that idea in mind when making storytelling decisions.
- Look for repeatable motifs in the script.
- Identify script problems as soon as possible and work with the writer to correct them.

Chapter

Lovely Layouts

In This Chapter

- ◆ Creating thumbnails
- ◆ Choosing camera angles
- ◆ Manipulating time

Designing the layout of the graphic novel is one of those steps that, in their haste to jump in and start making cool drawings, artists are sometimes tempted to skip. Don't, particularly if you're new at this. The possibilities for missteps in the creation of a page are endless. After all, you aren't just drawing one picture that makes sense on its own. Your panels all have to work together to tell your story clearly and entertainingly. A panel that's fine on its own can be disastrous for the rest of your page. Thinking things through in your thumbnail sketches can help you avoid problems and save you a lot of wasted effort.

Thumbs Up

There's no one right way to do *thumbnails*. I've used half a dozen different approaches on the same project, depending on who needed to see them, how much of a hurry I was in, and, in all honesty, what kind of pencil I had in my hand and what felt right on a given day. I drew the thumbnails reproduced at the end of this chapter on graph paper. Some people hate sketching on graph paper because they feel like all the little boxes clutter up their doodles. I like it

Thumbnails

Small quick sketches that are often no bigger than your thumbnail are called **thumbnails**. They have no intentional aesthetic value and are used for brainstorming or problem solving.

because it makes quick, accurate divisions of space easier, and how to divide up space is always a big concern for me on the comics page. Also, the blue lines tend to drop out or fade to a very pale grey when I make photocopies, which is handy. A final reason is sort of embarrassing, but I'll share it here because it could be a valuable tip. My studio is often hideously cluttered, and I lose important papers in it all the time. Blue lined graph paper is easy to spot in the midst of heaps of white paper. And because the only thing I ever use graph paper for is layouts, I'm less likely to lose them.

Make your thumbnails the same proportion as the actual page. I'm drawing *The Big Con* pages at 8 inches wide by 12 inches tall. That's a 2:3 ratio, which is fairly standard for the North American comics industry. Some other 2:3 ratios include 6 inches by 9 inches, 10 inches by 15 inches, and 4 kilometers by 6 kilometers. I'd advise avoiding that last one unless you own a good sized field and plan to ink with a tractor.

If you're desperate to avoid any math, you can find another rectangle that's in the same proportion by using the proportion shortcut. Just draw a diagonal line from one corner of your border to another. Any other rectangle on that diagonal is in proportion to the first one.

An easy shortcut to matching proportions.

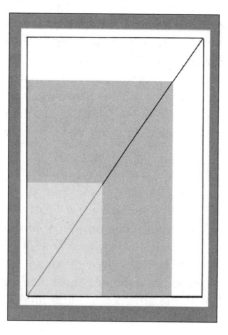

How big and detailed should your layouts be? Depends on who needs to see them. If they're for your eyes only, make them as tiny and obscure as you like. Just keep in mind that if you aren't using them immediately, you might forget that the broad squiggle with the wavy lines on page 2 is a bird's-eye view of Atomicus struggling to escape the tentacles of a giant squid.

If you plan to show the thumbnails to your writer, he or she will need a bit more detail. Label the characters, as I've done here. The sketches don't have to be tremendously clear because it's a fair assumption that your writer already knows the story being told. Still you can expect to get one or two phone calls asking if the bit on page 2 is a close-up of a mouth full of teeth or an establishing shot of the House of Representatives.

If the thumbnails have to be approved by an editor, it's a good idea to assume that he or she has had to read 15 or 20 other things since breakfast and remembers nothing about the story at hand. Try to keep your scribbles very clear and put in lots of labels and little marginal notes explaining what's going on.

When I make thumbnail layouts from a full script, I make sure to indicate where the lettering will go, too. In my thumbnails at the end of this chapter, you'll note that the caption boxes and speech balloons have numbers in them. That's because Nat was kind enough to number his captions and speech balloons in the script. We'll go into this more in the chapter on lettering. Those numbers make it easy for me to indicate where the word balloons need to go, and to spot potential placement problems.

Left to Right, Top to Bottom

One of the most frequent problems you'll run into is speaker order. In the Western world, our default way to read comics is the way we read everything else, left to right, top to bottom. We find it easier to read a comic if the word balloons are placed close to the speaker. Ideally a script should call for characters to be placed in the panel so that their position in the left to right lineup "just happens" to be the same order as their speech. The demands of storytelling being what they are, it rarely works out this way.

Even a simple and blah script can provide tricky complications for layout. Consider the blah script pictured nearby.

Nat Sez: Easy Redialoguing

A writer can solve the problem of changing speaker order without changing dialog. Take a look at the first figure showing the problematic blah script. You can move both of Rich's balloons to one panel. You can even have panel two be simply a shot of Louie, with Rich's dialog balloon pointing back to him in panel one.

A very blah but problematic script.

```
Panel one

1 Louie: BLAH

2 Rich: BLAH.

Panel two

3 Rich: BLAH?

4 Louie: BLAH.
```

What's the problem? The speaker order changed. Louie, the guy who speaks first in panel one is speaking second in panel two. But I want the reader to see them in the same order as they speak, and I want to group the balloons with their speakers. I could just make Louie and Rich switch sides, or flip the camera around and show them from the opposite angle. You can see me trying that in the first speaker-order doodles. But doing that violates an important rule: the 180-degree rule (I'll explain that in a sec). My preferred solution is shown in the second doodle. Use the reader's tendency to read top to bottom instead of the tendency to read left to right. Choose a camera angle or a composition to raise Rich higher in the panel. That way you can group him with his balloon at the top of the panel. Another solution: Ask the writer to rework the dialogue a bit.

What to do when speaker order is reversed.

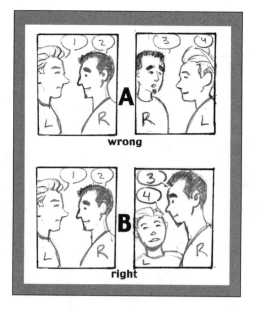

That 180-degree rule I mentioned is a very big deal. (It's also sometimes called the central-axis rule.) When drawing a scene with two or more characters, establish an invisible line between them. Keep Louie on the left side of that line, and Rich on the right. If you have to violate this, devote a panel to clearly showing the character cross the line. The thumbnails in the 180-degree-rule image show how the rule works.

Some examples of how the 180-degree rule works.

Calling the Shots

When you start breaking down each page into panels, you'll find yourself thinking like a camera operator. Nat named some camera angles at the end of Chapter 7: Wide shot, medium, close-ups. Those describe the distance of the camera from the subject. Here are a few others that refer to the height from which the scene is viewed:

- ◆ **High angle shot.** The scene is viewed from an angle noticeably higher than an average person's head. Good for showing the p.o.v. (point of view) of someone very tall, or hiding in a tree.

- ◆ **Bird's-eye view.** A really high angle. Can mean that the shot is from a great distance, or just that we're seeing the tops of people's heads. Good for showing the lay of the land, armies moving across terrain.

- **Low angle shot.** The camera is waist high or lower, showing the scene as if the viewer were crouching or just very short. Can make the subject seem bigger, more impressive.

- **Worm's-eye view.** An extremely low angle. The viewer is underneath the subject, looking up. Implies the utter subjugation of the viewer. While the bird's eye view is almost always used for objective, informational shots, this one is used either to show a specific character's p.o.v. or to create weird, disturbing effects.

Combine these beauties with the distance options Nat mentioned earlier and you'll see just how many possibilities there are for your panels.

The Shape of Things to Come

You've also got a wide range of shape options for your panels:

- **Squares and rectangles.** These are the default panel shapes, and with good reason. For at least a millennium, European visual artists have composed drawings and paintings and theatre sets and movie shots within these shapes. Your audience doesn't give them a second thought and will ignore the shape to concentrate on the content. And since you've also seen countless square and rectangular pictures, you've got a built-in sense for how they should be composed.

- **Circular panels.** I usually see these used for amusing, somewhat campy moments, or to evoke such a moment for ironic effect. Either way, they seem to identify a moment as somewhat out of step with the rest of the story being told. When used in adventure stories, they always remind me of TV commercials where someone stops midconversation, looks at the camera and says, "Wow! Now that's great coffee!" They do have a more practical use, though. Use them for p.o.v. shots seen through circular views like a rifle scope, a security peephole, a sewer outflow pipe, or a ship's portal.

- **Vignettes.** These are freeform pictures missing some or all of their borders, with empty spaces where things like floors or walls might otherwise be. These are often just used as a way to introduce some white space onto an otherwise crowded page. Vignettes can also psychologically remove characters from their physical context. Show Herbie Grubb standing on the curb next to his garbage truck, and he's just a sanitation worker talking to himself. When he hits the big point in his soliloquy, you vignette him, and suddenly, he is Man. Combine the vignetted figure with a prop or two for a scene that will feel more like the a stage play (where sets can be stylized down to a few basic objects) than a movie, (which is usually more literal, and requires more complete settings). Check out my thumbnails at the end of this chapter—page 8, panel four is a vignette.

You can compose your panels in any shape you want. Odd trapezoids, organic shapes, anything. They're harder to compose though, and unless you're really good at leading the reader's eye around the page, they can leave your audience wondering which panel to read next. Look at comics and graphic novels illustrated by Steve Bissette, John Totleben, and Rick Veitch for successful uses of eccentric panel shapes.

Because space on your graphic novel page is a scarce resource, pick shapes that match the subject being depicted. A long shape is great for showing a long subject—a river, a snake, a funeral procession, a sword. Look at the first panel of the first page of my thumbnails at the end of this chapter. I used a wide but short panel to show the convention center. If I'd used a taller panel, I would have had to either crop the sides of the building or leave a big area at the top of the panel showing the sky. You can see another in page 6, panel three. In that panel, The Bot is showing a kid how to swing his axe sideways, like a baseball bat. That required some horizontal space to show the full movement of the swing.

A tall thin panel is good for showing things like a skyscraper, a church steeple, a telephone pole and, of course, a standing person.

You can also layer panels, or parts of panels, over other panels. This can make for a lively design and is also a handy way to squeeze a little extra space out of a page. When a small panel is layered almost entirely over another, larger panel, that's known as an inset panel. Nat's script requested that panel two of page 4 be inset in panel one. Inset panels are particularly efficient in combination with *splash pages*. Any picture that takes up a whole page is likely to have some dead space. Arrange the panels so you can place the inset there.

I Before E, Except After Will

Will Eisner makes spectacular and inventive use of vignettes in his later graphic novels. Books like *Dropsie Avenue* and *To the Heart of the Storm* aren't just compelling stories, they're textbooks in the use of the vignette as a storytelling device.

Splash Page

A page with a really big panel that takes up most or all of the page is called a **splash page.**

Kubism

Some of the best uses of the inset panel can be found in the work of comics legend Joe Kubert. He evokes a sense of epic scale in his rugged melodramas *Tor* and *Abraham Stone* by using tight close-up panels inset in sweeping vistas.

Timing

On the comics page, we show time by using space. Here are some very general rules about depicting time:

- In the rhythm of a page, every panel is at least one beat. The more panels in a sequence, the longer that sequence takes.

- The longer a reader looks at a panel, the longer a stretch of time that panel represents. So panels with lots of words take longer to read, and thus feel longer. The same goes for panels with lots of interesting details or elaborate rendering.

- Wide panels read as longer periods of time than narrow panels.

- Panels that show a character moving through great physical distance suggest that a considerable amount of time is passing.

- You can give an effect of slow motion by using the same camera shot throughout a series of panels, breaking a brief moment down into briefer moments. The same camera technique can also show something close to real time or communicate the idea that a lot of time has passed. It just depends on the content of the panels. The following fixed-angle timing illustration shows examples of timing effects you can get with fixed camera angles.

- Disorienting changes in subject, composition, and technique can slow the reader down, forcing a pause to assess the new information, thereby lengthening the time a panel represents.

Fixed-angle timing. The conversation between the man and the typing girl takes place in something close to real time. The page of the room getting cleaner is more like time-lapse photography, and could represent days, weeks, or even months.

Graphic novelists usually do this sort of time-manipulation instinctively rather than consciously. To develop that instinct, read a wide variety of comics and graphic novels.

Composition

Composition is how you arrange the two-dimensional shapes and three-dimensional forms that make up your picture. The goal is to arrange your shapes in a way that communicates your meaning and leads the eye around the picture.

Composition is an important matter for any visual artist, and many long books have been written about it. To cover it sufficiently would take more room than we have in this entire book, much less part of one chapter. But here are a few useful principles:

- **Avoid symmetrical compositions.** These are a big problem for inexperienced artists. Symmetry stops a picture dead in its tracks. Save them for the occasional moment that needs to feel like a religious icon.

- **Three is a magic number.** Mentally divide your space into thirds both vertically and horizontally. Placing your subjects on these lines will create interesting, dynamic divisions of space. Dividing into fifths works, too.

- **Use contrasts.** Juxtapose big and little, straight and curved, vertical and horizontal, organic and geometric, sparse and busy, light and dark, smooth and textured, sharp and blurry, near and far. Remember that any time you put two things next to each other, your reader is going to compare them.

- **A bit of awkward tension is often a good thing.** Perfect harmonious compositions send a signal that everything is resolved. Let things lean too far in one panel and use the next to resolve the imbalance.

What If They Don't Fit Together?

Because of that "left to right and top to bottom" tendency I mentioned, some page layouts just don't work. In Chapter 7 Nat showed you some layouts where the reader will have a tough time telling which panel to read after the first. Sometimes the perfect individual panels just won't all fit together. This isn't a problem for web cartoonists, because they have an infinite canvas, but it's a constant problem for those of us who work on paper. This is another reason to do thumbnails first. It can be hugely frustrating to do a great pencil drawing on one part of the page only to realize that it's going to interfere with an important part of some other panel. Eventually you'll develop an instinctive sense of what can work and what can't. Until then, do thumbnails and make tiny mistakes instead of big ones.

The Little Version of *The Big Con*

These are the thumbnail drawings that I'll use to solve any problems I might have laying out *The Big Con*.

The Least You Need to Know

- ◆ Create thumbnail page layouts before you start penciling.

- ◆ Compose pictures that are dynamic, not static.

- ◆ Different panel arrangements will affect the reader's sense of time's passage.

- ◆ Arrange your characters so that their placement in the panel doesn't conflict with where the speech balloons need to be.

Chapter 14

Render for Real

In This Chapter

◆ Paper, pencils, and other tools

◆ Assembling reference materials

◆ Enlarging your thumbnails

◆ Working with bleeds

You've got a script, some nifty designs and model sheets, and a small pile of scribbly, nearly illegible thumbnail sketches. You're almost ready to begin drawing the actual story. In this chapter we'll look at some ways to make that go as smoothly as possible.

Some Art Supplies You Need

It's time to go shopping. Graphic novelists tend to be passionate about their art supplies, and can disagree fiercely about the advantages of one grade of pencil lead versus another. They're also quite conservative about their supplies. When something works, they stick with it.

There's no limit to how much a dedicated shopper can spend on supplies. Listed here is close to the bare bones minimum of what you should have, but there are plenty of options. Try them until you find something that's right for you. Then you can get weird and cranky like your peers and learn the joy of getting angry at confused art-supply store clerks.

Paper

Choose a paper that has a surface you like to draw on, that's sturdy enough for the type of drawing you plan to do, and that's affordable. That "sturdy" requirement can rule out a lot of otherwise terrific papers. If you're drawing in brush or pen and ink, or if your pages have to be shipped from one place to another, thin papers can buckle or tear, ruining your page and destroying all your hard work. However, if you're working only in pencil or marker, scanning the work yourself and sending it off digitally, you can use whatever you like.

The traditional choice for comic books and graphic novels is 2-ply Bristol board. "Board," in this case, means a sheet of sturdy paper. "Two-ply" means it's actually two sheets pasted together, which is why it's so sturdy. And "Bristol" refers to a place in England where the stuff used to be make. Two-ply is popular for a number of reasons. It's strong enough to pass from hand to hand to hand without getting banged up. It can take a lot of ink without buckling, but it's still thin enough to see through if you're using a light box (more on those in a bit). And best of all, it's cheaper than 3-ply.

Papers are available in different types of surfaces: "Hot press," "plate finish" and "smooth" all describe paper that's as smooth as glass. These papers don't grab pencil marks as easily as rougher papers, and when they do, they can be tougher to erase. Pens and brushes glide effortlessly across the surface of smooth papers, though the pen lines can take a long time to dry. Cold press or vellum papers are rougher. They're easier to draw on in pencil and easier to erase, but they wear out brushes more quickly. The surface can interfere a bit when you draw in ink, giving your line a texture you might not have wanted. Try different papers and see which works best for you.

Pencils

Pencils come in a couple of different forms. There are the standard wood ones that everyone grew up using in school. There are mechanical pencils into which you feed tiny little leads (which should, of course, be called graphites, but everyone says leads, so in the interest of consistency, we will, too.) And there are lead holders, which are like mechanical pencils, but use much thicker leads. Use whichever kind you prefer. I've used all three on the same page.

Lead is graded according how hard or soft it is. Here's the scale, from soft to hard:

Soft 6B•5B•4B•3B•2B•B•HB•F•H•2H•3H•4H•5H•6H **Hard**

Really soft lead gets your page dark and dirty very quickly. It smears easily and takes forever to erase. It can also build up a residue that makes it hard for ink to stick to the page. Using a very hard lead is kind of like drawing with the point of a steak knife. It leaves a very pale mark and, if you aren't careful, leaves a deeply incised groove in the page that can trip up your ink line.

Many graphic novelists use more than one kind of lead as they work. I like to use a 3H or 4H for lightly blocking things out. (I draw with the side, not the point, to avoid digging into the page.) Then I'll go in with an H or 2H for the rest of the drawing. Your preferences may be quite different, and may change from day to day depending on the paper you're using and how humid it is. Keep a variety of leads on hand. Mechanical pencil leads come in different thicknesses. The ones I see most often are 9 mm, 7 mm, and 5 mm. Before you buy any, check which size your pencil takes.

Mechanical pencils never need sharpening, but if you've got a heavy hand, the leads can break very easily, which can be frustrating. For wooden pencils, get a motorized sharpener, and keep a craft knife and sandpaper block handy for when it decides to stop working. If you're using a lead holder, you'll need a little barrel-shaped sharpener called a lead pointer.

A plentitude of pencils.

Leads for lead holder

Mechanical pencil

Lead pointer

Lead holder

Erasers

I use several kinds of erasers. A kneaded eraser is a little piece of gray putty that doesn't crumble away into nothing as you use it. It picks up graphite, and when it gets dirty, you knead it into new shape until it's clean on the outside. Put it down when you aren't using it, because it also absorbs skin oils, and that gets nasty after a while. The kneaded eraser is wonderful when you want to lighten your pencil marks without getting rid of them entirely. You can just drag it lightly across the drawing to do that.

Use a smooth white plastic eraser to erase pencil lines thoroughly. The standard 2-inch block shape is great for larger areas. When you need to be precise and erase the left eye on a gnome in the background, use a retractable eraser like the Sanford Tuff Stuff Eraser Stick. Don't use any kind of abrasive eraser for getting rid of pencil marks. They tear up the paper. If they're dry they leave a nightmarish pink stain on your work.

Electric erasers are low-level power tools, and are a lot more expensive than other kinds. ("Expensive" in this case means $70 instead of 70¢.) They're indispensable for one task, though. They can erase ink. If you buy one, make sure to buy the ink-erasing refills, because the other ones won't do you much good.

A drafting brush is a great thing to have on hand, too. It's just a big, soft-bristled brush for sweeping eraser crumbs off your drawing. Your hand doesn't do this job nearly as well, and the less skin oil you get on your paper, the better.

Make as many mistakes as you want.

Electric eraser

Drafting brush

White plastic erasers

Kneaded eraser

Rulers

The ruler I use the most when drawing is clear plastic, 18 inches long, and covered with a grid of thin red lines so that I can line up things in my drawing, even if the ruler is covering them. I also have an 18-inch metal ruler for when I need to cut a straight line.

A Bad Shave

Don't use a plastic straight-edge with a metal knife. The metal will cut the plastic and you'll be stuck with a not-so-straight edge.

These things rule.

Metal ruler

Clear plastic ruler with grid

Metal t-square

T Square

A T square is a straight-edge with a cross-piece at one end. To use it, butt the cross-piece up against the edge of your drawing board. Tape your paper in place, and move the T square up and down to make parallel lines. Get a metal one with ruler markings on it. It should be at least long enough to reach the full width of your drawing paper. Add a clear plastic triangle with a beveled inking edge and you're ready to draw perfect horizontal and vertical lines.

Tables

The most important thing about where you draw is this: You need a smooth surface that tilts. Most graphic novelists have professional-quality drafting tables. If you don't have the money or the space to set one up, get a good sturdy lapboard and brace it against something that won't move. There are two big reasons you want a tilted surface: your perspective and your spine. When drawing, you want to see the entire page from roughly the same distance. If you're upright and the table is flat, the top of the page is a lot further from your eyes than the bottom, and some strange distortions creep into your work. And to compensate for this, you'll find that you tend to lean out over the board, ruining your posture, and reshaping your spine into something like a question mark.

A graphic novelist, the idol of millions, using his lapboard.

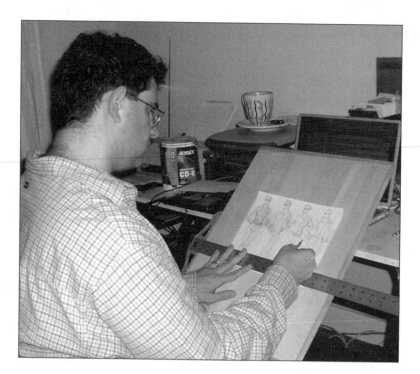

Light Box

There will be lots of times when you want to replicate a drawing. Say you drew the perfect face in your sketchbook, and now you want it on your final page of art. You could copy it, but you'd get the same results faster if you traced it. Two-ply Bristol board is too thick to trace through, unless you have a light box.

Shining light through paper makes it easier to see through. A light box is a translucent drawing surface with a light behind it. You can buy one in an art supply store, make your own, or improvise one by taping your paper to a window on a sunny day. (I briefly used a frosted Plexiglas window from a junk store, put a lamp on the floor between my legs and did my tracing using the glass like a lapboard. You can do this too, but please, please, *please* be careful and don't cut yourself.) For ways to make your own, type "make a light box" into an Internet search engine. There are dozens of sets of plans on the web. Look for ones that call for fluorescent light. Ordinary incandescent bulbs get hot too quickly.

Assembling Reference Materials

Reference falls broadly into two categories: the kind that helps you get the details in a drawing correct, and the type you use to improve your academic draftsmanship. No one has any quibbles with the first. The second can sometimes be troublesome.

Get It Right

As I mentioned in Chapter 11, getting details right is hard, but it makes an enormous difference in your storytelling. Your readers may not be able to accurately describe the uniform a chief petty officer of the U.S. Coast Guard wears, but they'll know when you've got it wrong. And is it an African or an Indian elephant that has the bigger ears? And what sort of support harness does a cave explorer wear when prusiking her way up a limestone wall using single rope technique?

In Hollywood, production companies hire experts to answer such questions. If you can find an expert who'll help you for no compensation other than the glory of Truth in Art, great. Otherwise, you've got books and the web. Gather pictures of everything you need to draw, but don't know how. Keep them in a file folder near your table. Tape the picture to your board while you're using it, and put it back in the folder when you're done.

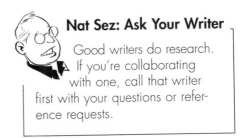

Nat Sez: Ask Your Writer

Good writers do research. If you're collaborating with one, call that writer first with your questions or reference requests.

Using Models

Reference isn't just for making your drawings more authoritative and accurate. It can make them better, too. This is a tricky thing, full of all sorts of aesthetic, moral, and even legal gray areas. Fine artists and illustrators have never hesitated to use live models. It's part of the tradition and (crude insinuations aside) there's never been any stigma attached to the practice. And from the earliest days of photography, artists of all sorts have used photographs as source material when they work. Making a complete drawing from life can take a long time, and some poses are difficult to hold. Even keeping the same smile on your face for 60 seconds is tough. A graphic novel can consist of hundreds and hundreds of pictures. Who has time to pose that long?

Photos are full of useful information for graphic novelists. You can certainly come up with four or five different poses to fit a description like "Bob sat in a chair" and if Bob does a lot of sitting, you'll run through them in a couple of pages. Shoot some photos of a model sitting in a chair, though, and you'll get poses you wouldn't have thought of, with lots of interesting things happening in the tilt of the head, the placement of the hands, how the feet arrange themselves, how the clothing wrinkles and how the light falls across the figure. And you'll save time when you draw from these photos, because you'll be able to interpret the anatomy instead of having to construct it from scratch. Many artists working in a wide variety of styles use the information in reference photos to help produce better drawings in less time.

For some reason, though, there are people who still regard drawing from photographs as "cheating." I don't think there is such a thing a cheating in art. There is plagiarism, though. An artist can get into trouble producing a drawing that's too close to a photograph that someone else took. Use information from published photos, but don't copy them directly. You're always safe if you take your own photos. If you're producing a close likeness of the model, though, you may want to get a model release. This is an agreement, signed by the model, that you have permission to use the model's likeness. (You can find standard release forms to photocopy and use in *Business and Legal Forms for Illustrators* by Tad Crawford.)

Judicious Usage

In his graphic novel *The Bloody Streets of Paris* Jacques Tardi rejects photo-reference for his characters, drawing them in a simple, almost blobby style. But he makes extensive use of photos for his backgrounds, which are elaborately detailed.

I won't tell you to use photos or not use them, but creating a graphic novel takes a lot of work, and I think it's foolish to automatically reject what can be an extremely useful tool.

Photo referencing doesn't automatically raise the level of everyone's work, though. It's hard, for example, to imagine that Charles Schulz's *Peanuts* would have been improved by it. Photos also offer traps to the unwary graphic novelist. I've seen nice, loose layout gestures turn stiff and posed when an artist tries too hard to make a drawing match a photo. Distortions in perspective creep into a picture. Sometimes when an artist creates a character out of the imagination, then uses photo reference to help with a panel or two, those panels look out of character. The effect is like a sudden switch of actors in the middle of a film. Clint Eastwood lowers his head to light a cheroot, the hat obscures his face, and when he looks back up, he's Buddy Ebsen. The camera cuts away, comes back, and there's Clint again. Not a good way to immerse your audience in the story, is it? Avoid making pictures that are too much model, and not enough character.

Photos are packed with visual information. Keep in mind that not all of it is relevant to your work. Your job when looking at that photo is to take what's useful and *discard anything else*. If your graphic novel is drawn in a clean, flat, decorative manner, then that beautiful light and shadow on your model is a distraction. Ignore it, or your readers will wonder why a film noir heroine suddenly walked onto the set of your Technicolor romance. And if you've been drawing clothing with a minimum of folds in the drapery, copying a real model's clothing too closely is going to make it look like your hero snuck off between panels to take a nap in his suit.

The axiom to remember is this: Use your photos, but don't let them use you.

Keeping It All Organized

Because I work on a lot of different sorts of projects, I have several big filing cabinets filled with thousands of reference photos. Keeping that many pictures organized isn't easy. Here are my broad categories, each of which may have lots and lots of subclassifications:

- Animals
- Art and architecture
- Disaster and law enforcement
- Entertainment
- Farm
- Flags
- Food
- Foreign (broken down into individual countries and regions, and sometimes into time periods within these)
- Guns
- Holidays
- Housing and decor
- Industrial design and ordinary objects
- Industry
- Magic and odd phenomena
- Maps
- Military
- Miscellaneous
- Money
- Nature
- People
- Period (as in "historical period," not punctuation)
- Regional USA (broken down state by state)
- Religion
- Science
- Sport
- Transportation
- Typography

Then there are the subcategories. You'll come up with your own divisions depending on what you have and what your needs are. In my file, the Transportation category (which covers only civilian transport, not military) breaks down like this:

- **Air**

   Aircraft

   Airports

   Balloons

- **Auto**

   2000s

   1990s (and so on)

- **Bikes**

   Motorized

   No motor

- **Boats**

   Motorized

   Sails, canoes, and rafts

- **Infrastructure**

   Bridges

   Signals

   Signs

   Streets

- **Miscellaneous**

- **Public**

   Trains and subways

   Buses and misc.

- **Trucks**

There's not a lot of room on manila folder tabs, so I abbreviate the names of each file. TRANSPORTATION/public/buses and misc. becomes TRANS/pub/bus & miscellaneous

Photos of people are grouped by gender, and then by pose. There are also categories for children, and for multiple-person shots like PEOPLE/couples/kiss & embrace.

When filing, anticipate the need a given photo is most likely to fill. Some are easy—a picture of a grizzly goes right into *Animals/mammals/bears*. Others are a lot tougher. You've got an illustration of a woman from 1800, wearing a nifty dress whose patterning you might want to adapt, sitting in a great design for a chair. Where does it go? *PEOPLE/women/seated* or *PERIOD/1800s* or *COSTUME/women* or *HOUSING/interiors/furniture/chairs?* Don't linger over these decisions—just file it where you think it has the best chance of being useful. As you build the file, there'll be some redundancy between folders. You'll also be surprised at how good your visual memory is at recalling where you stashed something four years ago.

> **Cheap Clips**
>
> Aside from the cost of the cabinet and folders, the photo file doesn't have to cost anything. Keep scissors handy as you read newspapers and magazines. When you spot something worth saving, clip it right then and there, and hide if the librarian yells at you.

Reference from the Web

The filing system I use was organized before the web. Many kinds of reference are now easily accomplished online. The web is particularly good at finding things like specific models of cars and airplanes. Just type "Spitfire" into Google's image search and you'll get dozens of great pictures. Other things can defy even the most dedicated searcher. With experience, you'll learn what you need to clip and what's easily available.

Blowing Up Your Thumbs

You've got tiny thumbnails and a big sheet of drawing paper. You need a bridge between the two. You could just eyeball and redraw the layouts on the page, but you've already done some nice composing in your tiny little scribbles, and it'd be a shame to waste time reinventing the wheel. The easiest way to transfer thumbnails onto your final sheet of drawing paper is to use a photocopier to blow them up to the final size and trace them using a light box. Here's how you blow them up to the right size.

Go to a photocopy shop. Take along a calculator and a ruler or borrow them from the person behind the counter. Punch the following into your calculator, *in this order:*

1. The height you want your page to be (in any unit you like—inches, centimeters, bullet lengths, whatever).

2. The "divided by" key.

3. The height of your thumbnails (in the same units as the first number).

4. The "multiplied by" key.

5. The number 100.

6. The "equals" key.

So if you want to draw a page that's 15 inches tall, and your thumbnails are 9 inches tall, you'd get this:

$$15 \div 9 \times 100 = 166.6667$$

There's your answer. You want to enlarge your thumbnails by 167 percent. (Just round off the part after the decimal. Photocopiers don't care about those little numbers, so why should you?)

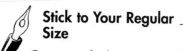

Stick to Your Regular Size

Once you find a size you like thumbnailing at, stick to that size and you won't have to recalculate what percentage to blow up your thumbnail sketches.

Bleed

A printed image is said to **bleed** when the image runs all the way out to the edge of the paper. The orange-bordered cover of this book bleeds, as do the gray-bordered pages marking Parts 1, 2, and 3.

If you drew your thumbnails in ink, the regular darkness settings will be fine. If you did them in pencil, most machines will lose some detail unless you push the darkness as far as it'll go.

Now just tape one of those enlarged photocopies to your light box, then tape your art board over that. Turn off the light in your drawing area, turn on the light box, and you're ready to trace.

Work lightly, and dig into the paper as little as possible. Turn off the box once in a while to see what your pencil lines really look like. They'll be a lot darker than you thought they were when they had a light shining through them from behind. It's common for light box tracings to look a little stiff and lumpy when you first start working that way. Don't worry. This isn't your final art, just a way to transfer your layouts.

Here's an important thing to remember: Photocopies often distort your enlarged image slightly, so rule out your image area in pencil on the board first. If you plan to let your images *bleed* outside the live area, measure the bleed area, too.

Letting Your Live Art Bleed

Printing presses need something to grab when they pull your paper through their works. The part they grab is apt to get a bit mangled by the process, so those edges are trimmed. Artists put *crop marks* on their page to indicate where this should happen. The tricky part is that paper moves around a bit as it's printed, so the trimming might not happen where you want it. The solution is to draw inside the live area on pages that don't bleed, and out past the crop marks on pages that do. You can read more about this and other production matters in Kevin Tinsley's invaluable *Digital Prepress for Comic Books*.

You'll notice that in the following bleed illustration, I drew the picture a little further out than the space cordoned off by the crop marks. That's so that when the paper is trimmed, the art will reach all the way out to the edge even if the trimming is a bit off target.

If you don't plan on letting your art bleed, just make sure to draw all of your pages at the same size. If you want to use bleeds, and someone else is publishing your graphic novel, talk to the publisher first. Sometimes bleeds cost more to print, and the publisher may have budgetary limits. If you're publishing it yourself, talk to your printer and find out how much extra, if anything, it will cost.

Crop Marks

Crop marks are small lines near the corner of an image. These marks show where the image is expected to be cropped (cut off) when the book is produced.

Some of the bleed gets trimmed away.

Crop marks

Live area is inside white lines

This part is trimmed away

This is the edge of the trimmed paper

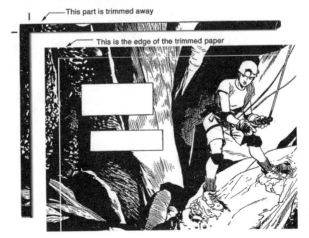

The Least You Need to Know

◆ Work at a tilted drawing surface.

◆ Art suppliers offer a wide range of options. Experiment and choose the tools that work best for you.

◆ Use photo reference to make your work faster and more accurate and to help avoid formulas. Don't replicate another photographer's work.

◆ Use a photocopier to enlarge your thumbnails, and trace them onto your final page using a light box.

◆ Talk to your publisher or printer before drawing art designed to bleed outside of the live area.

Chapter **15**

Drawing for Graphic Novels

In This Chapter

- Drawing with simple forms
- Using perspective
- Creating gestures
- Seeing light and shadow
- Penciling for an inker

Penciling is tough. Let's get that out up front. I know dozens of graphic novelists, and not one of them is ever happy with the work they do. It can take an artist years of effort just to acquire the most basic skills, so prepare yourself for some frustration.

It's not enough to know how to draw. You have to excel at a number of things at the same time. To tell a comic book story you have to unlock the mysteries of both form and content.

What the Job Requires

On the content side of things, you cast character types and in a way actually act out their parts by creating gestures and expressions for those characters. You make decisions about costuming, props, and set design, lighting for mood and for clarity, "camera" placement and focus, and pacing. Your choices determine the tone and character of the story—how light or how moody it is, its naturalistic or fantastic qualities. You can shift the meaning of a narrative with the change of the width of a line or two in a face and you can construct or subvert key metaphors just by shifting the viewer's angle.

The formal problems are an entirely different set of concerns, and you share them with every graphic artist. A panel isn't just a story unit. It's also a piece of two dimensional graphic design. And if you're drawing your panel in three dimensions, composing in depth, you have to carefully arrange the forms in space, as well. These arrangements have to work not only as individual panels but across the page and throughout the story as a whole. And the graphic novelist has to know when to keep things unified and when to blow the unity for expressive purpose.

Dealing with all of these at once is a lot like juggling. Juggling one ball is just a simple motor skill, two is a little tougher, three takes some practice. Each new ball you add increases the difficulty. A graphic novelist has to keep a lot of balls in the air.

How to Learn to Draw

A book this size can't teach you how to draw. Nor can a half dozen textbooks. You learn to draw by *drawing*. Pick up a sketchbook, a kneaded eraser, and an HB pencil, and spend some time drawing from life. You'll make mistakes, and the drawings won't be very good. That's fine. The work you do while learning to draw isn't art. It's exercise. You have to teach your brain how to observe line, light, pattern, and form. No advice or problem-solving technique that you read in a book will do you any good unless you've tried to solve the problem yourself.

If it'll hold still, draw it.

Some Good Books

Here are a few books full of lessons that can improve your drawing:

◆ *Drawing on the Right Side of the Brain* by Dr. Betty Edwards is a classic in the field of art instruction. That's because it works. Do the exercises in this book and you'll quickly get better at drawing from observation and will develop skills to improve your drawings from imagination.

◆ *How to Draw the Human Figure* is a fine collection of lessons adapted from the renowned correspondence school, Famous Artists School. The lessons in this book were prepared by some of the top illustrators of the mid-twentieth century.

◆ *Atlas of Human Anatomy for the Artist* by Stephen Rogers Peck offers a thorough analysis of the bony and soft-tissue structures that make up the human form. This a great book to keep with you when drawing from a live model. It's more than 50 years old and has been reprinted dozens of times.

◆ *Successful Drawing* by Andrew Loomis is another great book that's more than a half century old. Unfortunately, it hasn't been reprinted, and when copies do turn up they cost a fortune. It's such a useful book that I wouldn't be surprised to learn that overzealous art students have scanned it in its entirety and made every single page available for free download on the Internet.

Simple Forms

It's important that the drawing in a graphic novel be fueled by observation. Drawings carry their message by reminding their viewer of things from the real world. Unfortunately, graphic novelists almost never actually get to draw from observation. It's tough to cram a pirate ship into your studio, and Atomicus is usually too busy fighting The Neutron Mom to hold a pose for more than a minute or so. Artists, then, have to contrive their pictures, constructing them from imagination, reference, and their understanding of anatomy, perspective, light, and form.

For instance, I didn't have any cyborgs lying around the room when I drew The Bot's robot armor. As you can see, though, in the following picture, I was able to build the drawing out of boxes, wedges, tubes, and spheres. And you know what? That's how I draw almost *everything*. Anything a graphic novelist needs to draw can be built out of simple geometric forms.

Simple geometric forms are the basis of everything you draw.

This even applies to people. To construct a convincing figure, you first build a mannequin out of simplified forms, the way I do in the next picture. Many artists use an assortment of cylindrical and box shapes. Others work with amorphous forms. Several animators I know draw the torso as "a half-full sack of flour."

Use geometric or organic forms.

Learning to construct and pose the human figure means first learning to manipulate those simplified forms. The best way to do this is by drawing real objects in front of you, but you can jumpstart the process by spending some time tracing photographs.

Converting photos to mannequins will teach you how to invent your own figures.

Lay a piece of tracing paper over a good clear photograph of a person. Then trace over the photo, ignoring specific details, breaking the drawing down into basic forms. Don't worry about the subtle forms where things connect. If you're just getting started, don't worry about anything more difficult than tubes, balls, and boxes. Subtleties come with study and practice.

Depth

Unless your characters live in a highly stylized abstract environment, you're going to need to do more than just draw them flat on the paper. You'll need to create some kind of illusion of three-dimensional space. Depth creates visual excitement. Flatness can be elegant, but it can also quickly bore the reader. And many stories demand pictures that show how far away the coach is, or how close the Squirrel Hill Strangler is to his victim fleeing toward the apartment door. There are a number of techniques for doing this, including the following:

◆ **Linear perspective** is the technique that creates the most accurate illusion of depth. Its principles were first demonstrated in Renaissance Italy, and they haven't changed since then. Linear perspective works on the principle that the size of objects seems to diminish as they recede into the distance. Linear perspective seems difficult at first, but a diligent artist can learn everything he or she will ever need to know about the concept in a day or two. *Successful Drawing* by Andrew Loomis, which I mentioned earlier, is a great place to learn everything you'll need and more. You can also read a good basic explanation of it in *How to Draw Comics The Marvel Way* by Stan Lee and John Buscema.

This panel uses linear perspective, overlapping, and a form of aerial perspective.

◆ **Aerial perspective** (also known as atmospheric perspective) is an effect you've probably noticed. As things get further away, particles in the atmosphere make them look bluer and less distinct. (Remember singing about "purple mountain majesties"?) A color graphic novel can get this effect by using cooler colors in the background. In black and white, it's achieved by increasing the line weight, contrast, and amount of detail on the stuff you've drawn in the foreground. I'll talk more about this in the chapter on inking.

◆ **Overlapping** is the simplest way to create depth in a picture. It's also extremely effective. In the following group shot of three characters, it's unmistakable that the chairs are closer to us than the speakers, and that Yeo is in front of Terry and Derrick. Always be on the lookout for ways to have your characters overlap and be overlapped by part of their environment.

◆ **Larger objects** generally seem closer than smaller ones, particularly if there are no other depth clues.

◆ **Objects nearer the bottom of the panel** will sometimes appear to be closer than those at the top. A lot of non-Western and pre-Renaissance art works this way.

Acting Out: Finding the Right Gesture

Graphic novelists practice a silent art. Readers can't hear the words in the balloons, so what they say is only a small part of what your readers will learn about your characters. Most of the impressions readers form will come from what you show your characters doing. Consider the two panels of Terry and Derrick explaining things to Yeo in the next picture. In the first Terri is helpful and Derrick is mildly irritated. In the second, she's furious and Derrick is heartbroken. The words are exactly the same. It's the gesture that gives them context.

Coming up with gestures is one of the most enjoyable parts of illustrating a graphic novel. Most cartoonists have an urge to play-act, to perform in front of an audience. Gesture drawings are acting on paper. They're your chance to inhabit your characters, and even to ham it up a bit.

Gestures are a lot of fun to draw. Most artists scribble them out as either scribbly shapes or modified stick figures, then bulk them up to tube and box mannequins.

How can you get good at creating gestures? Do you have to ask? *Practice.* Keep a sketchbook with you and draw. Draw in the doctor's waiting room. Draw your co-workers at lunch. Don't worry about creating polished likenesses. With gesture drawings, the goal is to capture the essence of a pose.

The gestures you draw would affect how readers "hear" the lines.

Modeling Kley

One of the best artists to look at when studying gestures is the German illustrator Heinrich Kley. In Kley's scribbly, yet solid pen and ink drawings of people, animals and mythological beings he created the unmistakable impression of weight and movement.

Doing plenty of *real life observation* is crucial. People carry themselves in all sorts of interesting and revealing ways. Next time you're at a shopping mall food court, take note of how the people arrange themselves. You'll see the slumped shoulders of people trying to take up as little space as possible. There'll be teen boys and girls making all sorts of display postures, showing themselves to be bold, fierce, sensitive, and just plain available. There'll be workers and shoppers carting heavy objects, and you can see how their weight shifts to accommodate these loads.

There are a few formal techniques that will help you create effective gestures in your graphic novel, which I'll explain in the following sections.

Lay Down the Action Line

Build your full-body gestures around a single sweeping line that goes from toe to head. Start with the foot that's carrying most of the weight, move up through the hips and spine and up into the head. In my action-line drawings that follow you can see how I started with the single line, then scribbled it into something more like a human skeleton.

Try to make that first stroke capture the whole figure.

Exaggerate

As I noted earlier, your graphic novel doesn't come with sound. Gestures tell your reader how your characters are speaking, what they're doing, and how they're feeling. To make a 2-inch drawing communicate all that, you're going to have to indulge in a bit of exaggeration. How much depends on your story and your own instincts. Push things too far and you've got a bunch of loudmouthed hams hogging the stage. Don't push it far enough, and you've got a cast of sleepwalkers who never seem to move. Stand up from the drawing board and take the pose yourself. If you can't act it, you'll have a tough time drawing it. And you should know the reaction you want your readers to have. Making your drawings clear and lively will require a bit of exaggeration, making them funny enough to get a laugh will require a lot more.

Silhouettes with Negative Space

The pictures in a graphic novel are often printed very small, and the readers have to decipher a lot of them. Make their job easier by choosing gestures that read well as silhouettes. Look at the two pictures of Gene in the next illustration. In the first one, his silhouette is cluttered and difficult to read. In the second it's easy to see what he's doing.

Which silhouette nags like a Hollywood agent?

WHA...?

Negative Space

Negative space is the flat area surrounding the elements in your drawings. Negative space is important because it helps make the "positive space" (your drawing) read more clearly. *Drawing on the Right Side of the Brain* shows an excellent exercise in learning to see negative space.

When you can, position the body so that the elbows are kept away from the middle of the body. That creates an area of *negative space* around the figure that helps the audience read the silhouette more easily. It also gives an impression of movement, particularly if the hands are doing something interesting. Look for ways to keep the legs apart, too. It will lend your poses both clarity and dynamism.

Bodies Should Bend and Twist

Imagine the head, torso, and pelvis as blocks. Unless you're drawing a soldier standing at attention, a butler waiting for instructions, or a patient anesthetized upon a table, don't point all three boxes in the same direction. Look for spiral movements between the three, with the head leading a turn, the torso and shoulder following, and the pelvis playing catch up.

Don't line up the head, torso, and pelvis vertically, either. The three tend to tilt in opposition to each other. For particularly clear lessons about bending and twisting the major masses of the body, look at *Constructive Anatomy* and *The Complete Guide to Drawing from Life*, both by George Bridgman.

Is It Interactive?

Don't just pose you characters. Make them interact with their environments. Your princess will seem more exhausted by her circumstances if she's leaning on the Baron's stable door. When Big Nick loses his car keys, don't just draw him with his hands on his hips, squinting at the floor. Show him on all fours, tossing sofa cushions around and raising a cloud of dust.

Characters should interact with each other, too. It's a crowded world, and people touch or otherwise physically impact each other all the time. Here are some examples of interactive gestures to consider:

♦ Louanne puts her hand on Norman's knee, and Norm looks at her, amazed.

♦ Tom emphasizes his point by poking a finger into Mark's chest. Mark cringes backward.

♦ Mary tells Jane a lame joke, and elbows her playfully in the ribs as she does so. Jane cringes back, as if being tickled.

♦ Parker and Ford exchange high fives when they realize that their prank has succeeded.

♦ Maggie pulls on Lorene's collar, dragging her out of a party.

These sorts of gestures show your reader how the characters relate to each other. Dialogue is important, but it's the pictures that are your primary tool for making a relationship believable and interesting.

Let There Be Light

Light is an important tool for most illustrators and fine artists. Cinematographers can't do without it. Many fine graphic novelists don't give it a thought.

For much of the medium's history, going back to newspaper strips, cartoonists were restricted to the narrow range of possibilities of their era's printing technology. Their pictures were limited to a value range of pale newsprint gray to blotchy gray-black. Color, if used at all, was likely to be an ill-registered afterthought. And the paper on which pictures were printed was often cheap and coarse-fibered, leading to uneven reproduction. Cartoonists made choices based on what was available, and turned out work that ranged from hackneyed to sublime.

Those limits are gone. Anyone willing to pay for decent printing can have his or her work reproduced more faithfully today than Michelangelo's work was 50 years ago. You've got a much wider range of choices available to you when it comes to reproducing subtleties in hue, saturation, and value.

With such a range of options you'll do well to learn how light really works, and go from there to create your own stylizations. Break out your sketchbook again. Get a piece of charcoal or a soft lead pencil (4B is good). The exercise I recommend, which was frequently assigned by the great fine artist Thomas Eakins, is simple but effective. Get an egg out of the refrigerator, and place it on a flat surface on top of a sheet of white paper. Point one, *and only one*, light source at it. (The sun through a window counts as only one source, but try it at night with an electric light.) Your job is to draw the egg as realistically as possible. When you've done that, move the egg so that the light hits it from a different direction, then draw it again. Rinse, lather repeat. Why an egg? Drawing an egg's basic shape isn't much of a challenge, so you're free to concentrate on seeing how light shifts as it moves around the form.

Use Contrast

To translate a drawing with a wide range of tones to something that works in stark black and white, eliminate most of the gray. If it's dark gray, make it black. If it's light gray, make it white. Or find graphic equivalents for your gray, using hatching or crosshatching.

Handing Off the Penciled Pages

One of the stranger quirks of the North American comic book industry is the division of the illustrator's work into a small assembly line: a pencil artist and an ink artist. Working this way is, in my opinion, an artificial division, but it's common enough that I thought I should mention it.

Artists who intend to ink their own *pencils* develop a shorthand way of indicating their intentions. Some parts of a drawing may be worked out with infinite care, while others get only the loosest indication. The only rule is to do whatever works best for you.

When working with an inker, your penciled page is a set of instructions for what you'd like the finished work to look like. The more carefully you delineate everything, the closer the page will come to the way you would have done it. Some things will require more care than others, depending on your inker's strengths. You should put your greatest effort into drawing faces clearly, because that's where the split between the two creators' visions will show itself. Most inkers have their own palate of brush and pen strokes to indicate textural effects. When it comes to things like foliage, stone, and water, show the inkers what they're supposed to draw and how the light hits it, and they can usually take care of the rest.

WHA...?

Pencils

Pages of comics art that haven't been inked are often called **pencils**. An editor who asks to see your pencils wants to look at your art, not your art supplies.

The Least You Need to Know

◆ Keep a sketchbook and draw people and objects from life.

◆ Build your drawings out of simple geometric forms.

◆ Use linear perspective, aerial perspective, and overlapping to create the illusion of depth.

◆ Start figure drawings with a sweeping action line.

◆ Design gestures so that they read as silhouettes.

Chapter 16

Stylize Yourself—Finding Your Voice

In This Chapter

- ◆ A brief history of style
- ◆ Choosing a style or letting it choose you
- ◆ Experimenting with surface and structure
- ◆ Latching on to trends

What most graphic novelists mean when they talk about style is really just handwriting—the superficial mannerisms and habits that creep into an artist's work. I don't think that these things are worth worrying about. But every artist wants to create work that's uniquely his or her own. How can you accomplish this in a meaningful way? How does an artist find a style that goes beyond mere surface?

Looking Back at Style

Anyone summing up stylistic trends of the past century or so in a couple of paragraphs is bound to leave out many important people, put them in the

Style

Style describes the mannerisms, techniques, and attitudes that combine to make a graphic novelist's work uniquely his or her own.

wrong category, or understate their roles. When discussing something as ephemeral as *style*, it helps to have a few reference points mapped out. Pardon me for a moment while I neglect the graphic novel in favor of its parents and grandparents: cartoons, comic strips, and comic books.

Funny Stuff

Humor comics take their inspiration from a variety of sources. The main threads in their development seem to be satirical and whimsical.

At the beginning of the twentieth century, newspapers and magazines used cartoonists and illustrators to report and comment on the news and, in some markets, help sell their products to many people who barely knew how to read. In that world the cartoonist was a newspaperman, valued for the ability to quickly produce pictures that could tell a story or communicate a point of view to unsophisticated readers. Cartoonists caricatured the major figures of their day, mocked the public and private life they observed, and developed an increasingly sophisticated symbolic shorthand. The Sunday comics panel, as pioneered by R. F. Outcault in *Hogan's Alley,* evolved from this tradition of graphic satire, boasting lushly rendered pictures that were relatively realistic, and followed the rules of academic illustration, (unless an ethnic group was being caricatured, in which case things could quickly get grotesque). These comics were often crammed with interesting background details for readers to explore at length.

As the comics' popularity became obvious, (and as newspaper competition increased,) the role of the cartoonist moved from commentary to pure entertainment. Along the way, the public latched on to various cartoon characters, many of which became household names. These more absurd and whimsical cartoonists were influenced by decorative artists, children's book illustrators and, inevitably, their peers, their love of liquor, and their deadlines. They also developed an odd set of cartoon stylizations that are still seen today: banana noses, giant feet, big blobby hands, and so on. In 1907, one of these cartoonists, Bud Fisher, arranged his drawings in a row of boxes and published little gags about the same characters six days a week in the San Francisco Chronicle, becoming the first successful comic strip creator.

What Fisher and Outcault had in common, and shared with a number of other major talents of the day, was an interest in the amusing antics of disreputable people. From the beginning, many humor comics found their richest material in criminality, misbehavior, stupidity, and the low life.

Many, that is, but not all. Winsor McCay set the gold standard for the comic strip as a vehicle for fantastic imagery and ideas. His Sunday pages, *The Dream of the Rarebit Fiend* and *Little Nemo in Slumberland*, feature characters who find themselves caught in increasingly bizarre dreams until the last panel when the protagonist wakes up, shocked to find himself out of trouble and tangled in the sheets. The real treat of the strips was the wildly imaginative images and ideas, rendered with McCay's precise and elegant line work. McCay was also a master of linear perspective, which he sometimes used to move his readers through elaborately designed spaces. Other strips, like *Gasoline Alley* and George Herriman's sublime *Krazy Kat*, played interesting games with page design and color to create subtle moods, gentle whimsy, and moments of exquisite lyricism. Frank King's *Gasoline Alley* Sunday pages were sometimes designed around a single image, which was divided into panels by laying a grid over it, and moving the characters through the grid.

By the middle of its first decade, the path of comics split between those whose work seemed to demand respectability and those who would clearly have none of it.

Into the Drink!

Maakies, by Tony Millionaire, is a weekly comic strip about an alcoholic crow and suicidal monkey who make up the crew of an old-fashioned sailing ship. It recreates the lively pen and ink cartooning and lowbrow aura of the earliest days of the comics. The strip has been collected into two books: *Maakies* and *The House at Maakies Corner*.

Adventure Comics and "Serious" Illustration

Comic strips had played with melodrama in features like Elzie Segar's *Thimble Theatre* (where Popeye made his debut) but it was Roy Crane who made the transition from humor to adventure comics in 1924 with his strip *Wash Tubbs*. It was a fast-moving, fun strip illustrated in a zippy cartoon style. Five years later *Buck Rogers* and *Tarzan* debuted. Both featured characters that had first appeared in prose stories. Rogers was drawn by Richard Calkins in a mannered style that seemed to be an artistic dead end. Tarzan was drawn by Hal Foster whose work had a classical beauty and spectacular facility that sprung from the tradition of illustrators like Howard Pyle and Edwin Austin Abbey. Foster later created *Prince Valiant*, and established a tradition of comic strip classicism with a heavy emphasis on anatomical accuracy, fully realized environments, and scrupulous research. *Wash Tubbs* and other strips that followed, notably Chester Gould's *Dick Tracy*, pioneered a different approach that put cartoony or expressionistic characters in relatively realistic settings to tell stories where the object is the thrill, not the chuckle.

This was a major development. In his daily adventure strip *Terry and The Pirates*, Milton Caniff combined Foster's ability to create believable settings, a bit of Crane's cartoony character design, and a chiaroscuro technique he learned from his friend Noel Sickles, who was working on a strip called *Scorchy Smith*. Caniff made this technique his own, using dramatic lighting and bold compositions to create an unforgettable strip that felt a lot like a Hollywood movie on paper. The dramatic, high contrast pictures could be drawn quickly with a fully loaded brush and looked good no matter how badly they were printed. Caniff's stylizations became very popular with comic book artists, who coped with the worst deadlines and the most incompetent printing.

Will Eisner's *Spirit* also boasted a strong movie influence—notably that of Welles's *Citizen Kane*. In seven-page stories distributed weekly in newspapers, Eisner pushed the medium's boundaries in stories that are still available and still read more than half a century later.

Funny Animals

Talking animals were a big hit in animated cartoons, and it was only natural they'd find an audience in comic books as well. The most notable of these were the Walt Disney comics, particularly those written and illustrated by Carl Barks. His Donald Duck and Uncle Scrooge McDuck stories were characterized by his unusually diligent attitude toward researching his material and the realistically constructed environments in which the ducks had their adventures.

Subversive Humor

In 1952, the first issue of *MAD* magazine appeared. It was initially edited and written by Harvey Kurtzman, who also provided layouts to his artists. *MAD* was notable for its irreverent attitude toward the subjects it satirized (first comics, then the rest of popular culture, and finally the culture as a whole.) While *MAD* artists would work in a dizzying range of styles, they were all extremely solid craftsmen producing pictures that pushed at the boundaries of acceptable taste. Its greatest asset was the perception that it always seemed to be playing with fire.

Kurtzman and *MAD*'s influence can be detected in just about every major development in North American humor: notably *National Lampoon*, *Saturday Night Live*, David Letterman, Howard Stern, *Spy* magazine, *The Onion*, and many others, including the underground comics movement.

Underground comics, created by and for the counterculture of the 1960s, pushed *MAD*'s subversiveness considerably further. The most notable underground cartoonist was Robert Crumb, who married 1920s-style bigfoot drawing to psychedelia, an unrestricted libido, and a sense of rage and regret at the worthlessness of life as people lived it. His drawing used extensive pen-and-ink hatching to emphasize solid form and give his characters a slightly seedy, hairy look. That image of desperate, degenerate cartoon characters was extremely powerful, like an awful, but long-suspected truth revealed. Crumb's styles and strategies were imitated by innumerable artists with varying degrees of success. Talented from the first, Crumb continually worked at improving his draftsmanship. Over the decades, he brought in new influences from Breugel to Picasso to Thomas Nast.

Toward the end of the underground movement, Art Spiegelman created comics that emphasized an analytical approach—formal experiments that focused on the tools of cartoon storytelling: panels, balloons, sound effects, and so on. In 1980, he and Francois Mouly created *Raw* magazine, a bold, oversized anthology of post-modern experimental comics designed to place the medium in a fine-art context. In 1981, Crumb started *Weirdo Magazine*, which was resolutely lowbrow and stressed an unstudied, handmade aesthetic. The two magazines encompassed much of the range of *art comics* of the 1980s.

The start of the 1980s also saw the emergence of alternative comics, notably *Love and Rockets* by Gilbert, Mario, and Jaime Hernandez, who synthesized an enormous range of influences from punk rock to Archie Comics to Fellini to goofy monster stories. The best alternative comics were characterized by their interest in combining solid craft and accessible storytelling with personal expression. They tended to incorporate wiseass appreciations of the weirdness of popular culture. The subsequent generation of personal cartoonists, sometimes called post-alternatives, de-emphasize conspicuous displays of craft, replacing wiseass irony with raw sincerity or wistful detachment. Their strongest influences include Charles Schulz's *Peanuts* and children's storybooks. The most recent trend has been a combination of minimalist graphics and crude, willfully naive draftsmanship, sometimes called "cute-brut."

Nat Sez: Madly Influential

Mad is actually an example of how comics can influence culture beyond just comics. Some folks have credited it for helping craft a growing cynicism in the American public, and I agree with them.

Art Comics

WHA...?

As more cartoonists approach their work as a type of fine art, emphasizing personal expression rather than entertainment, critical jargon has appeared to label their efforts. The current term is **art comics.**

Adventure Art

Adventure comics took their lead from the newspaper strips. In addition to those I mentioned earlier, Alex Raymond set much of the tone in *Flash Gordon*. His figure drawing stressed his characters' muscularity and sexuality, and he developed lush brush techniques for capturing every ripple of flesh. He also shrunk the heads of his male characters a bit, to make their bodies seem more massive, a strategy later abused by generations of superhero artists. Later, he abandoned the fleshy romanticism of *Flash Gordon* for a more naturalistic and very heavily photo-referenced approach in *Rip Kirby*. *Rip Kirby* was drawn with brush and pen techniques developed for advertising art. The artist would photograph models, project the photos onto his page with an opaque projector, and trace the photo. This made it possible to turn out startlingly realistic images at the speed a daily newspaper strip required. It took considerable skill to do well, but the approach caught on and remains common today.

Jack Kirby worked on various adventure comics since the early 1940s, and his work was always identifiable for its combination of solid construction, deep composition, and wildly exaggerated action. In the 1960s, while illustrating comics like The *Fantastic Four* and *The Mighty Thor*, he reconceived the human figure into increasingly massive forms, moving it from heroic to godlike, while using exaggerated foreshortening to emphasize panel depth. As Marvel comics increased in popularity, Kirby became one of the most influential comics artists of the century.

Neal Adams married Jack Kirby's exaggerated gestures and foreshortening to the realistic surface of the *Rip Kirby* strip, and added some experiments with unusual layout. By the 1970s, this became the preferred style for upcoming adventure comics artists, and it's still with us.

The 1980s and 1990s brought us artists influenced by such disparate sources as avant-garde illustration and Japanese animation. The latter is undoubtedly the most important commercial trend today.

Factors That Influence Style

Graphic novelists are like most people, torn between the urges to stand out and to fit in. Nowhere is the latter more apparent than in the development of popular styles. A number of pressures combine to make trends, including the following:

◆ **Editorial pressure.** Sometimes publishers wish they were publishing a tremendously popular creator. Call him Joe Popstar. If Joe is too expensive, or too busy, or too difficult to work with, they are going to look for someone else who can reach Joe's audience, or lend that unmistakable Popstar aura to the publisher's line of books. Some will just come right out and say that they want Popstar-type stuff. Others make it clear by their publishing choices. Books that look like Popstar drew them get published. Books that don't, don't.

- ◆ **Commercial pressures.** Royalties are a big part of many graphic novelists' income. Imagine that graphic novels illustrated with thumbprint collages are now consistently selling a lot more copies than the last big trend: graphic novels drawn in ballpoint pen on brown paper grocery bags. Before long, dozens of creators will be walking around with one black thumb and telling cashiers that they'd prefer plastic to paper.

- ◆ **Admiration.** Some graphic novelists find themselves powerfully attracted to and influenced by the work of another artist. It's common, particularly if you encounter that artist at the right point in your life. You're filling up sketchbooks, trying to figure out what you want to say and how you want to say it. Suddenly you encounter the work of an artist who does it all and makes it look easy. "There are plenty of terrific comics out there, but Sam Henderson's *The Magic Whistle* is the one that really speaks to me." You study Sam's work and commit his every doodle to memory. When the time comes to say what you have to say, you're likely to speak with Sam's accent.

- ◆ **Technological developments.** Many stylistic choices are made as a way of coping with the limits of technology. Cartoonists who knew their work would be shoddily printed on cheap newsprint developed stylizations and techniques to keep their work readable no matter how badly the reproduction was mangled. As better printing becomes available, some artists develop new styles that take advantage of it. Artists who don't risk looking out of date.

- ◆ **Unconscious influence.** Artists in all media spend countless hours looking for ways to improve their work. They're trying to solve problems, iron out kinks, polish their surface, and refine their message. If you're diligent about this, you start to do it unconsciously. When you look at another graphic novelist's work, you may unconsciously latch on to something there and store it away for future use.

Should you try to fight this process? If you're gravitating toward a style that's trendy and lucrative, you probably won't feel inclined to change direction. But it's important to remember that you're in this for the long haul. Nothing is uglier or more embarrassing than yesterday's fads. And no one wants to be known for drawing like someone else.

On the other hand, if your current approach has repeatedly demonstrated itself to be universally unpopular, you may find yourself forced to make a decision: Either make some changes in your work, or adjust to having an audience that would fit comfortably in your apartment.

Taking Control of the Process

When pondering matters of style, it's natural to torture yourself with all sorts of unanswerable questions. "Why shouldn't I just do that cool trick with the nostril that Skip Rogers uses?" "Why do I draw like a third-rate Mike Ratko clone?" "Why can't I at least be a second-rate me?" "I know 28 different ways to draw a nose. How do I pick one?" "Why do I always put too many shadows on people in daylight?" "Why do all of my female characters look like Jack Lemmon in drag?" "Who," you may wonder "is driving this thing?"

Expanding Your Range of Influences

Take some control of your development as an artist by exposing yourself to a wide variety of influences. If everything you do seems to remind people of a prominent superhero artist, a popular line of greeting cards, or the illustrations in an eighth-grade health textbook, you tire of hearing about it, and your work stagnates. Two important things: First, quit looking at whomever or whatever you've been looking at. You've already swallowed plenty and the rest is just going to be stored as art flab. Second, get out of the house and look at something new.

Where do you go to do this? Hit the library. It's free. Read some art history. Visit a museum. Pick up magazines you don't normally read. Flip through illustrated books. When you find someone intriguing, use the web to find out more about that artist. You aren't buying anything yet. This is window shopping. I mentioned "unconscious influences" earlier. The goal of this wandering is to give that housebound brain of yours some fresh air so that it can start working on new possibilities.

Look for unfamiliar work that catches your eye and copy it in your sketchbook. What would a graphic novel look like drawn in this style? What changes would need to be made? If you spot someone with an eccentric ink line, apply it in one your own drawings. When something feels right, play with it a little more. Don't worry about producing drawings that anyone is going to look at. You're just trying to scrape a few barnacles off your brain.

The Real Question

When you find an interesting technique, don't just ask yourself *what* the artist did and *how* it was done. Ask *why*? What does that technique bring to the image or the story? Many artists copy something merely because it "looks cool," ending up with a work that doesn't work.

Too Many Options

For some graphic novelists the problem isn't too few influences, but too many. You can ape your favorite manga artist and you can produce a handsome photoswipe. You can draw angular, aggressive figures with bold brush lines and patches of solid black, but you also like using fragile pen lines to render minute organic details. You can draw like an animator from the 1920s or a fashion illustrator from the 1960s. And none of these styles seem to go together very well. It's frustrating, and you almost wish you knew a lot less, so you wouldn't have to constantly suppress all the other possibilities that are constantly occurring to you.

How do you decide how to draw? The late Gil Kane, a respected adventure cartoonist, once described himself as being like a small-engine airplane, overloaded with conflicting, irreconcilable influences, unable to lift off the runway. He had to jettison some influences before he could take off.

So how do you know which influences to keep and which to leave on the tarmac? Good question. Take a step back and remember that if you take art seriously, style is *not* a goal in and of itself. It's a means to an end, and that end is *communication*. Put your time and energy into figuring out what you want to communicate—what feelings, images, ideas you want to share with the reader. Identifying the central message of the story (the way I did in Chapter 12) helps, too. When you focus on what you want to say, you find that you have a goal in mind for each picture. Comparing your picture to that goal compels you to make changes. Listen to that little nagging voice inside and try to get closer to how each panel should feel. Here are examples of the sort of internal process that can take place:

- Maybe a change in picture-plane depth is called for? Sure, the photorealistic rendering on Suzy looks out of place when I put her against all those flat, distorted backgrounds, but the whole angst-ridden story is about how she's the only person who "sees what things are really like around here."

- Maybe a more conspicuous use of line would be appropriate? When Mucha does it in his posters, it really turns the subject from an individual person to an icon of beauty.

- Should these be bizarre or ordinary people? Would they be more or less familiar to my readers if I use broad caricature? How likeable would the characters be if I make them grotesque? Do I *want* them likeable?

- Suppose I want to stress something truly weird about the characters. They're sort of like gods come to earth. Maybe making them weightier will get that across. No, they just look clumsy. Maybe lengthening their proportions will get that effect.

- These people are just mindless, slogan-repeating drones. They need to be creepier, but when I use a lot of shadow on them, I lose the sense of the scene they're in. They're creepy in broad daylight. What will make them both ordinary and creepy? Maybe if I distort their hands a bit, they'll sort of feel like tentacles …

- Some sophisticated readers are always second-guessing the storyteller when they read. If I can't count on the suspension of disbelief, how do I get them to care about what happens? Maybe I have to entertain the part of them that's aware this is a story, as well as the part that wants to know what happens next. If I'm audacious and do something a storyteller simply shouldn't do, maybe that would do the trick.

Sometimes these decisions are made instinctively. To the extent that you're doing it consciously, base your stylistic choices on the story you want to tell. Is the depiction of light on solid form important to the mood you want to create? Should the story be funny? If so, is it an elaborate visual gag or is it a one-liner? Would believability be a plus or a minus? Are you illustrating a graceful moment or a spazzy, awkward one? Only you know what you want those pictures to communicate. Keep that in mind and over time, you'll find yourself instinctively nudging them in the direction they need to go.

Learn to recognize how other creators have answered these sorts of questions. Analyze your reactions to their results and try to figure out why a given technique would (or wouldn't) be helpful in communicating the stuff that's in your head. You may have to compromise if you find that the best solution is beyond your capacity as an artist. For some artists, these compromises form the bases of their styles.

You'll improve over time. Just keep asking yourself these sorts of questions. When you haven't gone far enough, you'll look at what you've drawn and feel inarticulate, cowardly, and lame. When you've gone too far you'll frown at your work and feel tawdry, exhibitionistic, and lame. If all is going well, you won't choose your style—it will, eventually, choose you.

Experiments Are Free

A great thing about sequential storytelling is that it doesn't cost much to produce a complete work. Other visual storytelling media require collaborators and costly technicians and materials to produce even the most rudimentary work, and the low budget will be painfully evident. But with a few dollars worth of art supplies and some talent, anyone, even you, can produce a graphic novel that's as good as the best ever done.

That doesn't just mean you're free to become a big success. You're also free to fail miserably, at no cost other than time, paper, and ink. Try writing and illustrating some short stories. Set rules for yourself and follow them.

Panels rendered in various techniques.

More techniques.

Experiments in Drawing Technique

Don't take how you draw for granted. Changing your basic technical approach opens up all sorts of new possibilities. Do a story with goofy, exaggerated cartoons, then try another with the most realistic figures you can muster. Eliminate lighting and work with contour line only, or eliminate line and work with solid areas of white, black, and gray. Set a rule that a story will be inked entirely with a pen. Then do the next one in nothing but brush. Pencil a page tightly, working out every part in advance. Then try laying down only the most minimal pencil indications and improvise the rest in ink. Work on different sorts of paper. Scan photos and distort them in Photoshop, then draw from the distortions.

Experiments with Subject Matter

Graphic novelists can get into a rut by writing only what they know they can draw. Push yourself. If your work tends to be explosive and dramatic, see if you can handle a scene that turns on subtle nuances of gesture. Have you ever drawn an animal story? See if you can capture a day in the life of a bird, or a dog. Never worked on a period piece? Any decent history book has two or three good story ideas on every page.

Nat Sez: Get a Push

If you're used to writing and drawing your own material, try working with a writer once. Someone else's script will present you with challenges you'd never have given yourself.

In *Vox*, a one-man anthology of experimental stories published by Pack Rabbit Press, Leland Purvis devised a type of storytelling he calls pentads. As you can see in the following example, the goal of a pentad is to tell a story with five wordless, seemingly unrelated panels that take on meaning only by their juxtaposition.

Can you decode the story from five panels?

Formal Experiments

Use a strict panel grid, then try an organic array of vignettes. Start every page with a shot of the same person or object but get further every time until the full figure or item is revealed. See what happens if you put dialogue in the gutters below panels rather than in balloons inside them. Are caption boxes opaque or semitransparent? What's the effect of breaking an action into each of its steps and scattering them throughout the story?

The Least You Need to Know

- Style emerges from your natural inclinations as an artist.

- You can influence your stylistic development by the artists you study.

- Concentrate on the story you want to tell and your art will change to meet its requirements.

A Bit of *The Big Con:*
The Penciled Pages

Back in Chapter 9 we showed you the script for a section of *The Big Con*. Here it is in pictures, brought to life by Steve's talents and his dangerously pointy pencil. In this form, the art is not meant for reproduction. In fact, every single line you see here will be covered up or erased before the job is done.

Even if the writer and penciler have already carefully reviewed the thumbnails, it's a good idea to review the pencils carefully. It is still much easier to make changes and corrections at this stage than later. The writer should not just look at the art but also review it against his script. This is the time to not only catch errors but also opportunities. You can fine-tune your dialog to better match the art and to take advantage of any wonderful detail that the artist has created. If the artist was working from a plot rather than a script, now is when you figure out what all the text should be.

Part 4

Polishing the Pages

Now that you've spent hundreds of hours drawing your graphic novel in pencil, it's time to erase all that work. No, wait, first you want to go over the pencil drawings with ink, and then you erase the pencil marks. I really hope you read that second sentence before doing anything drastic.

These chapters show you how to bring out your drawings in ink, creating texture and impact. You also see how to add word balloons, lettering, and coloring, turning a series of pictures into a finished comics story.

Old-Fangled Letterin'

In This Chapter

- ◆ Hand-drawn lettering
- ◆ Balloon basics
- ◆ Tools of the trade
- ◆ Sound effects

Hand lettering is a lot less common in graphic novels than it used to be. It's not as fast as computerized lettering, and it requires more skill. It's less flexible, too. It takes no time to correct a misspelling on the computer, several minutes if you do it by hand. (Some graphic novelists actually write dialogue as they digitally paste it in.) In addition, computer fonts are scaleable and easily distorted for expressive effects.

So why letter by hand? Many artists simply prefer the look of a hand-lettered page. There's no substitute for the warmth that subtle variations in spacing and handwriting can bring to a page. Doing your own lettering is particularly valuable because a page feels more unified when the natural stroke of your pen matches the line you ink with. Inking over a lettered page makes it easier to see that page as a complete piece of graphic art. Those blocks of lettering aren't just words on the page—they're areas of gray that need to be composed along with the other areas of gray, black, and white. Some graphic novelists who do their own lettering like to do so before they pencil. That way they'll know exactly how much room they'll have left over. (This is extremely important on text-heavy pages.) And finally, it's tremendously satisfying to look at a page and know that every mark on it was made by your own hand.

Tool Time

Hand lettering requires adding a few tools to your bin. All but one of those tools are also useful when you're penciling and inking.

T squares, rulers and triangles were discussed in Chapter 14. You don't have to buy new ones just for lettering. Use the money you save to buy extra copies of this book.

An Original Consideration

Some graphic novelists sell their original pages to fans of their work and art collectors. Hand-lettered pages are more prized by many buyers and, everything else being equal, can bring a bigger price.

Ames Lettering Guide

This is the best bargain in any art supply store. It's a piece of molded plastic the size of a credit card that costs about $2. It makes it easy to keep the space between lines of text consistent.

Technical and Fountain Pens, Pigment-Based Markers

When choosing a lettering pen, there are a few factors to consider. Technical (tech) pens are expensive and fragile and take a lot of time to clean if you aren't very diligent about maintaining them. They give you a line that's unchanging and mechanically precise. Fountain pens cost about as much as technical pens, but they're a little harder to damage and a little easier to clean. Also, the line you get from a fountain pen is slightly more flexible than that of a tech pen. Both of them are refillable with Koh-I-Noor Ultradraw waterproof ink. Don't try ordinary drawing ink in your expensive drawing pens. You'll clog them. With proper care, your pens can last years.

Pigment-based markers are cheap, but not refillable. They're less temperamental than fountain or tech pens, but when they're dead, they're dead. Some pigment markers fade a bit when you erase them. You can mitigate this by letting the page dry at least half an hour before erasing, and by using the Factis TK20 Technik eraser, if you can find one.

Fountain pens

Pigment markers

Ultradraw® ink

Tech pens

Some pens you can use for lettering.

There are still a few diehards out there who will call me a wimp for recommending you use these tools instead of a *real* letterer's tool: the Speedball C-6 dip-pen nib. If you do choose to use a dip pen for lettering, use a relatively thin ink like Koh-I-noor waterproof drawing ink. Dip only the tip of your pen into the bottle and make sure to wipe off the excess ink after every dip, unless you want to clean ugly blotches off your page.

It's your call. Choose whichever you're comfortable with, and get it in at least two sizes, one for regular lettering, one for bold. I like to use a .3 mm line for regular and a .5 mm line for bold. In Micron Pigma markers, that's an 02 and an 08. Experiment and see which ones you like. Just be sure that the difference between your regular and bold lettering is clear.

White Paint and Correction Pens

Now that digital correction is an option, these are a lot less important. For small mistakes, I use Winsor & Newton Permanent White gouache. (Don't use the Zinc White. It turns yellow.) Dr. P. H. Martin's Pro White is good, too. For larger mistakes, I'll make a patch or paste in the correction digitally. I've never had much use for Pentel's Presto correction pen, but some people really like it.

Ellipse Templates

I prefer the look of balloons that are drawn freehand, but if you don't have a steady enough hand to do it well, use a template. Look for the kind with little risers on the back. These will keep your ink from getting caught by capillary action and spreading underneath the template. If your templates don't have risers, make them by taping a penny on either side of the ellipse you're going to use.

Drawing the Alphabet

Many artists don't believe they're capable of lettering. They'll claim they have "terrible handwriting," or something like that. Doesn't matter. Lettering isn't writing, it's drawing. You are drawing one letter at a time. Any artist who can handle the human figure can learn to cope with subjects like the letter M, or even R or G.

Lining with Mr. Ames

That circular part of your Ames guide is a wheel. Go ahead and turn it. It's stiff, but it moves. Notice the numbers on the bottom of the circle. You use them to set how tall each row of letters will be. Line up one of them with the vertical line on the bottom part, next to the "A" in Ames. The bigger the number, the taller the row. For now, Pick 4. Then put a small piece of tape on it to make sure the wheel doesn't turn. Take a sheet of 2-ply Bristol paper, line it up squarely with your T square, and tape the paper down securely.

Lay the T square across the paper, near the top, and rest the Ames guide above the T square. Slide it over to the far right side of the paper.

The Ames Lettering Guide has lots of holes, but you need to use only a few of them.

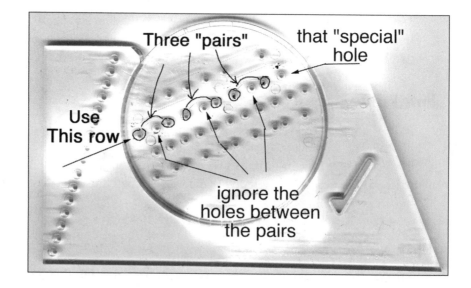

Find the second of four rows of holes on the wheel. It's highlighted in the holes close-up picture. Notice that there are three groups of three, and one by itself. Those are going to be your guideline holes. The other rows? Ignore them. Pretend they aren't there. Put them out of your mind.

Each of those groups of three has two holes joined by a curving line, and one in the middle. Ignore the ones in the middle. See the photo I've labeled for further clarification. We'll call the paired holes that remain, "pairs." Notice that we've left one special hole in the row that isn't part of any group. We'll get back to it later.

Your Ames guide should slide back and forth on top of your T square.

Get a sharp point on a hard lead pencil, (2H to 4H should do the trick.) Put the point in the top hole on the top pair. Now push down lightly and slide the guide across the T square, right to left. Hold the T square firmly, so it doesn't move. If your pencil is sharp enough, you'll find you've made a straight line across the top of the paper.

Now find the next hole in the pair, skipping over the one in the middle. (Ignore it. Pretend it isn't there. Put it out of your mind.) Put your pencil in that hole and slide the guide back to the right. Congrats. You just made a row.

Put your pencil in the top hole of the second of the three, pairs. Slide to the left. Move your pencil down to the other hole in that pair and slide to the right. Go to the third, bottom-most pair. Pencil into the top hole; slide to the left. Pencil into the bottom hole; slide to the right.

Congrats! You've made three rows of evenly spaced pencil lines. ("Evenly" in this case means big row, little row, big row, little row, etc. If they aren't evenly spaced you're probably not holding the T square squarely enough.) They should look like the picture nearby.

Now comes the tricky part. Remember that special hole at the end of the row of holes? Slide your T square so that the "special hole" lines up with the bottom line you drew last time. Check it by putting your pencil in, giving the guide a little slide and seeing if the mark lines up. If not, adjust and try again until it does.

All lined up? Stick your pencil in the top hole of the top pair and slide all the way across. Move your pencil to the next hole in the pair. Slide. And so on. Cover the page with rows, top to bottom.

You can get a bit fancier if you like, but a font of basic block capitals like this is easy on the hand and eyes.

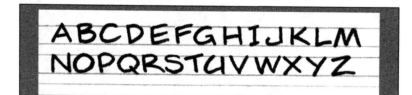

A, B, C, D, E ...

Using a sharp pencil, copy the text of this chapter, imitating the font reproduced in the preceding illustration. Use only capital letters. Fill the entire page.

Some things to watch out for:

- ◆ Keep the letters in each word tight together. The space between words should be about the width of the letter M.

- ◆ Make round letters like O, C, G, and Q reach slightly over their guidelines. Otherwise, they look too small.

- ◆ Be aware of the negative space that makes each letter readable. See the negative space picture for further clarification.

Once you've filled the page, get a pen. (No, not a ballpoint—fountain pen, tech pen, or pigment-ink marker.) Ink your letters: every word. Try to think of the letters as sets of pen strokes, not parts of a word. If you find yourself writing rather than lettering, slow down and draw the letters. Your wrist may hurt when you're done. Mine did the first few times, but it quickly gets a lot easier and more natural.

GOOD NEGATIVE SPACE

BAD NEGATIVE SPACE

GOOD　　BAD　　BAD

It's the negative space around your letters that makes them readable.

Placing Them on the Board

We already discussed balloon placement a bit in Chapter 13. Each panel should be read left to right, and top to bottom, and your readers should never wonder where to go next. Good placement should make that decision for them.

Lay down guidelines for where you want your balloons and captions to go. Give yourself plenty of extra lines above, below, and to the side. You may not need them, but it's easier to do extra than it is to try to line up your T square later on.

Tracing paper. Use it.

You can try out arrangements in pencil on tracing paper. Don't switch to ink until you're happy with the arrangement. Over time you'll get an eye for this. Until then, solve your problems in pencil.

Make sure everything will fit before you letter in ink.

Lightly pencil in each caption and balloon. Don't cover up a major character's head or any other important parts of the art. If your penciler was paying attention, there should be obvious places left for you to do your job. If not, just try to cover up as little important art as possible. You can also get a high-resolution scan of the unlettered panel, shrink it digitally and trace it. Smaller figures equal more room to letter.

Try to group your words symmetrically. If you're a little bit off track you can fix that when you ink the letters. If you're way off, erase the line of text, use the T square to touch up your guidelines, and try again.

Be Emphatic

You may be working from a script that specifies which words are **bold** or *italicized*, or ***both***. If so, do what the writer asks for. If not, or if you're writing the script yourself, keep these points in mind. *Italics* indicate that the speaker wants to *emphasize* something. **Bold** indicates that the speaker is **raising** his or her **voice** a bit.

Use the checkmark-shaped template on the Ames guide to rule italic guidelines. Then just tilt your letters to match the slant.

A consistent italic slant can be tricky to maintain. Use guidelines.

ABCDEFGHIJKLM
NOPQRSTUVWXYZ

FOLLOW ITALIC GUIDELINES.

Balloons and Boxes

Pencil your letters before constructing your balloons. Drawing a bigger balloon to fit the words is great. Using smaller letters to fit the balloon is bad. Don't cram a lot of text into a small balloon. Text reads more easily if it has some air around it.

Simian Letters

In the Cerebus series Dave Sim does some of the most effective experimental lettering ever attempted in graphic novels.

As I said earlier, freehand balloons look better if you can do them well. If you can't, use an ellipse template.

Point the pointers at the speaker's mouth. Don't let them *touch* the mouth though. It looks odd and can ruin the illusion of depth you've so carefully created.

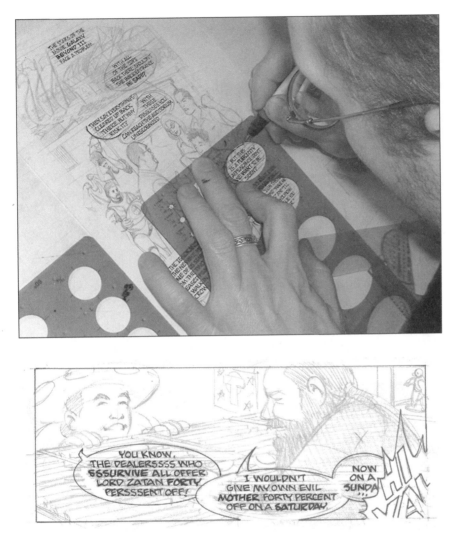

You can use an ellipse straight from the template or "build" a shape from parts of different ellipses.

The "Hi Yah!" from off panel interrupts the dealer's second sentence.

A word balloon can overlap another, creating an effect of one speaker interrupting another, as you can see in the inked lettering panel nearby. If you let a thought balloon overlap a speech balloon, it indicates that the thinker is ignoring the speaker.

Sound Effects and Clever Lettering Tricks

The number and kind of effects available to letterers is endless. Try to hear the sounds or the voices you are conveying. The more clearly you can imagine it, the easier it will be to translate into lines on paper.

Different fonts and balloon shapes make a big difference in the impact a piece of lettering has on a reader. See for yourself in the two pages of lettering examples nearby.

Change the line weight and you change the voice.

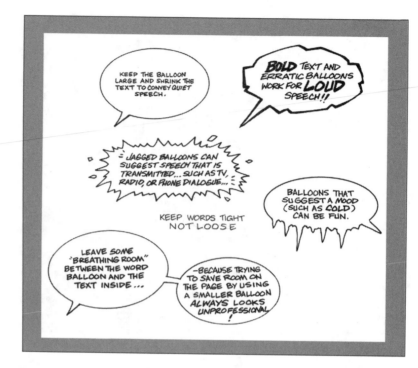

Study a variety of graphic novels to see what can be done with lettering.

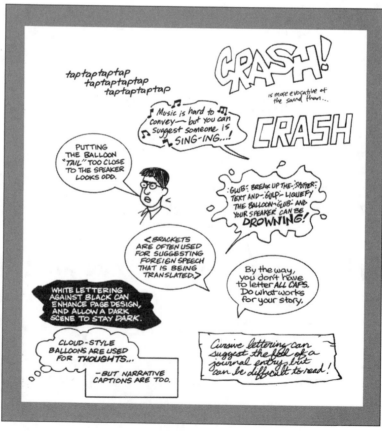

Read What You Can About It

There aren't many books on comic book lettering available. The best tutorial I've seen on the subject is in *How to Draw and Sell Comic Strips* by Alan McKenzie and Steve Parkhouse. Award-winning letterer Todd Klein is working on a how-to book on the subject, to be published in 2004.

The Least You Need to Know

- Use an Ames guide to keep your lettering straight.

- Keep the basic size of your balloon and caption lettering consistent throughout the graphic novel, varying it only for effect.

- Leaving negative space in a word balloon makes it easier to read.

Inking the Art

You're well under way. Panels and panels full of pencil drawings are on the pages in front of you. They tell the story, but they're smudgy and vague in places, and you can see the construction lines here and there. Those sorts of pencil drawings don't reproduce well and will distract from the story you're telling. It's time to break out the ink.

Inking can mean very different things. In the North American comic book industry, it's become common over the past 50 years to split the work of illustrating a comic book between several artists: a penciler, an inker, and a colorist. Many graphic novelists work this way as well, but it's increasingly common for illustrators to reject this assembly-line approach and do the complete job by themselves.

Which Way to Work?

There are advantages and disadvantages to splitting the job between a penciler and an inker. In some cases, you won't have a choice. A publisher may demand that the work be divided. In work-for-hire publishing, an artist is often a hired gun, brought in to do a specific job with little or no voice in how the work might be best served. At small-press publishers there may not be large enough budgets to hire additional artists. For self-publishers, there may not be large enough budgets to buy dented tuna cans or off-brand pasta.

The biggest advantage of working as a team is efficiency. Some artists find it easier to work only in pencil or ink. They may prefer the design work and imagination that penciling requires to the fine motor control and technical problem solving that's required of an artist working in ink (or vice versa). Some inkers have a real knack for handsome brush and pen work, or for lighting forms, but aren't interested in the grunt labor of constructing anatomy, designing gestures, or working out perspective. Milton Caniff, widely regarded as one of the greatest adventure cartoonists of the twentieth century, employed an assistant, Dick Rockwell, to pencil his comic strip *Steve Canyon*. Working as a writer/inker gave him control of the beginning and end of the process; he didn't need to handle the details in the middle.

Ink artists who love rendering pictures but aren't interested in choosing camera angles or laying out a page may prefer embellishing—working from someone else's penciled layouts but adding much of the detail—to inking or doing the complete job.

Paradoxically, the advantage to *not* working with an inker is also that it's more efficient. You're free to employ whatever shorthand you like in the pencils. Are those ovals a bunch of balloons or a crowd of well-wishers? Is that smear of graphite supposed to be a second rocket ship or is it the sky behind the first one? If you're inking yourself, you don't need to work these things out in the pencils. Similarly, you may have certain elements in your drawing that you can draw in ink with only the vaguest guidelines in pencil. If you're penciling for someone else, such ambiguities can be a recipe for disaster. Or comedy.

It's also a lot more financially efficient to do all the art yourself. It's hard to pay the rent illustrating your own graphic novel. But it's a lot harder if that money (and other sources of cash, like the sale of original art) has to be split between two people.

In the end, the choice is up to you. Do what's best for the story you're telling. At times in this chapter, I'm going to write as if I assume that the penciler and inker are two different people. If that isn't the case for your graphic novel, pretend that you've got multiple-personality disorder and let the inker-personality take over.

Your Job, Should You Choose to Accept It ...

Simply put, an inker's job is the same as everyone else's: to tell the story. Unfortunately, that isn't very helpful when you've got a stack of penciled pages in front of you. So, less simply put, an inker's job is to render the pencils so that they'll reproduce well, refining details and adding texture, depth and, in some cases, shading.

Inking is drawing. An inker needs to know how to distinguish between a construction line and an object line. A penciler uses construction lines to make sure a drawing is solid, and to avoid mistakes like having one eye higher on the skull than the other. Construction lines shouldn't be inked. An object line is there to define the form and should be inked. A conga line is for dancing and doesn't belong in your studio.

> **That's Al, Folks**
>
> Al Wiliamson's pen-and-ink drawing has set the standard for classical illustrative art in comics for almost half a century. *Al Williamson Adventures* is a collection of short stories, all of which are worth studying to see how he composes pictures and uses simple lines to render complicated forms and textures.

Ways to Get Better

You can learn ink techniques from other artists. Blow up and trace black-and-white pages by cartoonists whose technique you admire. Choose pages that contain a variety of settings and lighting conditions. Blow up these pages on a photocopier. An enlargement setting of 141 percent is usually a good choice, and will require a copier that can handle 11-inch by 17-inch paper.

On vellum (a high quality tracing paper) practice replicating the original inks. Try to match the construction lines exactly, feeling the form as you go. You don't have to duplicate every line that's part of a shaded area though. Just make sure that your lines follow the form in the same way, and that they build the same value of gray that's in the original.

Vellum is also good for practicing over photographs. Photocopy a photograph several times to increase the contrast, or use a computer graphics program to do the same with a digital photograph. See how high you can get the contrast and still keep everything recognizable. Then lay vellum over the high-contrast picture, and try to render it in brush. Keep the original, low-contrast image handy.

You can even get copies of other artists' pencils to practice over. Many large publishers will send you copies of some pencils if you send in a request, and some artists put scans of their pencils up on their websites, like the ones you'll find in the portfolio section of www.stevelieber.com, my website.

> **Give It a Dirty Look**
>
> Compare gray values by squinting at your pages and holding them at a distance or looking at them in the mirror. Blurring your eyes makes it easier to see an array of lines as a continuous tone. People who see you do this will think you are angry at the page and give you a wide berth.

The best way to get copies of penciled pages is by asking artists at conventions. Any good sized convention should have some artists as guests, and some may be willing to send you photocopies if you send them a big stamped, self-addressed envelope and a couple of bucks for copying costs. The less prestigious the artist, the more likely he or she will be willing to take the time to do this.

Tool Time

A lot of the tools inkers use are described in Chapter 18. Ink artists tend to be superstitious about their tools, and suffer horribly when an item they like stops being available. When you find an art supply you like, buy it in quantity.

Your Brush with Destiny

Brushes are a key part of many artists' toolkits. Unfortunately, they're also among the most expensive and fragile. A good sable brush can cost $20, and may last only a couple of months, depending on how well you care for it.

In 15 years of continuous drawing, I've found only one brush I like for inking: Winsor & Newton's series seven, number two sable brush. ("Sable" refers to the animal whose fur they use to make the brush.) Other artists I know recommend Raphael's watercolor sables, and I've even met people who use brushes with synthetic bristles. Try a few and see what works best for you.

Never, ever let ink dry in your brush. Ink that dries between bristles points them away from each other, ruining the brush's ability to come to a point. Rinse it in water after every few dips in ink. If you're going to be away from the board for more than a couple of minutes, clean it thoroughly with soap and water as shown in the brush care photos. Never leave your brush point-down in your water can—you'll mash the point into a weird shape.

The Winsor & Newton series seven, number two sable brush.

Good brushes are expensive. Treat yours well and they'll last a lot longer.

Twirl the brush in liquid soap, then use your thumbnail to scrape out dried ink, pushing up from the base

Use brushes that have lost their points to fill in areas of black, or to create textures that don't require control of every mark. They are useless for any sort of precise drawing.

Brushes are wonderfully versatile tools. A good brush artist can make a line as fine as a mouse's eyelash, then with just a bit more pressure, throw down bold, juicy strokes. Mastering brushes requires more practice than using other tools, but it's absolutely worth the effort. I found them enormously frustrating for my first two years of art school. Now they're my favorite drawing tool. There's no magic trick to getting good with a brush, but I find it helpful to visualize the line I want as I first let the brush's point touch the paper. Be confident when you lay down a brush line—it's a very sensitive tool, and your hesitations will register when you draw.

Brush Tags

Wrap masking tape around the ferrule (the metal part that holds the bristles) of your beat-up brushes and mark them with different colors. You'll find that different brushes are good for different tasks, and the colors help you keep track of which is which.

Dip Pens

There are dozens of metal pen nibs available, and they're all worth trying. One of the most commonly used is the Hunt 102 crow-quill pen. Its very firm point is easy for beginners to handle. As you use it, it becomes more flexible, so start with the finest lines on the page, then shift to the broader ones. Other popular nibs are the Hunt 108 and the Gillott series. Pen nibs are cheap. Buy a lot and experiment.

Traditional dip pens and a scattering of nibs.

Whatever nib you use, get used to cleaning it a lot. Get into a rhythm: Dip in ink, draw, draw, draw, swish in water, dry on cloth, dip in ink, and so on. Hold the pen with the concave side down and draw it toward you. You can't push a dip pen; it will spatter and ruin your life. If the line you need to draw is at an inconvenient angle, turn the paper.

No pen nib lasts forever. Some artists discard two or three a day. Sometimes nibs fail because they're clogged with dry ink or because the points aren't aligned anymore. You can try to get them working again, but if it continues to give you trouble, throw it out. Your time is worth more than a pen tip.

Rough or fibrous papers can shed little hairs that get caught in your pen tip and change your fine point into a sort of awkward brush. You'll find hot press papers (also known as plate finish) offer the least resistance to your pen line. They're more prone to smearing though, because they don't absorb the ink as quickly.

Markers

The Micron Pigma markers I mentioned in Chapter 18 are great for drawing, too. Markers make a deader (less expressive) line, but they're fast, and many artists have learned to coax a wider variety of lines from them. Some markers bleed more than others, so test them on the margin of your page before starting to ink. Some, such as Sharpies, can't be covered in white paint—they bleed right through it, leaving an ugly gray stain in the page. If you use this kind of marker, make your corrections with a patch, or (if it's a big correction) paste it in digitally. A number of markers are not lightfast, which means that over time, they fade to a fuzzy gray or purple. Keep this in mind if you plan to sell your original pages.

What Brand of Ink?

Drawing with good India ink is wonderful. At its best, it lays down a smooth, consistent line, covers large areas evenly without looking blotchy, doesn't fade much when it's erased, and is waterproof when it dries, so you can make corrections without worrying about the art bleeding.

I can't recommend one brand though, because ink producers keep changing their formulas. It's common to see anguished messages on message boards asking for "a better ink" because a reliable favorite brand has been taken off the market or replaced with something resembling instant coffee dissolved in ammonia.

The pigment in ink can separate, so before you start, screw the lid on firmly and shake the bottle for a couple of seconds. Inks thicken over time as the solvent evaporates. An ink that starts out too thin may get better if you leave the cap off. One that's just right may get too thick. Thin it with a bit of fresh ink.

I've been happy with FW acrylic-based black ink, and Winsor & Newton's Indian ink. Many artists fill ink bottles with the ink Rotring makes for technical pens. By the time this sees print, they may all be off the market. If the best at your local art supply store isn't good enough, post your own anguished message board request.

Changing the Pencils

Suppose you're inking someone else's pencils. When things look good all you have to do is follow the penciler's lead. But what if you see something wrong? Do you faithfully replicate the penciler's mistake, or fix it? This is a real minefield. It isn't always easy to tell where "style" stops and "errors" begin (and this applies to your own work as well as that of the penciler). A "correction" can produce a jarring discontinuity if a character suddenly looks different than it had before. You also have to juggle egos. Is a small improvement in the work worth the huge headache from dealing with your collaborator's hurt feelings? Will making a lot of corrections hurt your chances of being hired in the future? Or is not making the corrections more dangerous?

Talk to the penciler. Some are comfortable with inkers who bring their own abilities as draftsmen to the table. Others simply want someone to dutifully replicate every line they put down. Find out what he or she thinks about changes in general, and the changes you want to make in particular. Don't call every time you notice that the number of chevrons on Atomicus's robot arm is incorrect, but if you plan to crop a figure that had previously burst a border, either ask the penciler or check with your editor (depending on the nature of your arrangement).

If, for whatever reason, you can't get in touch to get approval for a change that you really think needs to be made, you have to decide on your own. For me, the matter is resolved by this principle: Your obligation is to the readers, not the penciler. Change what needs to be changed. But there's another principle to keep in mind before you perform surgery on another artists' work: "First, do no harm." If you aren't absolutely sure that your change will yield better storytelling, don't make the change.

Tangencies

Changes are always welcome when the pencils contain a *tangency*. Don't let these go. Usually you can nudge some part of the drawing a bit, preserving the penciler's intentions without changing anything significant. I did this to my own pencils in the following tangency example. In the pencil drawing, the Monk's right arm is placed so that it could easily belong to Gene! Before inking, I traced the arm so I'd be able to replicate it, then erased and redrew it in a better position.

WHA...?

Tangency

Tangency is a bad arrangement of the elements in a picture that ruins the illusion of depth or creates confusion by making unrelated objects seem to be connected.

Whose arm is that? Moving it a bit makes it clear.

Incomplete Pencils

Your penciler may give you layouts rather than completed pencils. If so, it's up to you to finish the picture. Keep the drawing consistent, matching what you've done before, even if your natural style is quite different. A slightly awkward drawing that belongs in the same world as its predecessors hurts the story less than a terrific drawing that seems out of place.

Ways to Ink

Everyone has a different way to approach the job, and one artist may regularly change the way he or she does things from project to project, or even one page to the next. The procedure I suggest here is just one way out of many:

1. Make good photocopies of the pencils before starting.

2. Lightly rub the entire page with a kneaded eraser to pick up any excess dirt or pencil dust. Don't erase the pencils!

3. Ink the panel borders, if the letterer hasn't already done so.

Adding black gives a panel richness and depth.

4. Ink the outlines of background objects with a light, relatively inflexible pen line. (A Hunt 108 pen is good for this.)

5. Ink the light side of foreground objects with a light pen or brush line. Keep your lines on the light side relatively thin.

6. Lay in areas of shadow with a bold brush line, as you see in the following spotting black illustration. If there are any large areas of black, leave them partially unfilled for now. Too much black ink can buckle or warp your page, making it hard to ink.

7. Add textures and transitional areas of gray. Work from the shadow into the light, keeping things as simple and uncluttered as possible.

8. Correct your mistakes with white paint or patches.

9. Squint at the page, holding it at a distance. Are the planes of depth clearly differentiated? Do your eyes go where they're supposed to go? Are the areas of black, white, and gray in proper balance? Correct as necessary.

10. Erase the page with a plastic eraser. Go back over any parts where the black ink faded to gray.

There are lots of ways to show the transition from light to dark.

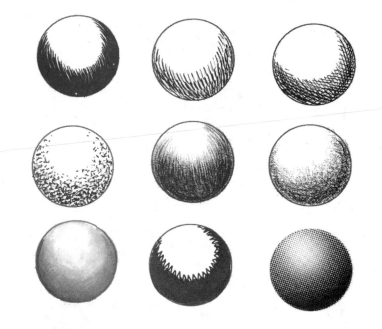

Transitions and Textures

There are several techniques for creating the illusion of light on form. The following rendering technique diagram shows some of the ways to transition from light to dark. Dry brush, hatching, crosshatching, stippling, feathering, gray wash, grease crayon, and digital tones are some of the options. Use the object's texture to describe light and shadow by drawing the texture where the shadow is and leaving the light areas open.

Hair, cloth, and shiny metal—one picture, different techniques.

Some artists prefer to let the outline alone describe the difference between materials. This can be tough for inexperienced artists but if you can do it, the results can be quite handsome.

Inking for Color or Black and White

When you're inking for black and white reproduction, you're creating something pretty close to finished art. You want to make pictures that feel complete and satisfying. When you're inking for color, this is still *sort of* true, but not entirely so.

Some artists, coloring their own work, or trusting their colorists to do a fine job, consider color to be a vital part of their picture making and storytelling. They can leave the job of completing the art to color. Others, less trusting, assume that the color they get will be in some way inadequate. They ink as if the page were going to be black and white, and think of the color as tinting, rather than an integral part of the art. One older artist summed up the difference to me this way: "This guy [a younger artist] draws that way because he knows the color will help him. We drew the way we did so that the color couldn't mess us up too bad."

How you approach drawing for color should depend on who the colorist is. Doing it yourself? Do as you like. Someone else? Look at other books the colorist has worked on and decide if you can trust this person to make your pictures complete.

Books on Drawing with Ink

The most important book you own is your own sketchbook. The work you do there makes you a more knowledgeable and confident artist, improving your pages. But there are some good books about inking, and I recommend picking up one or two of them:

- *The Art of Comic Book Inking* by Randy Martin
- *The DC Comics Guide to Inking Comics* by Klaus Janson
- *Dynamic Light and Shade* by Burne Hogarth
- *Rendering in Pen and Ink* by Arthur L. Guptill

The Least You Need to Know

- Take good care of your brush. Never let ink dry in it.
- Use a thinner outline on the lit side of an object.
- Use texture to show the difference between materials.

Chapter 20

A Bit of *The Big Con:* The Inked Pages

You saw this story in script form in Chapter 9 and penciled in Chapter 17. Here it is again, fully inked and hand lettered. Since our graphic novel *The Big Con* is going to be printed in black and white, this section is done and ready for press.

It's not too late to correct problems if you find any. The inker can fix small things with a little ink and Wite-Out, and the letterer can paste corrections over the existing lettering. If a whole panel needs to be replaced, it can be drawn on a separate piece of paper and then pasted over the original panel. Avoid comparing the inked version of your story to the script. The goal here is not make the final graphic novel match the script exactly, but simply to make the graphic novel good. If any problem isn't apparent from reading the finished pages, then it's not really a problem.

Chapter 21

New-Fangled Letterin'

In This Chapter

- Add text using your computer
- Design beautiful word balloons
- Get your lettering ready

Nat here. I've wrested this chapter away from Steve because he's such a good hand letterer that he doesn't need to rely on the computer. The same cannot be said for me. You can't read my hand lettering without a Little Orphan Nat Decoder Ring.

Digital lettering is not just for people who can't do it by hand. Using digital lettering means that the collectible original art page is left beautifully clean, uncluttered by word balloons. Hand lettering presents some problems when the comic is translated into other languages, since it's hard to resize the word balloons without touching up the art. There is no such problem with a digitally lettered page.

A digital letterer can actually letter a page at the same time that an inker inks it, making schedules easier to keep. In fact, several letterers can be working on the same graphic novel simultaneously, and so long as they're using the same fonts no one will know the difference. The same cannot be said for hand lettering, where each letterer's work looks different. Plus, the digital letterer can easily switch styles simply by switching fonts, helping the hero's words to look heroic while the snarling villain's words look snarlingly villainous.

Lettere Requirements

The stuff you need to do digital lettering is not cheap. Certainly, the hand lettering materials are much cheaper. However, most of what the digital letterer needs are things that many people have anyway:

◆ **A computer.** A faster and newer computer is always better, but most modern computers are powerful enough for the job. The graphic world tends to prefer Macintoshes to Windows-based machines, but either can get the job done.

◆ **A scanner.** The standard home scanner is good enough to get you started, although if you're doing a lot of digital comic book work you'll want a larger, tabloid-sized scanner that can scan full-sized pages of original art. Most of those cost more than $1,000. If you want a cheap one, go to www.mustek.com where some are under $200. The $200 scanner is not as good as the $2,000 scanners are, but that $1,800 can buy a lot of comfort.

◆ **Graphics software.** Proper professional letterers use Adobe Illustrator, because it has the tools to make delicate lettering adjustments. Unlike some other programs, Illustrator can store the text as outlines rather than dot patterns. This means that the text in your finished comic will be as sharp as possible. However, you can do very usable basic lettering with Photoshop, Paint Shop Pro, or other art programs.

◆ **Font files.** Computer files of *fonts* (lettering styles). As you'll shortly see, there are some fine points involved in choosing a font.

Hire Higher Quality

Computer lettering is a good talent to have, but if your time is of value, it may be worthwhile to hire an experienced, talented computer lettering service.

Don't spend the big bucks on the expensive stuff at first. Try doing it cheaply before deciding what parts you really want to spend the money on to upgrade. In fact, try doing it on someone else's computer to be ultimately cheap.

Founts of Fonts

Your computer has a bunch of *fonts* installed, most of which would make lousy graphic novel dialog fonts. Even the one called Comics Sans that comes with most computers makes a lousy graphic novel dialog font.

Most fonts are designed to look good on a page full of text. However, a graphic novel puts the text in the midst of a hand-drawn page. The fonts that work best are mostly those that look hand drawn. Even then, you want a font that matches the style of your graphic novel. There are fonts that look very serious, and others that look humorous and fun. There are even fonts that look like alien gibberish, if you have aliens in your stories or simply have dialog that's too lousy to inflict on the reader.

There are some very large commercial font companies out there, but your best sources for graphic novel fonts are folks who specialize in comics fonts. Go to www.blambot.com to find some free fonts and some not-free-but-fairly-cheap fonts. Head over to www.comicbookfonts.com to find fonts that are more expensive, but these are the ones that are made by and used by Comicraft, the most successful digital comics lettering company. You'll even find some good tips on computer lettering. Yes, they make it easy for you not to need their services. They're talented letterers, not financial geniuses.

Font

Most of us use **font** to refer to a specific typeface, such as Times Roman or Courier, but type professionals refer to typeface as a *font family*. To them, *font* means a specific typeface at a specific size, and the bold or italic version of that font is considered a different font.

In addition to dialog fonts, you'll want fonts for titles and sound effects. The fonts that come with your computer are okay for that, but again you should look at the special comics fonts.

You can even design your own fonts to meet your special needs. Many artists have a font designed around their own hand-lettering style, so the dialog really matches their own art style. You can pay someone bucks to digitize the font for you, or you can pay the folks who make Fontographer software big bucks for their program, then spend a lot of time learning the surprisingly subtle science of font design. Suddenly, doing actual hand lettering sounds like a good idea again, eh?

Pushing the Page In

I can't teach you the details of using your scanner, because every scanner is different and comes with its own software. You could go out and buy my book *The Complete Idiot's Guide to Basic Scanning for the Scanner You Own and 234 You Don't*, but you're probably better off using your scanner's manual.

You're going to need to scan your line art and then reduce it to the size you're going to print it. You want to end up with an image that's at least 600 *dots per inch* (a measurement of how precisely the image is reproduced) at the printed size. If you're drawing at actual printed size, set your scanner resolution to 600 dots per inch. If you draw at 50 percent larger than printed size, scan at 400 dots per inch. If you draw at double size, use the 300 dots per inch setting. If you draw at 600 times print size, set your mile-wide scanner to one dot per inch.

No Calculator Needed

Some scanning software lets you set the size and resolution that you want to end up with. The software then will automatically figure out what resolution it needs to scan the selected area at and resize the results as needed.

Scan the image in *grayscale mode*, which captures each dot of the image as one of 256 shades of gray, rather than in line art mode, which sees each dot as either black or white. Then use your graphics program to convert the art into line art (which some graphics programs call *bitmap*). When you do this, your graphics program will let you select how dark a dot has to be before it will be converted to black rather than white. Your lines will appear thin if you choose a high level, thick if you choose a low level. Experiment with it.

If you're making do with a scanner that's smaller than your art, you have two choices. You can use a good, clean photocopier with a reduction feature to make a copy of your art small enough to scan. You can also scan the art in portions, then use your graphics program to stitch it back together. Trying to line up two separately scanned sections exactly is tough work. Of course, if you're using panels laid out in clear rows with empty gutters between them, use those gutters as the edges of the scanning sections. You don't have to line up the blank space of the gutters nearly as precisely as you would have to align the lines in the middle of a drawing. And that's the end of my gutter talk.

Resize your art to the size you'll use for printing. If your graphics program has a re-sample option as part of its image resizing command, turn it off, because that would cause your image to become somewhat fuzzier. Save the image as a *TIFF* (*Tagged Image File Format*) file. Don't be tempted to save disk space by using the *JPEG* (*Joint Photographic Experts Group*) file format. The JPEG format degrades the image, and the printing company's equipment won't be able to handle it.

Putting the Text in Context

Bring the image file into the graphics program you'll be using for lettering. Use your graphic program's lock option to lock the image layer so you don't accidentally drag it later. Create a new layer for the type and balloons. Some programs will require you to create separate layers for each balloon, caption, or other piece of type. So even if your plot isn't deeply layered, your files will be.

Drag a text box into place in the area where you want the text to appear. Select the font and size that you're going to use, set the text alignment to center for thoughts and dialog, left for captions.

If you have the script in a word processor, you can copy the text right from the word processor and paste it into your graphics program. Otherwise, type it in, making sure that you don't make any spelling errors in your typing.

Then you can adjust the width of the text box. Changing the width changes how the text flows and how many lines the text takes up. Generally, you want to avoid lines in the middle that are much shorter than lines above and below them. You also want to keep an eye on what it is you're covering up. Don't be afraid to cover a part of someone's head, but don't cover up someone's face unless you drew it so badly that you want to hide it.

A Few Words on Little Letters

What is the right size for your lettering? You don't want it too small to read, or so big that it covers up most of your art. Most lettering is done with the size set to 6 or 7 *points*, but it really should fit the style of the art.

For dramatic work you can go as small as 5 points. This works particularly well if your art is highly detailed. Put that small a font on the more open art and it looks like you're trying to sneak by with the contractual small print.

Point

Font sizes are measured in **points**, and a point is approximately one seventy-secondth of an inch. The measurement of the font is based on the height of its capital letters.

Lighthearted work with an open, undetailed art style can support 8-point type. Open art work aimed at kids paired with very small amounts of dialog might even support 10-point type, but that's as big as you want to go. You need to leave some space for the pictures.

Do you have an overstuffed balloon? Don't reduce the font to a smaller point size. Save the smaller sizes to indicate whispering and larger sizes for shouting. If you really need to squeeze a few more letters into a word balloon, good graphic programs let you adjust the width of the lettering without adjusting the height. Set the width to 95 percent of the standard width to get a few more characters in. You can also experiment with adjusting the tracking, the spacing between the characters. This way, you're just giving your text a gentle squeeze, instead of an all-out squish.

If you find yourself squeezing text on the first couple of pages, you probably picked too big a font size. It's better to redo these pages now than to finish lettering half the graphic novel before you decide you picked the wrong size. You'll be tempted to just do the second half of the book in the smaller size, making it look like all your characters have laryngitis and have to whisper.

Capital Ideas

Traditionally, graphic novel dialog has been in all capital letters. The bold strokes of capital letters were easier for the hand letterers to write and some folks believe they make the text easier to read than graphic novels that use upper and lower case letterings. Other folks think the first folks are full of balloon juice.

Because of this tradition, many dialog fonts don't have lowercase letters. Type a lowercase s, for example, and you get an S. Type an uppercase S and you get an S, but one that looks slightly different. That way, typing in using a mix of cases will get you varying S's, making it look less mechanical and more like hand lettering.

The one place where you really have to watch your capitalization is with the letter I. If you use one of these all-capital dialog fonts, typing a lowercase i will get you a capital I that's just a straight vertical line, without the crossbars at top and bottom. Typing a capital I gives you a capital I with the crossbars in place. Traditionally, that cross-barred I is used only for the word I, as in "How many millions of dollars will I make off my graphic novel?" So even if your sentence starts with the word Illinois, you should type it with a lowercase i.

Blowing Up Balloons

Once you've placed all the text in a given panel, it's time to start drawing the balloons and caption boxes. Caption boxes are easy, since you just have to draw a white rectangle that surrounds the text.

For balloons, however, you're going to have to select a basic style of balloon to use in your graphic novel. As you can see in the balloon picture, there are three styles of computer-generated balloons that are commonly used.

Pick a balloon, any balloon.

The elliptical balloon has gained a lot of popularity, because it's easy to draw. However, because the top, bottom, and sides are nowhere near flat, you can't get text close to them, which means that the balloon is covering up art just to fill empty space. The rounded rectangular balloon is also easy to draw and fits text nicely, but its perfectly flat sides give it a mechanical look that clashes with some art styles. At this point, my personal favorite is a slightly more complicated style that I call the inflated ellipse, which looks more like the old hand-drawn balloons. Shouldn't all balloons be inflated?

In your graphics program set your fill color to white and your outline color to black. If you're using Adobe Illustrator, set your *stroke weight*, the thickness of the outline, to 1 point. Photoshop and some other graphic tools let you choose between drawing shapes so that they're stored as a grid work of pixels or as a vector shape, with the program storing a mathematical definition of the outline. Choose the vector shape option.

To draw an elliptical balloon, use your program's ellipse tool, dragging into place a balloon that covers the balloon text with just a little to spare around the edges. You don't want the balloon's outline to actually touch the text at any point. Just think of there being a protective layer of air all around your words. Dragging this shape takes a bit of practice, since you can drag an ellipse into place that covers the top, bottom, and furthest left and right text but still leaves some text sticking out along the edges.

Drawing a rounded rectangle is done in the same way, except you use the rounded rectangle tool instead of the ellipse tool. Start with the pointer just a bit higher than the highest part of the text and just to the left of the left-most part. Drag down and to the right, until the pointer is below the lowest of the text and to the right of the rightmost part of the text. Violà, you have your rectangle with those dangerous pointy corners removed.

The inflated ellipse takes a bit more time. Get the ellipse tool and drag it the same way that I described for the rounded rectangle. Don't worry if parts of some letters stick out along the curves between the top or bottom and the left or right of the ellipse.

Now, the shape of the ellipse is defined in your graphics program based on four points, one each at the very top, bottom, left, and right of the ellipse. Use the direct selection tool (usually represented by a white arrow) to select the point at the top, and two *handles* appear. These handles are lines with dots on the end of them. Point to one of these dots and drag it sideways away from the top of the ellipse, as you see in the following reshaping illustration. This pulls the curves of the ellipse out away from the center, making the sides flatter. Do this for both handles on each of the four points to swell the ellipse into one swell ellipse!

Press shift as you drag a curve handle to drag straight across.

Efficient folks make a few inflated ellipses and store them for easy reuse, either in a document that they can easily copy them from or as Adobe Illustrator symbols. Then they take all the time this saves them and squander it watching TV or curing diseases.

If you're using Illustrator, you now have a white balloon with a black outline. If you're using Photoshop, add the layer effect called *stroke*, setting the color to black and try a size of 6 pixels. You can experiment with the size later to find a size that works for you. If you're using one of the other mumbelty-thousand graphics programs out there, do whatever it takes to add an outline to the shape you've drawn.

Wagging the Tail

Next, add the *tail*, the part of the word balloon that points toward the mouth of the speaking character. For a dialog balloon, select your graphics program's pen tool. If you're using Photoshop, select the "Add to path layer" option so that the tail is on the same layer as the main balloon shape.

To make a straight dialog balloon tail, click the pen tool once inside the balloon, once outside the balloon, and another time inside the balloon, close to the first one. This makes a triangle.

To make a curved tail, point inside the balloon, hold down the mouse button, and drag outside the balloon. Click once outside the balloon to make the end of the tail. Then point back inside the balloon and drag inward into the balloon.

If you're using Illustrator, you now need to combine the tail and the balloon shape into a single item. Use the selection tool to select both the balloon shape and the tail. Open the pathfinder palette and click the "Add to shape area" button followed by the expand button.

Where Balloons Come From

Dialog balloon tails should point toward the mouth of the speaker, but the end of the tail shouldn't actually be in the character's mouth. The character isn't actually inflating a balloon.

The same technique that you use for joining the balloon to the tail also works to join two balloons. Breaking a long speech into multiple balloons can make it fit better in the panel. A new balloon can also serve as the start of a new paragraph, if you have a character who actually speaks in paragraphs.

Thought balloon tails are easier. Just draw a series of two, three, or four small ellipses, starting near the thought balloon and getting smaller as they head toward the brain of the thinking character. The first ellipse can actually overlap the edge of the thought balloon.

Once you have the word balloon drawn, go to the layer palette. On the list of layers, find the balloon's entry and drag it down so it's below the balloon's text entry. Now the balloon is under the text framing it, rather than merely hiding it!

Flattening a Balloon

Sometimes you want your balloon squished up flat against one of the edges of your panel. To make a balloon like this, place your text where you want it, then draw your balloon, letting it spill out past the panel.

If you're using Illustrator, draw a rectangle that exactly covers the panel. Select both the rectangle and the balloon. Open to the pathfinder palette. Click the "Intersect shape areas" button then the "expand" button. You'll have a new shape that includes only the area that was inside both the balloon and the rectangle—a balloon with a flattop cut.

For the same effect in Photoshop, select the layer with the balloon. Get the rectangle tool. Select the "intersect shape areas" option on the option bar. Use the tool to draw a rectangle that precisely covers the panel.

Bursting Out and Other Tricks

To draw a burst balloon for a shouting character, just use the pen tool. Go around the text, alternating between clicking points close to the text and clicking points farther away, to make a series of spikes. Put an extra long spike pointing toward the mouth of a shouting character— and hey, wouldn't you be shouting too if a big spiky thing just came out of your mouth?

That's not the only special effect you can do with the balloon. Some folks use transparency settings to make the balloon partially transparent. The goal of this is to better show the art, but it can also make the text harder to read and even change the impact of the dialog.

The better you know your graphics program, the more things you can find to do. Use stroke effects to create double-outlined word balloons for telepathy. Use roughening effects to create irregular balloons suggesting rough voices. Wobble the text of your drunken characters.

Sound effects, headlines, and signs are easy to add using the graphics program's text tools. With a bit of graphic program knowledge, you can blur the *whoooosh* of a flying jet, creating fading echoes of a *boom*, or skew the words *Peppermint Beer On Sale Now* so they look right on the angled billboard your artist has drawn.

They Lettered in Lettering

The book *Comic Book Lettering the Comicraft Way* shows a couple of comics stories and has Richard Starkings and John Roshell of the top digital lettering studio, Comicraft, explain how the lettering was done.

The Least You Need to Know

◆ Adobe Illustrator is the best program for lettering, but you can use other programs, including Photoshop.

◆ Put your text and balloons on different layers from your original image.

◆ Create your balloons and text in vector or shape mode, not pixel mode.

◆ Use a font and a size that match the style of your art.

◆ Combine the balloon body and the balloon tail into a single item.

Chapter 22

Colors Besides Black and White

In This Chapter

- ◆ Pick a pretty palette
- ◆ Choose your coloring tool
- ◆ Add color to your pages

A few years ago, graphic novel colorists were limited to just 64 solid colors. With the advent of computer coloring and affordable art software, you now have access to 10.3 million colors—that's the *big* box of crayons.

Wielding all those crayons correctly takes a special talent. That's why we (Steve and Nat) got together and decided to get a real specialist to write this chapter. Tom Luth came to mind immediately. He's a veteran colorist, having worked on Marvel Comics *Groo the Wanderer* comics and graphic novels. He has also worked for Image, on *Groo the Wanderer*, and for Dark Horse, again on *Groo the Wanderer*. It seems that wherever Groo wanders, so does Tom. Of course, he's worked on plenty of other projects as well. So here's Tom—treat him kindly.

Four Colors? Not Millions?

Almost all color graphic novels are printed using a technique called four-color printing. Each page is run through four printing presses, each of which adds one color to the page. The millions of different colors are achieved by overlapping various amounts of these four colors so that they mix in different ways.

This method of mixing colors is referred to as CMYK, with each of those letters standing for one of the four colors. C stands for Cyan, a kind of blue. M stands for Magenta, a kind of red. Y stands for Yellow, which is a kind of, well, yellow. And K? K stands for blacK. I kid you not.

You can't get every single possible color by using CMYK printing. Some people thinking about color get out those nifty Pantone color books that show a huge array of possible colors of ink, but those are specially mixed inks. Pantone shows you these beautifully bright oranges and vibrant violets that are outside of the CMYK *color space*, the range of colors that CMYK printing can give you. What kind of colors can CMYK give you? If you look through enough color graphic novels, you should get a good idea.

Don't Paint Yourself into a Corner

Folks who paint often approach coloring for graphic novels in the same way they would go about painting a picture, and that's all wrong. First off, your graphic novel art consists mainly of black lines. You won't be covering up the lines, but filling in between them and enhancing their effect. Details that would be delicate and beautiful in a painting will be overwhelmed by the hard black lines. If you add a lot of details, textures, or fancy shading, your colors will overwhelm the line art. In fact, the more detailed the line art is, the simpler your colors should be. Really detailed art should have just big flat area of colors. That's why colorists love detailed artists. Also, when you color, you're not just painting an image. The colors you place help to tell a story. Before you put a single color in, read the script. Your art should serve the intended tone of the work. Make decisions that support the story, above other artistic concerns. Artists sometimes make the mistake of getting caught up in cool details that detract from the main focus. Save the story by using color to downplay unimportant details and direct the reader to the important stuff.

Causing Contrast

Imagine a scene with Maurice and Minerva at the Café Flambé. The first shot may be a large panel showing a number of tables on a patio overlooking the ocean. We may not even see our couple, or, if we do, they are such a tiny silhouette we can't even see that Maurice is wearing a scuba suit. As the scene moves forward, you have to direct the reader's attention to the couple, because that's where the story is. How do you make our couple stand out in the crowd of diners and scuba divers? Contrast, making our couple so sharply different from the area around them that they stand out. There are four main types of contrast, as follows:

♦ **Contrast in value** deals with how dark or light the areas are. To work with value, think of your colored picture as a black-and-white photo. For our Maurice and Minerva example, make most of the areas of the patio and the things in front of and beyond the patio very gray with no very bright or very dark colors. Make Maurice and Minverva in strong black and white using very bright and very dark colors. Readers will focus right in on them.

♦ **Contrast in hue** is the relationship between warm colors such as red and cool colors such as blue. Usually (but not always) warm colors come forward and call attention to themselves while cool colors recede. Make Maurice and Minvera turquoise, and they will stand out against a picture made of cooler blues. Likewise a purplish red can appear cool, in contrast to warm reds, yellows and oranges. Be careful, because warming up a cool color or cooling down a warm color can leave you with a dulled color, and dulled color is, well, dull.

♦ **Contrast in saturation** is based on how bright or dull a color is. Pure, bright colors appear closer and grab attention, while duller colors recede into the distance. If Minerva is a very red red she will stand out against characters who are a not so red red, a not very blue blue, and so on. How do you make a not very red red? If you remember your color wheel from your school days, each color has a color on the opposite side of the wheel called its *complement*. Red's complement is green, so if you mix a little green in with your red, you get a dull red. Mix in more green than red, and you get a dull green. Orange and blue are complements, as are yellow and purple.

♦ **Contrast in detail** uses the eye's tendency to notice busy, detailed areas before simpler areas. If everyone else looks like they're wearing flat colored jackets, then all the shiny reflective areas of Maurice's scuba suit will draw the eye right to him.

You can can stick to using just one of these contrast techniques in a scene, or you can use several techniques at once to really catch the reader's eye.

Blocking Out Without Blacking Out

It used to be that to use the contrast in detail technique in a crowd scene, you'd color each nonimportant person a single solid color, or even just lay that color over the whole group. That's easy and still works, but it's not very subtle, and sometimes it looks like someone just dropped a big bucket of blue paint on the crowd.

Now with good computer coloring tools, you might still color them all blue, but with a variety of values and saturations. Make the waiter's shirt a little more blue, his face a little less blue, and he looks more human, while the reader's eye is still pulled first to Maurice and Minerva in their full color range. You can even fully color the unimportant items and then overlay them with a tint of, say, blue. Done carefully, it won't look like you're saying that these people are actually blue, but as a result of lighting and shade, they look bluish. Clusters of objects can be tinted warmer colors in sunlight or gaslight, and cooler in shadows. Use duller colors on distant objects.

Going Loco with Local Color

Local color is the actual color of an object. Apples are red, the sky is blue, the Screaming Purple Menace is purple. Mess with these colors but always remember that the color is there. If you're blocking things out as a solid color, this isn't an issue, but if you're blocking out by tinting, think about it. A red apple under a blue tint looks dark gray, because red and blue are close to being complementary colors. If gray won't work in your color scheme, cheat by removing a little yellow from the color mix of your apple. This makes the apple magenta, so the blue tint makes a color ranging from a deep burgundy to a red-violet. If you do this, reduce the yellow in all the tinted areas in the panel for consistency.

Showing Light and Shade

Where an object is in average light, use its local color. Use warm colors such as yellow and orange to highlight where light hits the object, and cooler colors like blue and purple for the shade. Moonlight is special, and blue highlights will show its odd glow.

Keep in mind the value of the colors. In highlight areas, make colors roughly the local color, in sharp contrast to the shadow area. In the following picture of the ball, the local color is the color right around the light spot. As you see on the lower right area of the ball, within the shadow you can lighten the color to show some reflected light. Don't try to use the full range of light, and don't go too much in detail. Indoor lighting is usually dull and even, without that much contrast between the light and the dark. You can make light harsher for dramatic, film noir-like effect.

Always remember where your light source is in the scene, and cast highlights and shadows accordingly.

A not very shiny ball.

Pick Your Crayons Carefully

The computer lets you use 10.3 million colors, but don't use them all. That makes your pages too busy, too messy. Pick a limited set of colors for your graphic novel. What's a good set of colors to use? That depends on what the graphic novel is like. *Goofy Guy and His Grumpy Pup* probably needs very light colors to match its humorous tone. Superhero material likes bright, bold colors, although a bit darker than humor material, with stark light and shadows. Drama and horror stories like *desaturated* (dim) color schemes.

Within your graphic novel, each setting can have its own color scheme. The scenes in The J. B. Sudsandsteaks Bar And Grill may need an orange, gas-lit look, while the offices of J. B. Sudsandsteaks III, Attorney-At-Law, will have a dull, blue-gray fluorescent lamp quality. The city streets may have a slightly desaturated look, contrasted with bright neon, and so on.

Try a palette based on the range between two complementary colors. Don't start with colors that are strong like a bright ultramarine blue and cadmium orange, or your palette will be suited only for a 1960s psychedelic poster. Start with duller versions like Prussian blue and burnt orange, and work toward a neutral from there. Now you have a range that allows for each color and all tints of that color, as well as every hue working toward a neutral by

Learn Color Theory

Do terms such as "split-complementary" and "triadic" confuse to you? Get a book on color theory. It will help you in picking color themes for your work.

Steve Sez: Show, Don't Tell

When talking about color, even experienced professionals can have trouble picturing what's being described. Line artists who want a specific palette or type of lighting should use visual aids. Find a photograph or illustration that has the effect you want, or capture a frame from a DVD.

mixing the two complementaries, and all the lighter tints of all these colors. You are not limited to just these colors, but add other colors slowly and carefully.

Colorful Computer

Check to make sure you have the computer you'll need for coloring. Although the Macintosh earned its reputation as an artist-friendly computer over the years, all the major software is now available for both Mac and Windows computers, so the Mac advantage is small. Adobe's Photoshop, the program used to color most graphic novels, is equally comfortable on both systems. Go with your personal preference. Get a lot of hard drive space, and a lot of RAM, whichever way you go.

I'm about to describe how to color using Photoshop, but you can use similar programs, although the commands will be slightly different. Photoshop is the king of the bitmap programs, which means it treats the page as a bunch of miniscule dots and keeps track of what color is in each dot. Other bitmap programs like Canvas, Painter, and the free program GIMP have their fans. Few colorists use Adobe Illustrator and similar vector art programs, where the colors are stored as shaped areas rather than as a series of dots. Much of the most groundbreaking work in computer coloring was done using the Codd/Barrett vector art system, but that was expensive and is now obsolete. But even bitmap programs like Photo-shop and Canvas now have some useful vector tools.

Vector Victory

Look at *Spawn Book 1* by Todd McFarlane for examples of Steve Oliff using the Codd/Barrett vector art system to great effect.

Putting the Page in Place

First, get the art into the computer. No, you can't fold it up and stick it in the CD drive. Nat covered the scanning stuff back in Chapter 21, so just flip back a few pages and you'll find it.

Resize the scanned art to the size and resolution the book will be printed at. To do this, set the rulers to the crop marks or borders on the page. From the Image menu choose the Image Size command. Uncheck the Resample Image checkbox. Type the exact measurements you want into the size fields. Put a check in the Resample Image checkbox and type the resolution you want to work at—say, 400—into the Resolution field and click OK.

The size is now right, but the image is gray, and you need pure black and white. You could do this quickly just by using the Threshold command, but there's a better way to do it. Zoom in 200 percent on a particularly detailed area. From the Image menu choose Adjustments, then Levels to get the dialog box you see pictured below. Put a check in the Preview checkbox. Alternate dragging the black point and white point sliders toward the center. You want to bring them together to meet eventually. As you slide them, watch what happens to the image. Your dark sections will get darker and your light sections will get lighter, and this affects the thickness of the lines. Try to bring those two sliders together at a point where the black lines aren't so thin that they break up, but the white space between them doesn't get clogged up.

The Right Size

Many American graphic novels are 6.625 inches by 10.20 inches, with the active portion of the art placed in a 6-inch by 9-inch area. Your own book may be different.

Level away your grays.

Some people use very high resolution line art, like 1200 dpi, and a lower resolution color layer to be composited later in a page layout program like Quark or Pagemaker. To work this way, convert the line art to bitmap and save it as a TIFF file. Then change your line art to 300 dpi for reference for coloring. Usually, though, you'll just keep the line art and colors together in the file, and work at a resolution of 400 to 460 dpi.

Copy this line art and paste it into a new channel, naming the channel "Line Art." This way, you can see the color to make sure you have painted under the line art adequately. If you're not comfortable working with channels, you can do it as a separate layer instead. Fill the original channel or layer with white. Eventually, the line art will become the black channel, but you want it "out of the way" while you paint, yet visible. Keep the line art channel unselected, but click on the "eye" icon on the channel or layer list to keep it visible.

Pretty Painting

Mark Waid and Alex Ross's *Kingdom Come* uses fully painted art rather than colored line art. If you paint your graphic novel, the publisher may peel your art off the canvas panel to wrap around the drum of a drum scanner. Protect your art by providing the publisher an expensive color transparency or use a flatbed scanner to make digital files.

Head over to the Image menu again and choose Mode, CMYK Color. Now, if you've been using Photoshop a lot, you're going to be tempted to choose RGB Color instead and work in the RGB—that's red-green-blue—color-mixing scheme that computer monitors use, because Photoshop has some neat tools and image-altering filters that work only in that mode. Avoid that temptation. You'll have to convert to CMYK in the end, and if you've been working in RGB you'll find that some of your colors just don't translate.

If you have something that you want to use an RGB filter on, copy it out to a separate document, run the filter on it, convert it to CMYK, then copy it back into the main document. Don't just switch your main document between RGB and CMYK mode, or you'll wreak havoc with the colors.

Flatting: Bad for Tires, Good for Colors

Flatting is the technique of filling shapes with general "flat" colors, before any shading or modeling is applied. These flat color shapes are the starting point for the rendering, and they provide a way to let you quickly select shapes with the magic wand tool. The flats don't have to use the real color you will finally color each area. Often flats are done as just five or six shades of gray, and a copy is kept in a separate "flats" channel, in case later selections need to be made.

If every shape in the drawing had just a simple closed and complete outline, selecting the areas for flats would be easy. Alas, it's not so. Oh, you will have some areas like that, which are easy to take care of. Use the magic wand tool to select the area on the line art channel or layer. Go to the Select menu and choose Modify, Expand. Enter 2 pixels as the amount to expand, and then use the paint bucket tool to fill the area.

Do you have shapes that are almost closed, except for tiny breaks? Go to the color channel and paint a little dot of the fill color to close up the break. Select the line art and color channels together. Click the magic wand to select the area, deselect the line art channel, and expand the selection and fill as before.

Most of the time, however, you're dealing with lines that are full of holes or crosshatched areas with lots of little cubbyholes. Use the lasso tool to select the area, or use the pencil tool to outline the area, then fill in the area. If you're using the lasso tool, be sure to turn off antialiasing and feathering, because those options create partially selected areas around the edges that may look nice but which won't fill with a solid color, making it hard to reselect. After you have everything selected, expand and fill.

Use the pencil tool to paint right on the color channel or layer. Make sure it is the pencil and not the brush. The brush may look solid, but it actually has partly shaded edges that will cause you problems later.

Start with large shapes, fill with a flat color, and then subdivide these shapes. It's easier to cut larger shapes into smaller sections than it is to paint each segment individually.

After you've flatted the page, click the magic wand on a flat to select it. Then you can fill the shape with the color you want.

Surrendering to Rendering

Next you *render*, meaning you add shaped highlights to give objects a sense of volume. Don't go overboard. Start in the background, adding simple *gradients* (color fades) and other effects as needed. In the foreground, add more detail.

Getting Cute with Cuts

Cuts is a technique in which you fill a shape with a dark shade, and then make selections with the lasso tool to create concentrically smaller shapes that you fill with gradients to create shading and sharp highlights. This technique is overused, particularly on people, because it makes everything look shiny, as you can see comparing the two balls in the following picture.

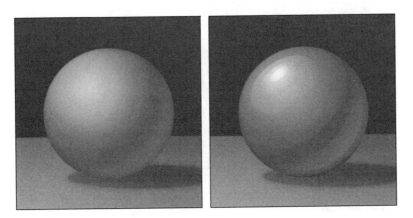

A not very shiny ball and a shiny ball.

To make cuts stand out, use substantial contrast between each new cut. To make cuts subtler, use more selections, and choose the antialias option on the lasso (it's okay to use, now that the flats are done), and build up gradually. You may want to add sharper contrast for the very last speck of highlight, depending on the desired appearance. In both cases, the technique seems to work best going from dark to light.

Diverse Examples

On the graphic novel *Fanboy* I colored several generations of comics artists, using different styles that match each artist's former work.

Beyond cuts, you can use the program's tools to add all sorts of fills, gradients, highlights, and textures. Spend a lot of time experimenting, and a lot of time looking at the work of other colorists to see what they did and what effect it has. Do you want to color with a soft watercolor look? A very precise linear look? A more abstract coloring scheme where the colors don't begin and end at the lines of the line art? It's all possible.

Attempt Advanced Tricks Carefully

As you master Photoshop, you'll find a lot of powerful tools. Once you know how to use filters, you'll be real tempted to do so, to make your work seem fancy. But as you can see in the texture picture, *fancy* is also *distracting*. Don't do it. You can use textures subtly by making them mostly transparent.

Some colorists use photos as surfaces in comics, like using a photo of a real brick wall to represent a brick wall in the comic. This can be done well, but it's risky. Readers' brains adapt to the drawn view of reality, and suddenly having a photo in there disturbs that sense of a drawn universe. Also, matching the lighting, perspective, and atmosphere of the art takes more skill and more time than you might suspect.

A fancy texture made with KPT Texture Explorer filter software.

Another no-no is using lens flares. *Lens flares* are the result of light refracting in a camera lens, and they aren't appropriate in most situations. Don't use the emboss filter to create depth, because it creates a style of illusion of depth that doesn't match the style of depth in the artwork. Learn and experiment all you want, but don't try a new tool on the final work just for the sake of using the tool.

And with that parting bit of advice, Tom dances off into the beautifully-hued sunset, forcing Nat and Steve to start writing their own book once again …

The Least You Need to Know

◆ Color graphic novels are printed using the four-color CMYK print system.

◆ Most graphic novels are colored using Photoshop.

◆ Coloring needs to serve the story and keep the reader focused on what's important.

◆ Choose a limited palette to match the style of the story.

◆ Don't get carried away with fancy rendering techniques.

Part 5

Bring Out Your Book

Your story is done. Now it's time to share it with the world. But how? Find a publisher? Publish the book yourself? Put it on the web? Carve it into cornfields so that it can be read from space? The possibilities are enormous.

This part of the book includes information on finding publishers and presenting your graphic novel to them. You will also see how to publish your graphic novel yourself and make it available to comic shops. With tips on how to drum up readers and build a following, you'll be ready for the big time. The only question is, is the big time ready for you?

23

Pretty Please Publish Me!

In This Chapter

- ◆ Prepare your pitch
- ◆ Pick potential publishers
- ◆ Protect your property properly

You've got your concept, your creative team, and all the knowledge you need to make your graphic novel. That's wonderful, if all you want is one copy of a graphic novel. If you want a lot of copies of your graphic novel and to get them into the hands of readers and even maybe make some evil, evil money off your endeavor, you'll need to work that out. The most obvious route to this goal is to find a publisher to bring your graphic novel to market.

Pitching in the Strike Zone

I've tried to get a lot of graphic novels published. It would have been nice if I could have phoned up a publisher and said "You don't know me, but my name is Nat Gertler, and I'd like you to publish my graphic novel. Could you please send me a big pile of money?" Alas, good things do not come that easy. You need to convince the publisher that your graphic novel will be wonderful, popular, and most important of all, profitable. The way you do that is to create a *pitch*, a presentation that describes your graphic novel in such a way that any durned fool—and even some intelligent folk—can see that this is a good project.

Now in some ways, the perfect pitch is to complete the graphic novel and present the whole thing. That way the *editors*, the folks at the publishing company who choose what to publish, don't need any psychic ability to know what the finished work will be like. They also don't need to trust that you will actually be able to get the work finished in a reasonable time. That's important, because a lot of would-be graphic novelist turn out to be would-be incomplete graphic-short-storyists.

The downside to the perfect pitch is that the publisher may love your concept and art but want it in a slightly different form. The publisher may want to print square graphic novels, or to serialize it in 22-page chapters. It would be a shame to start from scratch. Worse yet and far more likely, you may not find any publishers willing to put the work out. If you're not willing to publish it yourself, you'll be stuck with 128 beautifully drawn pages of drawer stuffing.

You'll need to have at least your writer and penciler in place to pitch a graphic novel these days. Few if any publishers will look at a writer-only pitch from an unestablished writer.

An Artful Warning

If your proposal is thick with art, put a piece of art on the cover. That way, the editor knows that your big pile of papers is not just a pile of words that make for slow reading.

If you're pitching the book in person, generally at a convention, your pitch will be a bit of conversation letting the editor know some very basic information about what sort of graphic novel it is and who you are, and a *proposal*, which is a description of your graphic novel on paper. If you're pitching by mail, your pitch will be just the proposal and a cover letter. In either case, the proposal is what sells the work. The spiel or cover letter just encourages people to read the proposal.

Different graphic novelists use different formats for their proposals. Here's a basic format that will work:

- **Cover.** This should have the title of the graphic novel as a nice logo, plus the names of the creative team and contact information for one of the members of the creative team. Don't list everyone's contact information. Pick the best conversationalist of the creative team, because this is who the editor will be calling to talk about picking up the project, if all goes well.

- **Character guide.** This is made of one-paragraph descriptions of your key characters, accompanied by drawings of those characters. Keep this down to two pages, unless you want to dedicate a single page to each character, with a single paragraph embedded in a large picture.

◆ **Plot.** This is where you describe the graphic novel. Keep this down to two pages. Start off with a description of the intended format, such as "original graphic novel," "six-issue miniseries," "to be printed, panel per panel, on a roll of toilet paper," or however you see it. Hit the key plot points, but don't get bogged down in the details. It's far more important to convey the tone of the story than to explain just how the giant singing gorilla got his own TV show.

◆ **Sample.** This is several consecutive drawn and lettered pages of the graphic novel. These don't have to be the first pages, although if you do pick the first pages you can put them after the cover and before the character guide. Don't automatically use the first pages, though. Pick a section that shows the style of the graphic novel and shows off the artist's strengths. It doesn't have to be long. Four good pages is enough for someone to start liking the graphic novel.

Your cover letter should be brief, introducing the proposal with a single-sentence description of the work's genre and another describing its target audience. For example, you could say "The enclosed proposal is for an original graphic novel called *The White House Wheel*, a taut political thriller about a hamster who becomes president. The audience for this is a cross between the sort of adult political fiction fans who watch shows like *The West Wing* and 12-to 18-year-old boys who own hamsters." If the creative team has any particularly impressive or interesting credentials that would serve the work, mention them briefly in the cover letter. "The artist, Juanita O'Sullivan, was the head storyboard artist on the film *Hamster with a Vengeance*. The writer, Grover Cleveland, served two nonconsecutive terms as President of the United States."

Be sure to include a stamped, self-addressed envelope with your proposal. It probably won't get used if the publisher is interested in your book. Acceptances are generally phone calls. Rejections come back to you by mail.

Picking Publishers to Pitch

There are a lot of companies publishing graphic novels these days. Most are small companies. Some are self-publishers—people who write, draw, and publish their own graphic novels—who probably aren't looking for other people's work to publish. Others are large, well-established companies that generally work with well-established creators. An unknown creator who wants to sell an original graphic novel to an established publisher will not only have to knock their socks off but also snap their suspenders, unhook their bra, and cause their bow tie to spin around. You can find a list of graphic novel publishers in Appendix A of this book.

Not So Prosaic

There are plenty of books and articles about how to sell your prose novel to a publisher. Don't read those books and assume that the same rules apply to selling a graphic novel. For example, new graphic novel creators rarely if ever use an agent to represent their work. Also, graphic novel publishers are more accepting of *simultaneous submissions*, proposals sent to more than one publisher at a time, than prose publishers are. If you are submitting simultaneously, mention that fact in the cover letter.

You don't want to try to go after every publisher at once. Doing so will just sap your energy and keep you from focusing on the publishers where you really have a chance.

The trick is to get to know what kind of graphic novels each publisher puts out. It will do you little good to try to sell a political thriller like *The White House Wheel* to a publisher that specializes in serialized and collected superhero tales. That story about vampire ninjas fighting ninja vampires isn't going to catch the attention of the Lovey-Love Romances line.

Go to a well-stocked comic book store and the graphic novel department of your bookstore. Find graphic novels that are similar to what you want to do. Note who the publishers are.

Many publishers now list their website address on their books, either on the title page or the back cover. Get those addresses. Visit their websites. Most publishers that are open to submissions will have a link on their site marked "submissions guidelines." This page will tell you what they're looking for and what format they want to see it in.

Some publishers' websites will tell you that they don't look at "unsolicited submissions." This means that they won't look at any proposal you happen to send them; they only look at proposals that they ask you for. Since they've never heard of you, this means that there's no way to get them to look at your proposal, right? Wrong. What you have to do is ask *them* to ask *you* if they can see your proposal. You send them a *query letter*, which looks a lot like the cover letter described earlier—a one-sentence description, a mention of who the target audience is, and a statement of any outstanding background you bring to the work—and add on a simple request for permission to send them the proposal. Find out the name of the submissions editor or the editor in chief of the line, and address it to that person. Be sure to include a self-addressed stamped envelope. If you never hear back or get a "no thank you" note, then the publisher doesn't want your proposal.

Go Outside the Lines

These days, a lot of big nongraphic novel publishers are itching to experiment with graphic novels. If you know prose publishers that publish work similar in content to your graphic novel, pitch it to them. This is a particularly good way to go if your graphic novel is the sort of thing that would sell better in bookstores than in comic shops.

But ahhhh, if that self-addressed stamped envelope comes back to you with a "yes" inside, then you no longer have an unsolicited submission! Put that proposal in a big envelope, write "requested submission" on the outside, add on a big wad of stamps, and stuff it in the mailbox. Oh, and you want to put the address on there, too. It helps.

Convention Contention

Major comics conventions are great places to meet editors, and lousy places to actually try to make a deal. Conventions are crowded, noisy, and if all is going well, the editor is far too busy to read or seriously consider a pitch. The best you can hope for is to get a bit of attention.

Introduce yourself to the editor. If you can honestly compliment one of the editor's recent publications, do so. That helps show that the two of you share beliefs of what makes a good work. Explain to the editor that you've got a proposal, give the one-sentence description of the tale, and open up the proposal to show some of the art.

If the editor is interested, don't just hand over the proposal. Proposals get lost at conventions. Ask if you can mail the proposal to the editor after the conference. A "please do" response means that you not only get to mail it in, you can mark it "requested submission," possibly getting it read before the huge *slush pile* of submissions that editors usually use to soundproof their offices.

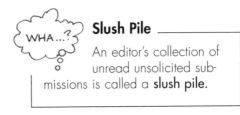

Slush Pile

An editor's collection of unread unsolicited submissions is called a **slush pile**.

Don't be surprised if you never hear back from most editors. Reading the solicitations is considered the least important part of an editor's job. Wait at least four months before you follow up. Some folks prefer to call editors on the phone, but editors are hard to get on the phone and when you reach them, they're not likely to know which proposal you're talking about. It's much easier to e-mail the editor, who can then respond when the time is available to grab your proposal and give it another look.

Honor an Offer?

Eventually, if all goes well and you eat all your vegetables, you may hear from a publisher who wants to publish your work. This should be a very happy moment, but perhaps a scary one as well. For just a little while, you have to set aside being an artiste and instead become a businessperson.

Publishing companies are companies, and for the most part they are neither evil nor charitable organizations. They want to make money, but if your work is good and sells they want you to make money, too. That way, you keep doing projects for them and keep making money for everyone.

Publishers have different ways of paying out, and those differences make a big difference in how much, when, and even whether you get paid. Even artistes know that getting paid is good.

Page Rate Can Pay Great

A page rate is, as the name implies, a rate of money that you get paid for each page of the graphic novel that you turn in, generally paid within a month after the material is submitted. Depending on how you cut the deal, the entire creative team might get a chunk of money when pages are completely done, or each member of the team might get paid when each has completed his or her individual job. The writer might be getting paid for the script to page 42 while the penciler is working on page 10 and the inker hasn't even started.

The big advantage of a page rate is that it's the surest money in the business. You actually get money while you're working on the material, which makes life a lot easier. And if there's a financial problem with the publisher, when it stops paying for work, you simply stop working. It's not a wonderful situation, but it's a lot better than completing an entire graphic novel and only then finding out that the publisher is going to leave your wallet as empty as a mime's dialog balloon.

The biggest downside to a page rate is that it's hard to get one, at least a sufficient one that will cover your expenses while doing the work. The larger, well-funded publishers can offer it, but many of the smaller ones can offer only relatively small payments, if any. Also, the money usually comes at a price, as page rate jobs generally require you to sacrifice more of your rights. What rights? If I answered that now, you wouldn't have an incentive to read the section of this chapter on rights, just a couple pages away.

Steve Sez: A Bird in Hand

I strongly recommend that artists working on graphic novels try to negotiate some sort of page rate. As I noted earlier, assume you'll take 10 hours to draw each page. Can you afford to do that much work in exchange for the possibility of a payday at some point after the work is completed, printed, and distributed to stores?

Royalties Can Be Royally Wonderful

A *royalty* is a chunk of money paid for each and every copy of your graphic novel that is sold. Multiply a good royalty rate by a good amount of sales and you can get a good pay rate. As long as the book keeps selling, you keep making money.

Of course, the downside is that you don't get the money until after the book is complete and published, copies are sold, and the publisher's accounting department has a chance to track the relevant information and cut a check. And you're gambling on your work. If the book sells poorly, you don't make much money. That's true even if the failure is not due to the quality of your work. If the publisher decides to experiment by publishing the book on Swiss cheese instead of paper, the holes will be in your bank account.

A lot of deals mix a page rate with a royalty. That way, you have some money up front and get to keep at least that much if the book does poorly. When you make a deal like that, the page rate is called an *advance*, since the publisher is advancing you some money against your royalties. If you have a deal for a royalty rate of $1 per copy and an advance of $5,000, that means that you get your $5,000 before the book is done but you don't get any royalty on the first 5,000 copies sold. You may never see another copy sold.

Many royalties are stated in terms of a percentage of the sales price of the comic. Keep an eye on whether it's a percentage of the *cover price*, the price that the stores sell the comic for, or of the *wholesale price*, which is what the publisher charges the distributors for the book. The wholesale price varies, but it's generally around 30 to 40 percent of the cover. A deal for 8 percent of the cover price is actually better than one for 15 percent of wholesale, and either is better than a kick in the teeth, even a *really good* kick in the teeth.

Profit? What Profit?

Some deals, particularly with smaller publishers, pay you a percentage of the profit that they make off of the book. The downside to this is that there often isn't any profit. In order to make a profit, the book has to sell enough copies to pay for all the printing, shipping, advertising, and various other expenses involved in production. So not only are you not making money up front, you may have to wait a long while before the book is profitable and you get a check. You may have to wait forever.

The upside to the profit deal is that once a book starts making a profit, you should be making more per copy than what you make on a royalty. Sell a lot of copies, make a lot of money.

Or at least, that's the theory. When you get the contract, look very carefully at how the publisher defines profit. Make sure there is a clear definition of what expenses can be deducted from the book's income. You want to make sure that only expenses directly related to your book are included, such as printing, shipping, advertising, perhaps paying a designer, and

Play Detective

Talk to some of the publisher's existing creators and see if they have any problems or concerns. Even long-surviving publishers can start having payment problems. Small new publishers without any track records are very risky.

so on. If they start charging you for the overhead of running their company, convention expenses, or other things that serve anything besides the production and promotion of your specific book, it's time to start being very wary. Perhaps you need to renegotiate. Perhaps you need to run away fast.

You also want to have the ability to verify both the expenses and income that the book is generating. You need the right to have an accountant audit the printing expenses and the sales if there seems to be a problem. Otherwise, you're trusting their word on their profit. That's only wise if you like giving away thousands of dollars. And if you do, e-mail me! I could use thousands of dollars.

Right and Wrong Rights Deals

Whenever you cut a deal with a publisher, you're selling them some of your rights. At the very least, you're selling them the right to print copies of your graphic novel. Other rights you may be offering include the rights to …

- Publish any sequels to the graphic novel you create.

- Sell foreign publishers the right to publish your graphic novel.

- License out your graphic novel for TV, movies, and similar use.

- Create or license products such as T-shirts, toys, or statues featuring characters or other elements from your story.

If you make a graphic novel featuring publisher-owned characters, you're almost certain to sign over all those rights. In fact, those deals are usually *work for hire* deals, which means that the law considers the publisher to be the creator of the graphic novel. With that, the publisher can do any dang thing it pleases. If it wants to spray-paint your work on the sidewalk and charge people to play hopscotch on it, or turn it into the first Eskimo opera on Broadway, the publisher has those rights.

If you create a completely original graphic novel, you're in a better position to keep control. On the other hand, the more money the publisher pays you, the more control it expects. This is particularly true of page-rate payments.

How much control you're willing to give up is up to you. You really have to know yourself. Once you've completed your 250-page autobiographic epic *The Deepest Part of My Dark, Dark Soul*, would you be shattered if anyone were to use the material in other ways? Or would you be thrilled when they turn it into an animated sitcom with your mom depicted as an axe-wielding hippo, so long as you got a check from it?

Sometimes, it can actually be beneficial to give up the TV and movie rights, so long as you have a deal for a sizable chunk of whatever the publisher makes representing the rights. Some publishers are quite good at making TV and movie deals, making this profitable. Make sure you get cuts of any licensing money made on any front. If the publisher's making money off of your creation, you should be as well. If you're not comfortable with looking at contracts, find yourself an entertainment lawyer.

When possible, you want to get *rights reversion*. That means the rights you give the publisher come back to you eventually, generally when your work goes *out of print*. By getting the rights back, you can at least hope to find someone else to publish it, someone who can actually make money with the work. The publisher who put out *The Road to Perdition* got the movie rights as well, but it let the book go out of print and the rights reverted to the creators. When the movie was made, the creators got all of the movie money, even though the original publisher ended up reissuing the book. Now that was one sad publisher, but it made for happy creators.

> **Out of Print**
>
> A book is considered **out of print** when the publisher doesn't have copies to sell to stores and has no immediate plans to print more. Rights reversions are often based on when a book goes out of print. Be careful, because with the new print-on-demand technology, a publisher can keep a book in print forever without tying up much money.

The Least You Need to Know

- Your proposal should include descriptions of characters, plot, and intended format, as well as some finished pages of art.

- Learn what type of books each publisher publishes, and focus your efforts on appropriate publishers.

- Turn an unsolicited submission into a solicited one by sending a query letter.

- Be patient and understand that reading the slush pile is often on the bottom of the editor's list of things to do.

- Page rates are surer money than royalties or profit participation.

- Protect the rights that are important to you and make sure you get paid for the ones that aren't.

Chapter 24

Releasing on the Cheap

In This Chapter

◆ Should you skip making a profit?

◆ How can you make printed copies cheaply?

◆ How can you put your work online?

If you read the last chapter and immediately found a publisher, you can skip the rest of this book. If you haven't found a publisher but have a few thousand dollars set aside to invest in yourself, you can skip to the next chapter. But if you fall into the great in-between, with the people who are having trouble getting published but still want to put their work out in front of people's eyes, then this is the chapter for you.

Limiting Losses Rather Than Gathering Gains

The techniques in this chapter aren't about making money. You'll have a hard time making any profit through these methods, much less making enough money for the necessities of life, like caramels and dental floss.

No, these methods are designed to keep you from losing money. If you go through a normal printing method, you can expect to be out thousands of dollars before you ever get your ink-stained fingers on a single copy of your 64-page black-and-white graphic novel. You'll probably have to sell more than a thousand copies to break even, even with no other expenses. With the methods we tell you about in this chapter, you won't need to invest the cash. You won't get financial success, but you can get artistic satisfaction. You can get readers. You can even get experience that will help you make the next project better, and make it financially worthwhile. Don't just shrug this off. Look at your work. Is it ready for the big time? Does it really look like something that people will readily pay 10 or 20 bucks for? There's no shame in saying "no." Almost everyone starts trying before they're good enough. Often, the ones who don't realize they aren't good enough yet are the lucky ones, because they keep on trying until they are good enough. Then they look at the early attempts they had been so proud of, dig a hole in the backyard, and bury them under a foot of dirt.

But even if you recognize that your work's not big-time ready, go ahead and do it anyway. Put your inspiration and sweat into it. Just don't toss your money at it.

Photocopicomics

Most folks releasing graphic novels on the ultracheap print them using a photocopier, because it's cheap. In fact, it's free if you use the copier at work when no one is looking.

Of course, in this digital age, you don't have to use a photocopier. In fact, if you're using digital lettering, you've already got the whole thing in the computer and might as well print it on your laser printer. Think twice about doing a full-color work and printing it on an inkjet printer, because the price per page for color ink is quite high—unless, again, you use the one at work.

Check Those Charges

Before you copy a bunch of copies, check the prices at your local copy shops carefully. The price per page can vary by 100 percent between shops. See whether you get a price cut with 100 copies, whether that has to be 100 copies of the same page or 100 copies total, and whether they charge for collating.

Most folks doing photocopied graphic novels serialize them in the digest format, the size of a standard piece of paper folded in two. This format can easily handle 32 pages of work, or even 48 pages, but when you get longer than that you start getting things that are hard to staple and hard to get to lay flat.

The tough part of putting together a digest is making the original version you bring to the copier. You need to copy your art onto your *masters*, the set of pages that you'll photocopy to make your copies. You need two pages on each side of each sheet of paper. They have to be arranged so that when you fold them, they make a complete comics pamphlet, as you can see in the following page arrangement diagram.

Page arrangement for a 16-page installment.

If you want a different page shape, simply use legal paper. When folded, it comes closer to being square than illegal paper does.

Other folks, looking for larger pages, simply copy the graphic novel page for page on full-sized sheets of paper, stapling the left edge together making a simple book. This doesn't look as smooth, but you can get greater length. Staples are still your limitation, unless you want to pay for fancier binding.

Whichever format you choose, try using heavier paper for your cover pages. This feels right, and makes the finished work easier to hold open.

A Stapler Is Staple

Whichever photocopied format you use, you're going to need a stapler. Ah, but you already have a stapler, right? But sorry, your stapler isn't good enough. You suffer from inadequate stapler syndrome.

Your standard stapler is designed to tack together a few sheets of paper at the corner. If you want your work to be short and badly bound, that will do. But you, of course, dream of better things.

If you're working with digest format, you'll need a stapler that can reach the center of the page. For standard digest format, that's a reach of 5½ inches. If you're using legal paper, it's 7 inches. Either of these is beyond the reach of the standard stapler. A good office supply store will have special ultralong staplers that can reach a whole foot or so for around $20 to $30.

If you're using whole-page pages and have more than a few sheets at a time, you'll need a real heavy-duty stapler. That's a different stapler, but will run you a similar price. Your copy shop may have such a stapler available for public use.

The copy shop may even offer appropriate stapling service, but such specialized stapling is never as cheap as you think it ought to be. At least, not if you're a cheapskate like me.

Don't Tack Tackily

If you're making one-page-per-sheet comics, make sure you staple down through the front cover, leaving the smoother end of the staple on top. Staple at least ¼ inch from the edge, since otherwise the pages may rip easily from the staples. That means leaving at least ½ inch between the stapled side of the pages and the start of the art. The thicker your book is, the more space you lose in the valley between stapled pages.

Put two or three evenly spaced staples in each copy. Try to keep them both parallel to the edge and the same distance from the edge. Otherwise, the pages will be apt to crumple and fold when the comic is opened. Even a cheaply made comic needn't be a cheaply made comic. Except by definition, of course.

Stapling digest comics is a little tricky. Most of the extra-long staplers have an adjustable slider you can set for the depth of the staple, but you shouldn't rely on it. Instead, compile your pages and fold them first. Pinch the fold and run your fingers along it, to make the crease sharp. Open the pages back up, and aim your staples to go in through the front cover, right on the fold. Two staples give you the best result. More staples won't make your book hold together any better, and it would only go to further line the pockets of the international staple cartels who have a monopoly on all the staple mines.

Hand-Sell Your Handmade Handiwork

Most comic book distributors don't want to deal with photocopied comics. In order to get your work to readers, you'll have to try some more direct selling methods.

The best way to reach people who are into graphic novels is to buy table space at a comics convention. Some conventions are really for the mainstream superhero collector, and you're not likely to do well there. Some are full-range comic shows, and even have reduced rates for *small press*, which includes photocopied works as well as low print-run, standard-format comics. And some shows specialize in small press and alternative works, and at these places you'll be treated as a normal part of the scene rather than as the freak that we all know you really are. Check out Appendix B for a list of comics conventions.

You can also reach out to the small press crowd via magazines aimed at that group. A number of magazines target readers of small and alternative press of all forms, sharing news, reviews, and ordering information. The granddaddy of these magazines is *Factsheet Five*. Other such reviewzines pop up and disappear faster than plastic moles in an arcade game, but if you head down to your local alternative newsstand, you may find a few that you can send copies of your work to. With luck, you'll get a good review and dozens of orders via the mail, although then you'll have to deal with packing and shipping them off.

Local comic shops may be willing to carry your photocopied works, particularly if they carry alternative comics or if you're a regular customer. Most will take a handful on a consignment basis, which means they'll put them out and then pay you for any copies they sell. A fair deal is a 50-50 split; if they sell the book for two bucks, they'll give you one. Make sure you get a receipt for the copies that you deliver to them. That way, when it comes time to collect for the copies they've sold, you just have to count how many copies they have left to know how many they've sold. Another victory for the miracle of subtraction!

Raven's Route

Leyla Lawler started *Raven's Children* as a series of photocopied digests, a system that allowed her release the material and get feedback as she worked on it. Then she collected the first five installments into a professionally printed graphic novel.

Online Outlets

In this Internet Age a lot of people skip printing altogether, putting their graphic novels on the World Wide Web. There are a lot of advantages to this. The web gives many millions of people easy access to your work. All they have to do is find out about it, click the mouse, and *wham!* they're reading it. You can work in color without racking up the hideous expenses of color printing or the complicated worries about trapping.

If your goal is a web-based graphic novel, you really should design your work around the screen. Some people deal with this by doing horizontal pages, as with the sample picture from *Nowhere Girl*. Other folks avoid the limitations of the "page" concept altogether. Scott McCloud is a leading champion for avoiding the page metaphor. At his www.scottmccloud .com website you'll find tales told as huge single pages that you simply scroll through, and even one where you see one panel at a time and click on it to fly through the panel into the next one.

Nowhere Girl, *at www. nowheregirl.com, uses a wide page to fit the screen.*

(© 2003 Justine Shaw.)

If you take a look at a variety of web-based comics, you'll find that they use varying levels of technology and complexity. Some are done very simply with HTML, so that you read the page, click on something to move to the next page, then the next page's image downloads while you wait. For dial-up users, that wait can take a while. A graphic novel like *Nowhere Girl* uses preloading tricks, so that while you're reading one page, the computer is already downloading the image for the next page so that the moment you click for the next page, it appears. Still others use a program like Macromedia's Flash to make graphic novels with full sets of page-turning controls and interesting added features. Spend some time exploring, and you're apt to find a site that functions in a way you'll want to copy. And even if you don't, you'll have spent a lot of time reading comics, and that's not a bad way to spend a day.

Millions in Viewers, Pennies in the Bank

Online graphic novels are a great way to make a lot of fans, even make a lot of friends. They're a pretty poor way of making a living, though. Web readers love free things, but aren't nearly so fond of paying for things. Still, there are ways to try to crank some money out of the web, and at least cover your expenses and with luck have some left over.

Until recently, attempts to charge for reading an individual story have failed, because readers didn't want to pay much and there weren't good ways for the cartoonist to try to collect just a small amount of money. People are now having some small success with the system found at www.bitpass.com for charging *micropayments*, small charges from a few pennies up to a dollar for reading. Of course, you should give people some small free sample before you charge them, to convince them that your masterpiece is worth the few pennies you're asking for.

Other people take a tip from street performers, turning to asking for tips from the people who enjoy their work. Some use the services of www.paypal.com to accept their tips, while others use Amazon.com's tip jar feature to collect money. Either of these works okay for tips of at least a dollar. A very small percentage of people actually tip, though. Most people prefer to get things for free for some reason.

Selling stuff is a good way of making some money. Some creators sell their original art, which means that the graphic novel serves as both a story and a catalogue showroom. Other creators sell products featuring characters and artwork from their graphic novel. A cool T-shirt with your character on it can serve as both an income source and an ad for your work.

Most folks offering character products use Café Press, a service where you can upload your designs and build your own store page. They take the orders, print up things like T-shirts, mugs, calendars, and caps one at a time when people order them, ship them, collect the money, and give you a cut. You won't make as much per shirt as if you had a thousand shirts printed up professionally and sold each one off, but you also don't risk ending up with an empty bank account and a garage full of Tommy The Diabetic Turtle T-shirts. Surf over to www.licensablebeartm.com to see an example of Café Press in action.

Print-on-Polite-Request

All these solutions are fine if you just want to get your story out there. But if you really want a book in your hands? One that looks like a book? One that feels like a book? One that you can womp spiders with? Then it's time to start looking into print-on-demand publishing.

Print-on-demand (or *POD*) uses a high-tech process that can print small quantities of a book relatively affordably. The individual books aren't nearly as cheap per copy as if you printed several thousand copies the normal way, but the main cost in a big print run is a first copy that costs thousands of dollars. Print-on-demand has a much lower startup cost.

Demanding Print Outlets

Currently the cheapest way to do print-on-demand is through Café Press, the same folks who print one-off T-shirts and mugs. They'll print one-off books with absolutely no startup charges. A single copy of a hundred-page graphic novel will run you about $10. You can order copies for yourself or you can sell copies through your website at a markup—charge $15 a copy and pocket $5 for yourself, or charge a million bucks a copy and pocket $999,990 per copy. You probably won't sell many copies, of course, but imagine if you sold even five!

> **Beware of Paying Publishers**
>
> Sites like xlibris.com and iUniverse.com offer print-on-demand and distribution services for a price. These folks can get your book listed on sites like Amazon.com, but they're ineffective at getting books into bookstores and they don't even try to reach comic book stores. They charge hundreds or even thousands of dollars for services that do little for graphic novelists.

A number of printers out there will use print-on-demand technology to print a small order of your book—a hundred copies or so. This is still cheaper than printing a full run of a book, although now you're stuck with finding your own ways of distributing the book. Go to www.opm.com for a site where you can get a hundred copies of a small hundred-page graphic novel for a couple hundred bucks plus shipping, or check out www.BookSurge.com for a POD service that includes some distribution but with reasonable and affordable up-front costs. However you find a printer, get the print shop to show you samples of books it's printed with pictures in them before committing. You don't want to get your book back and discover that it's about black furry blobs talking to gray furry blobs, unless your graphic novel is *The Great Blob Debates*.

Demanding Print Formats

Print-on-demand printers won't let you hand them a stack of drawn pages and say "print this!" Usually, they need everything electronically delivered. Different printers vary in the formats that they'll take covers in, but the interiors will have to be delivered as a *PDF* file. That stands for *portable document format*. This is quite popular with printers because the file has everything they need completely formatted. The printer won't make decisions about what will be in your book, that will all be in the PDF file. A few years ago, you would have needed to spend hundreds of dollars on special PDF-making software, but now there are affordable solutions, so long as you already have a computer.

You're also going to find that print-on-demand printers only print certain fixed sizes. Look into the printers and what they have to offer before you draw 200 perfectly square pages, only to find that the printer doesn't offer any square formats and you'll end up with a lot of blank space on each rectangular page.

Because of the way that they bind the pages together, print-on-demand printers have length limitations. Any one of them can do a book that's 100 to 200 pages, but you may need to research some more if you're doing larger or even smaller sizes. Some will handle 480 pages just fine but balk at doing 48. And any print-on-demand printer can handle black-and-white, but some don't handle gray tones well and many won't do color.

The Least You Need to Know

- Photocopied serials, web-based graphic novels, and print-on-demand won't make you a fortune, but they keep your losses down.

- Photocopied works are generally hand assembled and stapled.

- Small press conventions and alternative press magazines are good places to find readers for photocopied works.

- Web-based comics can reach a lot of people, but it's hard to squeeze money out of them.

- Design your web-based comics specifically for the web.

- Print-on-demand lets you publish books with small print runs, then go back for more as needed.

Chapter 25

Put It Out Yourself: Printing

In This Chapter

- ◆ Who will print your pretty publication?
- ◆ What do you send to the printer?
- ◆ How do you check what the printer sends you?

So you've decided that you want to publish yourself, and that you're going to invest your money in yourself and do it up in real commercial style. This doesn't mean you want to throw your money away. You probably want to spend it wisely and get your book to look good. Of course, if you just want to throw your money away, I've got a bucket right here. (Hey, Steve, hands off! That's *my* money bucket!)

A Single Spurt or Slowly Serialized?

The big first question is: Do you want to go right to issuing your work as one big book, or would you rather serialize it in individual issues? On one hand, this is an artistic question. Some stories really work best being serialized, but some really don't. Serialization interrupts the reading experience, which makes it great for works with cliff-hanging moments but poor for works that want to be read straight through at a single sitting.

On the other hand, this is a question of desire. If you grew up reading *X-Men*, *Archie*, or even *Love and Rockets*, you may have a real love for the comic book pamphlet or you might see the respect for graphic novels as coming from their square-bound form, and view the traditional format as something that makes hard work seem disposable.

But as anyone with three hands can tell you, the third hand is the most important one. In this case, the third hand is business. To make money on this venture, you need to think like a businessperson. But it's tough to see the right thing from the business standpoint.

Many folks assume they can put out a series of pamphlets, keep themselves going by bringing in a bit more than printing costs on each one, and then make the real money from the ongoing sales of the eventual book-format collection. Unfortunately, these people often discover that its not so easy to make even a little money off the pamphlets, and they can run through all their money before the entire series is run, leaving them with an incomplete work and no money to print the book edition.

Although printing a single black-and-white pamphlet is a lot cheaper than printing a black-and-white book, printing ten or even six issues of a comic book is a lot more expensive than printing a book that collects all the issues. This is because the most expensive part of printing most black-and-white works is printing the four-color cover. For the book, you have to pay for printing only one cover. A six-issue series obviously needs six covers, because you can't just use the same cover again and again without confusing folks. The cost adds up.

Scientific Business

For *Two-Fisted Science* and *Dignifying Science*, multi-artist anthologies of true tales about scientists, Jim Ottaviani preceded each square-bound edition with a single pamphlet containing a story from the book. That way, people could affordably sample his work without Jim tying up a lot of money in a whole series of pamphlets.

Calculating the effect of working in both pamphlet and book form is tough. Some people will buy the pamphlets instead of the book. Some people will avoid the pamphlets as long as they assume the book will come out. Some people will buy the pamphlet, and, if they like the work, buy the book to have a more permanent format. And the pamphlet can help build the reputation of your work. Some stores are wary of ordering a book by an unknown publisher but will be more willing to order pamphlets, then order the book if the pamphlets sell well.

If you ask three "experts" whether you should put out pamphlets or go straight to the book, you'll get four different answers. My best advice is to publish the pamphlets only if you're aiming at an audience that is used to reading pamphlets. If you're doing *Captain Arachnid and the All-Bug Squad*, for example, your pamphlets may well outsell your book. But if you're doing a story aimed more at the bookstore audience, putting out pamphlets will waste your money.

Pick a Perfect Printer

There are thousands of printers out there, but you're really best off dealing with one that handles comic books or graphic novels regularly. These folks understand the special needs of publishers in the comics field. They know the things that can go wrong, and they're used to shipping to the distributors. Local printers may seem convenient, but you'll find yourself having to work through a lot more problems.

The main North American printers for independent comic books and graphic novels are as follows:

- **Quebecor World Lebonfon** (Quebec, Canada). Quebecor is the world's largest commercial printer, so even though it's the biggest printer in the comics field, comics are a small part of its business and its website is not friendly for comics folk. Instead, phone Patrick Jodoin at (514)494-5443 or e-mail him at sales@lebonfon.com.

- **Brenner Printing** (Texas). Surf over to www.brennerprinting.com for more information. Brenner handles both color and black-and-white material for smaller publishers.

- **Morgan Printing** (North Dakota). Its website at www.morganprinting.com has its contact information and a guide to what you need to provide the company.

- **Preney Print and Litho** (Ontario, Canada). Contact information can be found at www.preneyprint.com. Preney is best known for doing affordable black-and-white printing on newsprint. For samples of what it's good at, look at the issues and collections of *Cerebus the Aardvark*.

Cheap Runs

If you want fewer than 1,000 copies of your black and white book or pamphlet, check out www.icomics.com/hbps for the low prices of Harold Buchholdz Print Services. Harold won't give you many options, and he accepts only all-ages material. If you have racier material or want color printing for pamphlets, check out www.firstwaveprinting.com.

Some publishers go with overseas printers, particularly when looking to find cheaper routes to getting hardcover or full-color graphic novels. This makes sense after you've been publishing for a while, have a fair number of books coming out, and can become good at both predicting how many copies you'll need and dealing with the printer. For your first book, however, you'll be better off dealing with people who speak your language.

Contact printing companies you're interested in and ask if they have a price sheet. Most folks used to printing comic book pamphlets will send you not only a price list but also samples of comics they have printed to show the different types of paper they work with. Different paper costs different prices.

Some of the price sheets will include prices for square-bound books that are the same width and height as the pamphlets. Not all printers include that information, and even with those that do you may want different paper, different size, or other special things. In that case, you'll have to ask for a quote.

"I Quote, Therefore I Am"

A *quote*, short for *price quote*, is simply a statement of the charges you'll be billed for printing your book. In order to provide you a quote, the folks at the printer need to know some things about your book. No, they don't really care if the lovers get together at the end or if Sinister Charlie really does conquer California. They need to know how many pages your book is (counting both sides of each sheet as separate pages) and the size of the pages. They also need to know whether the interiors of the book are in color or black and white. If it's black and white, are you providing the interior as computer files, or are you sending the actual art for the pages? Color pages have to be provided as computer files. The printing folks need to know how many copies you'll want to print, although they don't need the exact number—ask for the minimum you're planning to print and for the *marginal copy cost*, which is how much it will cost to print each additional copy.

They also need to know what sort of stock—that's paper—you want your graphic novel printed on. Actually, you need to pick two types of stock, one for the interior and one for the cover. Paper varies in a lot of ways. There are gloss papers, which are shiny, and matte papers, which are not. Papers vary in thickness, in graininess, in color, and even in how they feel in your fingers. They also vary in the amount of bleed through. That may sound like the horrific effect of a paper cut, but actually it is the ability to look at a page and see the print that's on the other side of the page, as you can see in the accompanying image. Bleed through can be caused by two things: ink actually soaking deeply into the paper, and bright light shining through thin paper and reflecting off the next page.

> **Perfect Paper Picking**
>
> Did you see the graphic novel *HeliCatterpillar* and think "that looks just like what I want!"? Ask the publisher which printing company put it out. Tell that printing company you want your graphic novel on that same stock as *HeliCatterpillar*.

> **Steve Sez: Ask the Artmonkey**
>
> Artists who have been published before have seen how their work reproduces on different sorts of paper, and they've probably noticed the same when looking at other artists with similar styles. Get your artist's opinion.

Look at this area under bright light to see bleed through.

Don't assume that the whitest paper is the best. Very white paper creates a stark, photo-copied look, and many black-and-white graphic novels look better on a muted color such as beige or cream. Really bad graphic novels would look better printed on black paper, so you wouldn't have to see the art.

Pricing the Price

The price quote or price sheet will show a basic printing price. For a book, it might say that printing 1,000 copies costs $3,000, and then each additional copy will run you $1 to print. So if you want 2,000 copies, it will cost you $3,000 for the first thousand and $1,000 for the second thousand, so it will run you $4,000 total, right? No, because that's just the start of the costs.

Somewhere else, you'll probably see something that says tolerance +/–5%. What that means is that they're really not going to try to print 2,000 copies, but rather 5 percent more, making 2,100 copies. That way, if something goes wrong with printing some of the copies, they can still promise to get you at least 1,900. This also means that you have to be prepared to pay for 2,100 copies, bringing your potential total to $4,100.

Then there's an additional cost for creating the *films* of your pages, listed as a price per page. For a black-and-white book this may cost $10 per page if you provide the physical art, or $7.50 per page for digital files. So if you have a 100-page graphic novel provided as art, there's another $1,000, bringing your total to $5,100. The films for the color book cover are more expensive because each of the four CMYK colors needs its own sheet, so it will run around $100 for the whole cover. That's $5,200 bucks.

Some printers are willing to store your films in case you want to reprint the book without paying that $1,000 all over again. Otherwise, you'll want the films shipped to you at a slight added expense. Ah, but let's say you get off easy and the printer will store them for you. So you're still at $5,200.

Films

Films are the negatives of your pages, traditionally used in the printing process. Some new printing systems don't use films.

Now you've paid to get your books printed, which is all great and wonderful, except now you just have a pile of books at the printer. If you want copies of the book to get to you and to the distributors, you'll have to pay for shipping. The printer will do an up-front shipping estimate by adding 10 percent to the total cost of printing. That $4,000 price has become $5,720.

And sadly, that may not be the end of the money you give the fine and gorgeous folks at the printer. If you're overprinting your book for long-term sales, you may want to keep the extras in the printer's warehouse, for an additional monthly fee. Otherwise, you end up with a living room full of boxes, which is no good even if you try to use them as furniture.

Pre-Press with Success

Printing isn't magic. You have to send your printer all the contents of your graphic novel to print. If you're doing a black-and-white graphic novel, the easiest thing for you to send is the actual art. The printer will photograph it to make the films, and will print from those. Even if you're doing digital lettering, you can print out those pages on a laser printer. If you don't own a laser printer, you can get access to one at most modern copy/business centers, some libraries, and even some dentist offices if you do it when the dentist isn't looking.

You can submit the outside covers as a single computer graphic image in TIFF format. Make sure the image is larger than the actual cover by about an eighth of an inch on all sides. That way, if the cover stock isn't cut in exactly the right place, you don't end up with blank white nothingness at the edges of your cover. If you're doing a book, remember to include the width of the book's spine in your cover measurement. How thick will your spine be? Ask your printer! Printers love answering questions. It's so much easier to help you not to make mistakes than to fix mistakes later.

Digital Helps You Dig It All

If you're doing digital lettering, your lettering will look better if you submit your book *electronically*, as computer files either uploaded or burned onto a CD-ROM. If you're doing digital coloring, then digital submission is a must.

To put together your graphic novel digitally, you need a page layout program. This sort of program helps you design each page, placing the images there, adjusting the size, and adding some text. Currently, the most popular is QuarkXPress, but some folks use PageMaker or In Design. Ask your printer what programs it supports. None of these programs is cheap, and all of them will take a while to learn to use.

Modern graphic programs can put out files in umpty-gazillion different file formats, give or take eleventeen. Most of your favorite formats are useless here, however, because the big fancy printer computers don't understand them. You can count on them to understand two formats. For coloring or other things that you've worked on in Photoshop or another bitmap program, stick with *TIFF* files (that's *Tagged Image File Format*). Save pages lettered in a vector program like Adobe Illustrator in the *EPS* (*Encapsulated PostScript*) format, and make sure to use your program's option to include or embed fonts in the file. If EPS gets too confusing, you can use the vector program to export a TIFF file, but your lettering won't look quite as sharp.

Some people actually use three separate files when dealing with colored pages. They remove the original black line from the coloring and save it at about 400 dots per inch. Next, they save a version of just the black line at 1,200 dots per inch, to make sure the line is sharp. Finally, they save an EPS file with just the lettering by going into Illustrator and turning off the visibility of the line art. In the page layout program they make a pile out of those three files, putting the color on the bottom, the line art on top of that, and the lettering on top. It's extra work, but it's the best way to get the sharpest possible line and lettering, which can be important if you're doing detailed work.

Do It by the Book

There is far more to preparing your graphic novel digitally than can be covered in a chapter. Luckily, Kevin Tinsley covers it all in his book *Digital Prepress for Comic Books*.

Postscript

Postscript is a *page description language,* a system of encoding the information about what a page is supposed to look like. The high-end printing devices that your printer uses understand Postscript. *Postscript fonts* are font files with the information about the letter shapes encoded in a way that can be understood by Postscript devices.

If you do use your page layout program to add any text, use PostScript fonts. The font information is encoded in a way that the printer's expensive tools understand. If you use TrueType fonts or some other sort of font, it may look great on your screen and even from your computer's printer but can come out like gobbledygook when the books hit the printing press. Or, if you mean it to look like gobbledygook, it may come out looking like Walt Whitman poetry.

After you've got everything all put together in your layout program, use the collect or export command to put out a version where all the relevant files are in one directory. When your program asks you which types of files to include, check every option. Don't assume your printing company has the same font files as you do, because it doesn't. Burn a CD-ROM with the files in this directory. Put the cover in a separate directory on the same CD-ROM.

The printing company will probably give you a couple pages of suggestions to help you prepare the book for printing. Listen to those suggestions. Ask questions if you don't understand. It's better to *look* stupid than to *be* stupid.

Complete Idiot's Guide to Dummies

Whether you submit your book as digital files or as physical art, you should send the printing company a *dummy*. No, they don't need a mannequin or a Guy Fawkes. What they're looking for is a handmade copy of a your book. If you're sending physical art, you'll probably use a photocopier's reduction feature to get the art down close to the printed size. If you're setting it up digitally, print the page on your computer printer. If possible, print on both sides of the paper, or else you'll have to tape your pages together. Don't worry about using the same size paper as the final book, or trimming off the excess edges. Staple the pages together.

The printing folks use your dummy to make sure the pages aren't in the wrong order. That's not much of a problem with digitally prepared books but can be a real risk for books sent in as pages. For digital books, if the printing folks see something weird on their output, they can check your dummy and make sure that it's the weird thing you intended.

In addition to the art or CD-ROM and the dummy, the printing company wants you to send in a signed order sheet that includes the paper types and the print quantities. Often, you can just sign a copy of the quote and send that in.

And that's not all you have to sign. You also have to sign a check, or at least a credit application. Most printers will give you 30 days to pay as long as you have some record of paying your debts. If you're going for credit, send in your credit application a few weeks before you intend to send in the book, so that the printer has time to check and approve your credit.

The Proof Is in the Proof

You send in your dummy of the graphic novel and the printer usually sends back its dummy—but the printer calls it a *proof* or perhaps a *sherpa*. This is your last chance to catch mistakes. If the printer makes a mistake and you catch it now, then the printer has to fix them for free. If you catch mistakes that only you made, you can get them fixed, although in some cases your fixes will cost you money. But if you miss mistakes now, you've got a problem. Suddenly, you'll find yourself the proud owner of 4,000 copies of a book that has three copies of page 27 and no copies of pages 40 and 95.

Depending on the printer, you'll get the proof either as a computer printout or as *bluelines*, an odd-looking pile of your black lines printed in blue on yellow pages. Make sure your pages are all there and in the right order. Check to see that nothing is badly tilted. Make sure no text is placed too close to the edge of the page, otherwise a slight change in the cutting position will leave your characters cut off in midsentence.

Don't worry about uneven shading and odd shadowing on bluelines. The process of making a blueline can leave a mottled darkness, but that doesn't mean your blacks won't be black and your whites won't be as white as new gym socks.

If you're doing a color book, you might get a color key for the interior pages, a full-color proof where you can check for color problems. Such color keys aren't cheap to make and a printer may charge extra for them, so you may need to skip this unless you're rich or paranoid or both. If you are both, your money may be better spent on Gertler & Lieber Brand Space Alien Repellent.

You'll almost certainly get at least one proof for your color cover, possibly two. You'll at least get a color guide, a sharp-looking color reproduction of your cover that actually looks a little better than your finished cover will. Use this to check that your colors are reproducing as you intended.

The position guide is a trimmed and folded version of the cover, to show you exactly where the printer intends to cut and fold the cover. This may be produced on a very different printing system, so don't use it to judge the colors, unless the printer gives you just one guide that is meant to be used as the color guide and position guide.

> **Be FedExpecting It**
>
> If you're not constantly at home (or wherever your proofs are being delivered), ask your contact at the printer to call you when the proofs are being shipped. That way, you know to be home when the package arrives, and can respond quickly to the proofs.

Proofs often come to you via overnight delivery service. When you get the proofs, look over everything carefully but quickly. Printing companies usually want you to respond the same day, so that they can make any necessary fixes and get on with the job. You may get the cover and interior proofs separately, because they'll be printed at different times and on different presses.

Your proofs will often come with a form that has to be signed and faxed back, on which you list any corrections that are needed. Remember, when you sign that approval, any blame for any mistakes you missed is now yours. Even though you must do it quickly to avoid your printing being delayed, you should still do it with care and fear. A trembling signature is a sign that you take this responsibility seriously.

The Least You Need to Know

- Don't be too optimistic about your ability to publish your graphic novel both as a serial and as a book.
- Get price quotes from several experienced printing companies before picking one.
- Quality and convenience should be considered in picking a printer, not just price.
- The paper that best matches your book may not be the whitest or the most expensive.
- Send the printing company your art or CD-ROM, a dummy, an order, and payment.
- Check your proofs carefully for page order and placement, then quickly return the approval to avoid delays.

Chapter 26

Put It Out Yourself: Distribution

In This Chapter

- ◆ How do I get my graphic novel into comic shops?
- ◆ What do I tell the distributor about my graphic novel?
- ◆ Can I get it into bookstores?

You have thousands of copies of your graphic novel sitting in genuine cardboard boxes in your living room. And somewhere out there, you hope, are thousands of readers who want to have a single copy of your graphic novel in their living room, cardboard box not included. If you wanted to, you could hire Madam Louella, Comic Book Distribution Psychic, to divine the names of all of those thousands of people so you could mail copies right to them, but Louella isn't cheap and her accuracy is in doubt. Instead, you're better off dealing with distributors, companies that can offer your books to the stores.

Diamond: A Gem of an Operation

The main distributor you'll deal with is Diamond Comics Distributors. They are the heavy hitters in distributing to comic book stores. This is because they have the exclusive right to distribute the works of the four largest publishers to the *direct market*. You could theoretically run a comics shop without dealing with Diamond, but most of your day would be spent answering questions with "no, we ain't got that." So every single comics shop deals with Diamond, and a huge portion of the shops don't use any other source for graphic novels.

Direct Market

The **direct market** is the stores, primarily comic book shops, that buy comic books and graphic novels on a *nonreturnable* basis. That means that once the store gets the book, you get to keep the money, even if the store never sells it.

A company with a near-monopoly status could make them sloppy and tough to deal with, but in Diamond's case it's not much of a problem. They are conscientious, they know their field, and they can be very supportive of small publishers as long as the work is of commercial quality. If you've got a product that's worth selling, Diamond will help you sell it, but realize that they can do only so much.

Pitching on the Diamond

The first step in getting Diamond to carry your book is to send it a copy. Don't worry, you don't have to have the book actually printed. In fact, you really shouldn't have the book printed yet. Send a photocopy or computer printout of the completed work to Diamond's purchasing department. Go to vendor.diamondcomics.com for contact information and other information on dealing with Diamond.

Don't Dis Diamond

Some would-be publishers resent that Diamond refuses to carry some graphic novels, but Diamond is providing a needed service. The stores don't get to see your graphic novel before ordering it. Ordering a book that's too ugly for anyone to buy hurts the store, and things that hurt stores hurt the distributor and all the other publishers as well.

In addition to the photocopy, Diamond wants to know the format of the book, so you'll explain how big the pages will be and whether it's hardcover or softcover. If you're serializing the work and Diamond sees the photocopy is 24 pages and is called *Thus-and-Such*, Issue 1, Diamond will assume your work's a pamphlet unless you say otherwise. Diamond will also want to know the cover price of the book, which is the price you'll print on the cover and that most stores will sell the book for.

Diamond will also want to know your *terms of sale*. Basically, that means you're telling Diamond what portion of the cover price you expect to be paid for not only the work you just showed them but also every future work you ask Diamond to carry. Diamond won't tell you the terms; it's your job to tell them. It's your choice to make.

But I'm about to tell you your terms. Your terms are *60 percent off.* That's right, that $20 graphic novel you're publishing? You get only $8 for it. And suddenly, you realize why it's not easy as pie to make a living in the graphic novel field. Why charge only 40 percent of the cover price? If you offer that as your terms, Diamond will charge the retailer about 55 percent of the cover price for the book, keeping 15 percent in return for distribution services. The retailer charges 100 percent, using the 45 percent profit to pay for rent, employees, all the books they bought that didn't sell, and cream-filled cupcakes.

If you charge more than 40 percent, Diamond's going to feel there isn't enough profit for the stores in carrying the book. You'll get the answer "thanks but no thanks". Charge less than 40 percent and Diamond gladly passes the discount on to the retailers. However, the retailers that actually order from smaller publishers are used to paying that 55 percent. Oh, they'll tell you that they'd rather pay less, but it's not likely to make enough difference in the number of copies they order to make cutting the price worthwhile.

Running Diamond's Bases

Once Diamond accepts your book, you'll have to properly *solicit* the book, which means giving Diamond all the information it needs to offer the book to stores. This begins a several month process in bringing your book to the market. Let's say you want to release *The Deadly Art of Bonsai* in April. Here's the schedule:

- By mid-January, you have to e-mail Diamond a solicitation, which includes the a scan of the cover, plus the title, price, format, name of the printing company, the names of the writer, penciler, and inker, and a 50-or-fewer-word description of the book, designed to sell the work: *Bonsai is an ancient power that can reduce mighty trees to near nothing. Will young Bradley Goldfarb use his new power to avenge his family, or to win the heart of the girl he loves? Perfect for fans of* Sashimi Sword *and* Feng Shui Warrior.

- In February, Diamond sends all of the comic shops a copy of the monthly catalog *Previews*, including a listing and picture of your book.

- By the end of February, all of the comic shops have to send their orders to Diamond.

- In mid-March, Diamond adds up all the orders and sends you the total, including a list of how many copies you have to send to each of Diamond's warehouses.

- Sometime during the last week of March or hopefully at least a week before the last Wednesday of April, your books reach the Diamond warehouse. If they arrive more than about a month later, the books become *returnable*, which means that stores that have trouble selling them can send them back to Diamond, and you'll have to refund some money. That's bad. Keeping money is good.

- A month after getting your book, Diamond ships you a check.

If you're serializing your graphic novel as pamphlets, you'll have several issues going through the process at the same time. As such, you have to be able to handle several issues in your mind at a time. If you have problems handling all the issues in your mind, consult a psychiatrist.

For the first three issues of your serialization, Diamond needs to see the full content of the issue as part of your solicitation. That way, Diamond knows the work is actually done, and stores won't be ordering something you won't bother to finish. Many folks get confused and scared by this, because Diamond tells them this in a confusing way. I've seen people spend a lot of money or give up altogether because of a misunderstanding. They think you have to have all three issues done before you solicit the first one, or even that you have to have the issues printed. Neither is true. Just send a photocopy of issue 1 when you solicit issue 1, a photocopy of issue 2 when you solicit issue 2, and a photocopy of issue 3 when you solicit issue 3. Once you've done that, you've conned Diamond into believing you can actually deliver on your promises.

After stores get their copies of your work, they may place reorders, asking Diamond for more copies. If enough requests are generated, Diamond will reorder the book from you. If your book seems to be one which stores will want to keep in stock for a long time, Diamond may make your book part of their *Star System*, which is their system for handling ongoing reorders.

Direct Distributors on Parade

Although you absolutely need Diamond to carry your book, it's not a marriage. You don't have to be true to them. You can deal with other distributors on the side, and it's not cheating. Other distributors can reach other stores and generate more sales, more readers, and more money, three categories in which *more* is definitely better.

Solicit the other distributors at the same time that you solicit Diamond, and include a full photocopy of the graphic novel or issue you're soliciting.

FM: No Static at All

FM International is a direct market distributor, much like Diamond although much smaller. Its customers are a mixture of shops that carry comics as a sideline and full-range shops that place part of their orders with FM due to the better discounts it offers, even though you get paid the same portion of cover price as you do with Diamond. FM's order is likely to be around 5 or 10 percent the size of Diamond's order.

FM has a website at www.fminternet.com that you should check out for more details about the company. Send your solicitation information, a photocopy of your story, and terms of sale to FM International Inc., P.O. Box 259804, Madison, WI 53725-9804. If Diamond is willing to carry your work, FM almost certainly will as well. FM is friendly and eager to carry whatever possible, to make up for not carrying the large publishers who are exclusive with Diamond.

Cold Cut: Deli Delight

Cold Cut Distribution is a different sort of distributor. The folks at Cold Cut don't mean it to be the distributor that dealers turn to first. They want stores to turn to it *second*. Cold Cut deals strictly in reorders, keeping in stock many pamphlets and books that Diamond doesn't have, and offering comic shops generally better discounts on reorders.

Because Cold Cut doesn't seek store orders before ordering copies from you, you will get a quite conservative order at first. Then, as stores reorder from Cold Cut, Cold Cut will reorder from you to keep copies in stock, until the orders come so slowly that your book is no longer worth carrying and goes out of stock.

Send a photocopy of your comic to Submissions Director, Cold Cut Distribution, 220 N. Main St., Salinas, CA 93901. In fact, you can wait until the book is printed before contacting Cold Cut if you want to send a printed copy; that way the submissions director can evaluate the package as well as the content. After he decides whether to carry your work, he'll talk to you about terms. You can go to www.coldcut.com for more information.

Last Gasp: A Breath of Fresh Air

Last Gasp isn't so much a comics distributor as a book distributor with a range that includes graphic novels. If you go to www.lastgasp.com and check out the catalog, you see a range that is very special. You may think the folks at Last Gasp carry all sorts of things, but they really don't carry *all* sorts of things.

Last Gasp sells mainly to alternative bookstores, so what it carries is alternative and *underground* books. Sex, drugs, and rock and roll all have a place in its catalog. Underground comix, tattoos and conspiracies, gay culture, and geek chic, radical artists and flying saucers are also there. Last Gasp is more likely to carry a graphic novel about a space alien who's mistaken for Santa Claus and becomes a rock and roll star than to carry some standard superhero tale.

Underground Comix

Underground comix are black-and-white comics focusing on drugs, sex, and human concerns. Last Gasp got its start as a publisher of this kind of material, which thrived as counterculture items in the 1970s.

Will Last Gasp be willing to carry your book? You can probably make a good guess, but don't. Instead, solicit your work, and let Kristine at Last Gasp tell you whether she wants it or not. She may surprise you. The terms are 60 percent off, paid in two months. In at least some cases, Last Gasp carries books on consignment, which means you get paid only after the books are sold to a retailer. Send a copy of your printed book to Kristine, Last Gasp, 777 Florida Street, San Francisco, CA, 94110.

Dealing with Dealers

Some retailers are always going to be happy dealing with distributors. If your book sells well enough, however, you're apt to find a few dealers who will want to deal directly with you. By cutting out the middleman, you can charge more than you charged the distributor and still have the store paying less than the distributor's rates. This leaves the distributor having to eat the store-brand macaroni and cheese rather than the more expensive type shaped like Spongebob Squarepants.

The biggest downside to dealing directly with dealers is that the effort can be a real interruption. For a distributor, servicing the dealer is their constant job and they build their world around it. If you start selling directly to dealers, however, you'll probably have to deal with about one order every week or so, depending on how your book sells. You have to pack the books to make sure that everything is well protected, be-cause receiving a bent book can make a usually happy-as-a-clam dealer turn as irritated as an oyster. You also have to get the package to the post office, which may be part of your normal routine but for some people it's a big interruption. Generally, the dealer pays once the books arrive, which means that you're trusting the dealer for the money. Also, some of the books you sell direct to the dealer are ones which they would have ordered through Diamond anyway. The fewer you sell through Diamond, the less seriously Diamond take you, and the more likely they'll choose not to carry your work.

Still, it can all be worth it. It's not just that you can reasonably charge dealers 50 percent of cover price instead of the 40 percent you charge the distributor, it's also because you're building relationships with retailers, and those relationships can be very helpful for later projects. You really want retailers, especially the key independent-friendly retailers, to be on your side.

You'll also have to face the question of charging for shipping. The best bet is to make the shipping free if the dealer orders at least some amount, say $30 worth at wholesale. That encourages upping orders to reach the free shipping level, and it saves you from figuring out what to bill. Of course, you have to limit the area that you're willing to provide free shipping to, or you'll lose money sending copies to the four pointiest corners of the globe.

Be careful about making up your deal on-the-fly. If you offer a deal to one retailer that you don't offer to others, word will get around, and the other retailers will wonder why you're playing favorites. Of course, retailers don't mind you playing favorites, so long as they're the favorite.

Plus, it's very handy to get your local comic shop to be your buddy. The store can be a good resource in times of need, the folks there may even promote your work to their retailer friends, and some shops give sizable discounts to friendly creators.

> **Conventional Wisdom**
>
> Sales are usually slow during the last hour of a comics convention. Go around to the dealers at the con and offer them your book. The dealers are flush with cash, you don't have to deal with shipping, and it's that many fewer books for you to drag home.

Get Yourshelf in Bookstores

These days, comics shops are only part of the equation for graphic novels. Bookstores are the other part, and for some graphic novels they are the biggest part, outselling the comic shops several times over. So bookstores are an attractive outlet, but they're tricky to deal with. They're used to dealing with humungous publishers. Remember, the Harry Potter books alone outsell, by a good margin, all graphic novels combined.

Bookstores are going to be interested in books. They won't be interested in serialization pamphlets. Don't even think about entering the mainstream magazine distribution market with your pamphlets. That is an expensive morass that has destroyed otherwise successful publishers.

ISBN: It's Something Bookstores Need

The first step for getting into the bookstore market is getting an *ISBN* (that's the *International Standard Book Number*) for your book. That's the number that you see on the back cover of many books, generally over a bar code that looks like a design for an electronic zebra like you see in the picture.

The zebra on the left is the ISBN code, while the zebra on the right is a price code.

But, alas, you cannot buy an ISBN. They will not sell you one.

They will, however, sell you ten. That will run you about $225. Ten thousand ISBNs will run you $3,000. That may sound like a bargain compared to 10, but you're not really planning on putting out 10,000 graphic novels, are you? Surf on over to www.isbn.org for information on the ISBN and an application.

You'll probably want one of those zebra codes as well, so you can send secret messages to zebras. There are places online that will generate a graphic file with your code for about $10 to $25, but there's a cheaper option. Your printing company may be able to generate the code for you and add it to your art, so long as you leave a nice white spot on the back cover for it. Otherwise, head over to www.cgpp.com/bookland/isbn.html for a site that generates the bars for free.

When you get your ISBN, you'll also get information about adding your book to the ISBN book listing. That will get your book listed in all sorts of online book guides, such as the listings at some online bookstores.

Look, a Nook for Your Book

Once your book is in the ISBN directory, bookstores will have all the information they need to order your book. But that's just like saying that because you have the phone book, you have all the information you need to call the National Campaign For Calling Everyone "Myrtle." Stores can order from you, but the only time they will is if a customer comes in, requests the book, and expresses a willingness to wait for weeks to get it.

In order to get bookstores to seriously consider your graphic novel, you really want some middlemen in place. Distributors put out catalogs of upcoming releases that bookstores use to order from, just like in the comics fields. What's different from the comics field is that there's another middle-man, the wholesaler, who buys from the distributor and sells to the bookstores. Big bookstore chains like Borders have their own wholesalers. Smaller chains and independent bookstores rely on wholesalers with names like Ingram and Baker & Taylor and Fred the Amazing Cheez Doodle. Well, names like that.

There are a number of distributors that handle some graphic novel publishers. That doesn't mean that they'll automatically take your book on, however. First of all, they don't want to deal with just a book, they want to deal with you as a publisher, and they generally want an exclusive deal, so you don't reach the bookstore through any other distributor.

> **Amazin' Amazon**
>
> Amazon.com will carry your graphic novel on consignment, no distributor needed. Go to www.amazon.com/advantage/ to learn about this system. It's really handy, because you can steer people looking to order individual copies to the Amazon site. Amazon takes credit cards, and handles the shipping, so you have much less to worry about.

Most graphic novels reach the bookstore market through one of three distributors. Warner Books has their own distributor, which handles DC Comics but isn't likely to handle you. Client Distribution Services (known as CDS) carries Marvel, Tokyopop, Crossgen, and a couple of others. You can find out more about CDS at www.cdsbooks.com.

And then there's Diamond. Yes, the same Diamond that serves the comic book stores has a separate division for reaching bookstores, Diamond Book Distributors. You can learn more about this division at www.diamondbookdistributors.com.

And there are many other book distributors out there. Most of them will be at least a little wary about a single-title self-publisher. But it never hurts to ask.

Hardcovers, Softcovers, and Hard Realities

The sad, sorry truth is that the bookstore market, with all its potential for great sales, is harder to deal with than the comic book shops. It's not just that you're dealing with stores that are less interested in what you're doing, although that's often true. It's that when a bookstore buys your graphic novel, you haven't really sold it yet.

Bookstores stock their stores with returnable books. This means if someone buys your book at a bookshop, it really is sold. But if the book sits on the shelf for a while and the store decides the space would be better used for something else, the book is sent back. You get a slightly battered book, and the bookstore gets a refund. Worse yet, you actually have to pay the distributor money for handling the return. You end up with less money than if the store had never wanted it in the first place.

Luckily, most copies don't get returned. In the book industry as a whole, less than one in four copies is returned. At the moment, graphic novels are running at lower return rates than most books, with some publishers citing return rates around one in twelve.

Another hard part of the bookstore biz is that you have to plan further in advance. Distributors put out three or four seasonal catalogs each year, announcing a full season ahead of time what books will be coming out. Add in the distributor's lead time in making the catalog, and you'll find yourself needing to have the details of your book ready up to nine months ahead of time. Now, that's not all as dreadful as it seems, because you can miss being in the seasonal catalog and still be in the monthly catalog with just a few months' notice. But you'll be missing some promotional opportunities if you do so.

The Least You Need to Know

- Diamond Comic Distributors is the main supplier of comics to comic book stores.
- Solicit Diamond, Cold Cut, and FM to find out how many copies they want to order.
- With complete graphic novels, you're likely to see ongoing reorders.
- To get your book into bookstores, it has to have an ISBN code.
- A book distributor is key to getting stores to actually order your books.

Chapter 27

Promoting and Publicizing

In This Chapter

- ◆ How do you get people to want your graphic novel?
- ◆ Where should you advertise?
- ◆ Which conventions are right for you?

Your graphic novel may be the wonderfullest, perfectest, most grammar-bendingest thing ever published. But people will know that only if they read it, and they'll read it only if they've heard of it. With dozens of new graphic novels hitting the shelves every week, few stores order everything, so readers won't even stumble across your book unless the stores have heard of it and expect people will want it.

Press. Release. Repeat.

The best and cheapest way to get the word out is to take advantage of the press. A handful of e-mails, faxes, and even a few pieces of old-fashioned put-it-in-the-mailbox mail can get information about your book before the eyes of tens of thousands of graphic novel readers.

A press release is your way of informing media outlets about your book. Some places will cast your press release aside. Others may use your information as the basis of an article. But the comics press has a number of outlets that will simply publish the press release you send them, letting you get exactly the message you want out to the public, unimpeded by the pickiness and demands for honesty that would come from more rigorous outlets.

What to Say

The point of a press release is to make your book sound interesting. That's very different from what makes your book interesting to read. It's not a matter of subtle concepts and nuance. It needs to be an idea that people can grasp quickly. It may not be enough to sell them on the book, but at least it will get their attention. This can come from a number of categories:

- **Content.** The series *Little Laps* is set in the exciting world of midget car racing.

- **Format.** The book *The Hole Truth* is the first graphic novel printed on real Swiss cheese.

- **Creative team.** Jane Superstar paints the cover of the first issue of *Sans Gorilla*.

- **Synergy.** The upcoming mystery *False Killer Whale* is written by a marine biologist.

A press release should read like an enthusiastic article. First you start off with information for the reporter or editor who has to deal with this:

> For immediate release

> For further info, contact Iggy Ologist, 805-555-0100, iggy@unfathomprod.com

This way, the editor knows the press release can be run immediately (as opposed to being embargoed until a certain date), and if it inspires a full article, Iggy's the guy to reach out to. Next up is a headline, in all capital letters.

> THE FIRST FISH MYSTERY WITH ACCURACY

Follow that up with a subhead, a secondary headline that explains or adds to the first. This can be a bit longer.

> Real marine biologist writes graphic novel *False Killer Whale*

After that, it's time to get into the body of the article. The first paragraph should be short, three sentences or shorter. But that small amount of text should carry the heart of the information. A reader who reads just the first paragraph should take away what's memorable about the book, as well as the title.

Unfathomable Productions announced today a new graphic novel, a mystery set below the waves. *False Killer Whale*, written by a marine biologist with more than 12 years experience studying undersea life, is a 96-page private-eye tale with deceit, danger, and a shamus named Shamu. This lushly colored tale hits store shelves in August.

That wasn't hard. Now readers know who the publisher is, what the title of the book is, what's interesting about it, the format, and when it's coming out. After that, it's time to flesh out not only detail about the hook of the story, but also other key details about the project. It's also time to make it seem more comfortable and chatty.

"When I sat down to write a graphic novel, I remembered the old advice 'write what you know,' and what I know is marine creatures," explained Iggy Ologist, writer of *False Killer Whales*. "There are actually very complex societies and social interactions beneath the waves, with creatures speaking, vying for power, and yes, even killing one another. So a detective story seemed a natural in that setting."

Realize that no one was actually interviewing Iggy. In fact, Iggy wasn't speaking out loud. Iggy wrote the press release himself. You're allowed to invent quotes for yourself. And remember, it's supposed to read as if the magazine running the piece wrote it, not you, so don't use *I* or *we* except within a quote. Nat says that talking about yourself in the third person is not only okay, it's actually fun. And Nat is so wise, you should all listen to him.

The book and movie world has had big success with fish-based mysteries, or "fishteries" as the fans call them. *Wat'ry Grave* spent three weeks on *The New York Times* best-seller list and *Finding Nemo's Stolen Watch* was an all-ages box-office success. "Bringing the form over to comics was the logical next step, and I wanted to include a more realistic sense of sea life to make it even more interesting," explains Iggy.

"Finding artist Winter McLeod was fate. Her years at the Sequential Art and Scuba Institute prepared her for telling stories with fish. And her second career as a police sketch artist has gotten her deeply familiar with the criminal physicality."

The plot is a classic noir-style tale. When Danny the Dolphin is found dead, Willie the Killer Whale quickly confesses. But there's something fishy about the confession. Who is Willie covering for? Billy the Blowhard Blowfish? Or is Tina the Tuna not as dolphin-safe as she seems?

If you have some place for readers to get more information, send them there.

The Unfathomable Productions website has a several-page preview of the story, along with interviews with the creators and other vital information. The URL is www. unfathomprod.com.

Then you wrap it all up with the technical details.

> *False Killer Whale* (ISBN 0-9847-632) is a full-color 6"x8" graphic novel priced at $16.96. It ships in August from Unfathomable Productions, distributed by Diamond Comics Distributors, FM International, Cold Cut, and Rosemund Book Services.

Include some graphics from the story, both in black-and-white for print outlets and in color for better print outlets and websites. Pretty pictures will sell your book at least as effectively as pretty words.

Don't feel you need to squeeze every bit of good news into a single press release. If you have enough good information for two press releases, you can follow up the first one with a second one a month later. That way, readers get more exposure.

Who to Tell

You should send your press release out to the weekly comics newspapers like the *Comics Buyer's Guide* and *Comic Shop News.* Send it out to the comics magazines, although you should realize that every magazine has its own tone and you may want to steer the press release toward it. The snobs at the *Comics Journal* aren't apt to be interested in the fact that your graphic novel has a limited edition hologram cover, and the superhero-loving folks at *Wizard* aren't likely to care that your story is inspired by Molière and your art inspired by Moiré.

> **Turnaround Time**
>
> Weeklies and monthlies don't get the press release in one day and have it in the issue that goes out the next. As a rule of thumb, a press release you send out today will appear three issues later.

Some of the magazines will run your stuff, some won't. The easiest place for an unknown publisher of unknown creators to get a press release released is online. A number of websites specialize in comic book news, and most of them want to carry as much news as possible. They don't have the printing cost limitations of a magazine. Go around to sites like Newsarama.com, ComicBookResources.com, and Comicon.com. Check out the e-mail addresses of the folks who post press releases in their news or press release sections, then e-mail your press release to them.

Then there are comic book discussion sites that don't have news coverage. Go to these and post your press release as the first message of a new discussion. Make sure you post in the correct discussion section and put *[HYPE]* before the title of your press release in the discussion board's title field. Otherwise, you may tick off the board's regular users looking for a discussion and finding hype instead. The hype warning isn't needed at the CBIA, where the savvy retailers know that you're hyping anyway.

After you get your press release posted on one of these sites, keep going back to that site for a while. People may end up responding to your press releases, talking it up, asking questions, and so on. Getting yourself involved in these threads is a good way to get people excited about the book, and to feel like they know you personally. And you can always count on the occasional bozos who will talk down about your book simply for the joy of being nasty. Feel free to ignore them. The folks who read the discussions generally know these folks for who they are.

But that's all just the comics scene. If your book has hooks beyond the comics field, spread the word other places as well. *False Killer Whale* might make only a ripple in the comics field, but there could be a tidal wave of interest if you send your press release to *Modern Aquarium*, *Fishery Mystery Magazine*, and *Water World Daily*.

The CBIA

The **CBIA** (Comic Book Industry Alliance) is a discussion board primarily for retailers, with publishers and creators encouraged to talk to them. Go to www.thecbia.com for more information.

Use the Newspaper

Send press releases to your local paper, particularly if you're not in a big population center. Editors love the local-boy- (or girl or marmoset)-makes-comics angle.

When to Release

The most important time to spread the word to comic shop customers is shortly before the issue of Diamond's catalog *Previews* comes out with your graphic novel listed. A lot of comic book store orders these days are generated from readers *preordering*, seeing a book in *Previews* and telling their retailer to get it for them.

Comics retailers send in most of their orders during the last week of the month, so reminding them of your existence during the prior week is a good idea. Don't hit them afterward with a "you should have ordered this" message, or they'll just hit you with a "you should have told us sooner" response.

Outside of the comics field, you want the press information to hit when the book is actually available. You want people to see the coverage, go to their bookstore or comics shop, and actually be able to buy the book. The problem is that for a new publisher, most stores won't have ordered your book, so a lot of people may come back from their quest empty-handed. Don't let that stop you! People asking stores for a book they don't carry is a good way to help stores figure out "we should carry this book." They'll realize it's a good way to make money, at least the smarter ones will. There will always be a few retailers who will tell 75 people in a row "we don't carry that book. No one wants it."

Adding Ads

Advertising is an expense. Expenses are bad. Advertising in the right way to the right audience can build sales. Sales are good.

The most popular place to advertise graphic novels is in *Previews*. Diamond will sell you ads there. The ads aren't cheap, but comic book stores and the preordering customers will see your ad at the time they're figuring out what to order. With an ad, you get a half page or a full page to show off your graphic novel to good effect, in addition to the small cover shot and blurb that *Previews* normally runs. *Previews* has some strong limitations on ads, not letting you list your website or do anything else that would encourage people to order directly from you rather than through a retailer and Diamond.

The same magazines and websites that you send your press releases to all sell ad space, and the advantages there is that they will generally let you push direct customer sales. If an ad can drive someone to mail order your graphic novel from you, then you get all the money. If someone orders your book from a retailer, then you get 40 percent. After spending a few hours with the calculator, I find that "all" is better than "40 percent," although the overhead effort of handling individual orders should not be underestimated.

Don't just throw money into advertising without thinking about it carefully. If you have a $10 graphic novel and you spend $800 on a *Previews* ad, the ad will have to generate 200 additional retailer orders just to break even, and that's not counting the additional printing and shipping costs for those 200. On the other hand, the difference between a store ordering zero copies and a store ordering one copy can be much more than one copy. The store that orders one copy and sells it quickly will reorder another copy, and keep reordering copies as long as they sell. A store that doesn't order in the first place will never reorder.

If you're serializing your *I was a Vampire for the CIA* graphic novel, the most important issue to advertise is issue 1. Sell folks issue 1 and they're apt to order issues 2, 3, and so on, as long as they're enjoying the blood-sucking tale of political intrigue. If you skip advertising issue 1 and then try to advertise heavily on issue 3, you're asking people to come in during the middle of the story, when you've already revealed that the werewolf is a double agent. It's a much harder sell.

The Conventions of Conventions

Comic book conventions are good places to go to, be seen, and get the word out, as well as to sell a few copies. Conventions range from small local dealer-oriented shows that are only worthwhile if you happen to live in the area all the way up to big national conventions that attract tens of thousands of people per day.

It is hard for the publisher whose book is not yet out to justify the expense of buying a table or booth space at a convention. Smaller publishers generally depend on actually selling their materials to make conventions worthwhile, and some publishers even find that such shows are their biggest profit center. They spend their summers bouncing from convention to convention, often to the disappointment of their spouses, who are sure that they're out there seeing the exciting sights and having wild times. In reality, they're seeing an endless string of convention centers, cheap hotel rooms, and airports.

If you want to promote your upcoming work at a convention, there are several options available to you. One is to take advantage of *artists' alley*, an area at the convention set aside for comics creators where the tables are generally cheaper or even free. There your artist can display the pages from the upcoming work and hand out fliers for it while chatting with folks, and can often cover expenses simply by doing sketches for a fee. Comics fans aren't nearly so eager to see writers in artists' alley, and almost no one wants to buy an original paragraph.

If your book is out, you can still go the artists'-alley route if you want, but you should seriously consider buying an actual dealer's table or publisher's booth. At some conventions, artists are allowed to sell only art at their table, not published books. At other conventions, the artists'-alley space is less desirable space, reached only by people who want to buy original art. Paying for space will get you more in the flow of customers.

Steve Sez: Tales from the Art-Side

As an artist at a con, you have to be "on" nonstop—tracking time, money, and the availability of schmoozable editors, holding and prioritizing multiple simultaneous conversations, trying to remember names, being funny, hustling up the next gig, escaping friends for a couple hours of sleep, critiquing insightfully, and dodging crazed babbling fans, all while sketching decent drawings for your potential customers.

Put Info in Your Infomercial

Unknown creators talking about unknown projects won't draw much of a crowd. If you give a talk about creating graphic novels or another larger topic related to your work, the audience may become interested in you and your work. Would you have bought this book if it was entitled *Why You Should Buy The Big Con*?

Another angle to take is to see if you can give a talk at the convention. The smallest conventions don't have talks and the largest ones usually have too many better-known people who want to give talks, but a medium-sized convention may be in need of anyone it can get to fill its small auditoriums.

Many of the talks at conventions are panel discussions, where a group of supposedly knowledgeable people discusses some topic in front of an audience. If you can get on one of these panels, do it, but only if you're actually knowledgeable about the topic and can present yourself well. I've seen too many folks embarrass themselves by getting on the panel and having nothing to say. That won't build your sales or your self-esteem.

Autographing Like a Superstar

When you publish your own graphic novel, you may do a lot of autographing. Unfortunately, at first you'll be autographing checks. The printing company, the shipping company, and the magazines that take your advertising will all want to see your pretty autograph.

Once the book is out, however, it's your chance to do signings in comic book stores and bookstores. You can autograph like a famous person. If enough people believe you're famous, that's how you become famous.

Contact bookstores and comic shops within driving range. You don't want to set up signings at two shops that are close enough to share customers, but at least at first that probably won't be a problem. If you know the shops in your area, you know which ones do signings and which do it well. You may find some stores that would do well with a signing but never even thought about it. Let the retailers know that you're available for signings, and that you're willing to have them carry your books on a consignment basis on the day of the signing. That means the retailer doesn't have to risk ordering a lot of your book, but there will be plenty of copies for anyone who shows up.

Arrange the signing at least a month in advance, to give the retailer time to publicize it. Then, don't count on the retailer doing the work to publicize your visit. Especially if you're local and covering all expenses, the store has no money at risk and sometimes will not do anything to promote the signing.

Send signs to the retailer weeks in advance, with a picture of the art from your book and saying *Iggy Ologist will be signing his new graphic novel* False Killer Whales *here September 31st.* Make up a master copy of a flier for them to put out, again announcing the signing but including the store name and location. The retailer may copy this to hand out, or just ignore it, but you're far more likely to get a flier out there once you've shown the retailer it's something you expect.

A week before the signing, go to some of the online comics discussion sites and mention your upcoming signing. Mention it on your website. Get the word out any way you can, because the more people who show up at your signing, the more you sell on that day, and the more the retailer will believe you're a big name whose work should be ordered heavily.

Write Right

Get your hands on good *signing pens*, pens that writes well on slick book covers, unlike most writing pens. Many signers use Sharpie brand markers, while others use metallic ink pens.

Steve Sez: Give 'em a Taste

Produce a simple, cheap giveaway for your signings. A photocopied booklet or signing card with some teaser art or behind-the-scenes info is great. (Think "DVD extras.") Include your cover, your web address, and your ISBN. Add the store's logo and contact info on there, too, because a store that hosts your signing is a store you want to promote.

A normal signature, a more efficient practiced signature, and a designed signature for Mr. Otto Graph.

Before the signing, practice your autograph. I know, you've been signing your name for years, but you rarely have to impress people with it. You may want to develop a special signature just for signings. As you can see in the above signature picture, it doesn't have to be readable, as long as it has enough readable letters for people to tell which member of the creative team signed the book. It can even be something that looks more like a design than like handwriting, so long as you can reproduce it quickly. This won't matter to you early in your career, but if you ever get to where you're signing hundreds or even thousands of autographs, this will save your wrists.

At the signing, be gracious and charming, even if it is poorly attended. Sometimes that happens even to famous creators, even when the signing was properly promoted. Maybe the signing conflicts with another event, or the weather is too miserable to go out, or the big evil robot Dethpuppi is holding everyone at bay several blocks away. Whatever the reason, don't growl too loudly at the store owner. Remember, you want this retailer to order your next project as well. The good news is that very few people see you have a bad signing, while lots of people see you have a good one. That helps your reputation.

Before you collect the money for any copies that have sold, offer to sign some more for the retailer to sell to people who missed the signing. That's just that many more copies sold.

And do take a moment to look around the store. Look at all the fine comics and graphic novels on the rack, and enjoy the fact that you've added another piece of enjoyable graphic literature to the world.

The Least You Need to Know

- Press releases are a cheap way to spread the word about your book.

- Your press release should have an interesting title and key information in the first paragraph.

- Advertising sells more books, but not always enough more to make it worthwhile.

- Conventions offer opportunities to create new readers and turn existing readers into real fans.

- Signing sessions at stores can win you a following with both readers and retailers.

Graphic Novel Publishers

Many publishers put out graphic novels. The following are important ones in the graphic novel field at this point. However, new players emerge all the time and the existing players often change direction. Don't assume that the publisher you're interested is open to submissions. Go to their website and check their submission guidelines before sending them anything.

AiT/PlanetLar

Type of material: Cinematic original graphic novels.

Address: 2034 47th Avenue, San Francisco, CA 94116

Website: www.ait-planetlar.com

Alternative Comics

Type of material: Mainly original graphic novels in alternative styles.

Address: 503 NW 37th Avenue, Gainesville, FL 32609-2204

Website: www.indyworld.com

Dark Horse Comics

Type of material: An eclectic mix, heavy with licensed properties. Mostly serialized, some original graphic novels.

Address: 10956 SE Main Street, Milwaukie, OR 97222

Website: www.darkhorse.com

DC Comics

Type of material: DC is best known for superhero material (Superman, Batman, and so on), generally serialized and then collected. However, DC also does significant original graphic novels, including nonsuperhero material.

Address: 1700 Broadway, New York, NY 10019

Website: www.dccomics.com

Fantagraphics Books

Type of material: An unlikely mix of artsy material and porn.

Address: 7563 Lake City Way NE, Seattle, WA 98115

Website: www.fantagraphics.com

IDW Publishing

Type of material: Serialized-then-collected horror and crime stories.

Address: 4411 Morena Boulevard, San Diego, CA 92117

Website: www.idwpublishing.com

Marvel

Type of material: Primarily superhero (Spider-Man, Hulk, and so on) and everything is serialized first. Marvel has done original graphic novels in the past, and that may happen again.

Address: 10 East 40th Street, New York, NY 10016

Website: www.marvel.com

Image Comics

Type of material: Heavy on superhero and action material, but interested in other things as well. Mostly serialized, some original graphic novels.

Address: 1071 N. Batavia Street, Suite A, Orange, CA 92867

Website: www.imagecomics.com

Oni

Type of material: Hip alternative material, mostly serialized, some original graphic novels.

Address: 6336 SE Milwaukie Avenue, PMB 30, Portland, OR 97202

Website: www.onipress.com

SLG Publishing

Type of material: A mix of material leaning toward humor. Mostly serialized and then collected.

Address: P.O. Box 26427, San Jose, CA 95159-6427

Website: www.slavelabor.com

Top Shelf Productions

Type of material: Mainly original graphic novels in alternative styles.

Address: P.O. Box 1282, Marietta, GA 30061-1282

Website: www.topshelfcomix.com

Graphic Novel Conventions

Comic book conventions are great places to find collaborators, talk to editors, and sell your work. Many comic conventions are held each year in the United States and Canada, ranging from small shows with a handful of dealers in a church basement to shows that fill major convention centers with tens of thousands of creators, dealers, and fans. Larger science fiction or gaming conventions also often offer comics programming.

Listed here are some of the larger and more important annual conventions. For a fuller list of conventions and schedules for the current year, pull up www. comicbookconventions.com in your web browser.

Full-Range Conventions

These conventions cover a full range of the comics scene, from photocopied small press materials all the way up to the biggest mainstream superhero work:

- **Comic Con International: San Diego** (summer, San Diego, California), more commonly known simply as "The San Diego Comic Con," is the huge granddaddy of the convention scene. This goes beyond comics to include a lot of film, TV, and animation material. Unspeakably huge. For more information: www.comic-con.org

- **Wizard World Chicago** (summer, Rosemont, Illinois). After buying out the long-running Chicago Comicon, Wizard Magazine used this as a basis for running mainstream-oriented but still broad-ranged conventions around various major cities. For more information: www.wizarduniverse. com/conventions

- ◆ **MegaCon** (winter, Orlando, Florida). For more information: www.megaconvention.com

- ◆ **Mid-Ohio Con** (fall, Columbus, Ohio). For more information: www.midohiocon.com

- ◆ **Motor City Comic Con** (twice a year, spring and fall, Novi, Michigan). For more information: motorcityconventions.com

- ◆ **Baltimore Comic-Con** (fall, Baltimore, Maryland). For more information: www.comicon.com/baltimore

- ◆ **WonderCon** (spring, San Francisco, California). For more information: www.comic-con.org

Alt/Indy Conventions

These conventions shy away from the big mainstream superhero material to focus on small press and alternative content. It's easier to avoid getting lost in the shuffle at these shows, all of which are better known by their acronyms than by their names:

- ◆ **SPX, the Small Press Expo** (fall, Bethesda, Maryland). For more information: www.spxpo.com

- ◆ **APE, the Alternative Press Expo** (winter, San Francisco, California). For more information: www.comic-con.org

- ◆ **MoCCA, the Museum of Comic and Cartoon Art Art Festival** (summer, New York City, New York). For more information: www.moccany.org

- ◆ **SPACE, the Small Press and Alternative Comics Expo** (spring, Columbus, Ohio). For more information: www.backporchcomics.com

Other Resources for Graphic Novelists

Your reading doesn't end here. There are a number of other fine books, magazines, and web resources that will help you create your graphic novel. For books that may be out of print, try used book dealers or your local library.

Books

Comics and Sequential Art by Will Eisner: Eisner didn't just produce one of the first graphic novels, he also wrote one of the first serious textbooks on their creation.

Drawing the Head and Figure by Jack Hamm: Hamm crams an enormous amount of useful information into his books. Get them all.

Figure Drawing For All It's Worth by Andrew Loomis: Loomis's many books are the gold standard of how-to-draw books. Of course they're all out of print. Used copies will cost you hundreds of dollars, and library copies are frequently stolen. If it wasn't wrong to recommend violating the copyright, I'd suggest you borrow them by interlibrary loan and make cover-to-cover photocopy sets.

On Directing Film by David Mamet: This short book by the acclaimed playwright, screenwriter, and director is full of advice about visual storytelling that graphic novelists will find valuable.

Panel Discussions: Design in Sequential Art Storytelling by Durwin Talon et al.: Interviews with comic book illustrators, with a strong emphasis on their artistic process.

Panel One: Comic Book Scripts by Top Writers by Neil Gaiman, Kevin Smith et al., and *Panel Two: More Comic Book Scripts by Top Writers* by Scott McCloud, Peter David, et al., both edited by Nat Gertler (yes, the co-writer of this book you hold in your hands): These books reproduce complete comic book scripts for published comics—a useful resource for artists who want to practice on a professional script and for writers who want to see how others do it.

Perspective! for Comic Book Artists by David Chelsea: This is a textbook in comics form on the art and science of perspective. It's not easy to make perspective, with its complicated diagrams, fun to read about, but Chelsea succeeds.

The DC Comics Guide to Pencilling Comics by Klaus Janson: Janson's book reflects his years of experience as a teacher and adventure cartoonist.

The New Comics: Interviews from the Pages of The Comics Journal edited by Gary Groth and Robert Fiore: This book contains thoughtful interviews with some of the most important graphic novelists of the last 50 years.

Understanding Comics by Scott McCloud: McCloud's thoughtful comic about how the comics medium works is considered a must-read by most cartoonists.

Magazines

There are a number of magazines that are aimed at the graphic novel reader, and some of those include frequent articles on creating graphic novels. The following magazines are aimed primarily at creators.

Draw, published by TwoMorrow Press, and *Sketch*, published by Blue Line Productions: Both target graphic novel artists with interviews and tutorials.

Write Now!, published by TwoMorrow Press: Interviews with and articles for graphic novel writers.

Websites

The World Wide Web is the greatest single informational and conversational resource ever. This proves as true for graphic novelists as for anything else.

www.comicbookresources.com, www.newsarama.com, www.comicon.com, www.sequentialart.com: Fan-oriented sites with news, reviews, and discussion, all of which can be handy when it comes time to promote your graphic novel.

forums.delphiforums.com/comicspros/: Even a small graphic novel credential will qualify you for this discussion board, which is often less about the medium than you would expect.

www.thecbia.com: The Comic Book Industry Alliance discussion board is primarily a hangout for graphic novel retailers. It comes in handy for self-publishers when it comes to promoting your works and when seeking advice about what makes a book marketable. Simply lurking here will give you an education on the reality of the graphic novel business.

www.comicbookconventions.com: A list of almost all of the upcoming comic book conventions.

www.the-master-list.com: The Master List attempts to list every comic bookstore in the United States, which makes it handy if you're planning on sending out mailings or looking for stores in a given area where you can do signings.

www.balloontales.com: An online guide to digital comic book lettering, done by people who know what they're talking about.

Index